Manegold of Lautenbach

Liber contra Wolfelmum

D1608390

DALLAS MEDIEVAL TEXTS AND TRANSLATIONS
1

Manegold of Lautenbach
Liber contra Wolfelmum

TRANSLATED WITH INTRODUCTION AND NOTES
BY

Robert Ziomkowski
(Cornell University)

PEETERS
PARIS – LEUVEN – DUDLEY, MA
2002

Cover illustration by kind permission of the Badische Landesbibliothek, Karlsruhe. MS. Rastatt 27, fol. preceding 1r, shows Manegold of Lautenbach with Bishop Gebhard of Salzburg, the addressee of his *Liber ad Gebehardum*

Library of Congress Cataloging-in-Publication Data

Manegold, von Lautenbach, ca. 1030-ca. 1112.
  [Liber contra Wolfelmum. English & Latin]
  Liber contra Wolfelmum / Manegold of Lautenbach ; translated with an introduction and notes by Robert Ziomkowski.
    p. cm. -- (Dallas medieval texts and translations ; 1)
  Includes bibliographical references and index.
  ISBN 9042911921
    1. Wolfhelm, Abbot of Brauweiler, d. 1091. 2. Scholasticism. I. Ziomkowski, Robert. II. Title. III. Series.

B734 .M3513 2002
189'.4--dc21

                                                                            2002074986

© 2002 – Peeters – Bondgenotenlaan 153 – B-3000 Leuven – Belgium.
ISBN 90-429-1192-1
D. 2002/0602/113

For Laura

inscienciis tam multę & uarię spes sunt ut nisi sps
pietatis adsit cui regulam dirigam. cor hominis pra-
uum. & inscrutabile prius sit ueri simili ratione
seduci. & nisi sobrietate quadam intelligentia re-
frenetur aliquando inaltum elata ipso tandem tumore
in inmensum crescente rumpetur. quandoq̃; uero sini-
strorsum nimis adima deuergens intenebras fatui-
tatis submergetur. Gaudebat hoc animus apli sps sci
gratia illustratus. qui inter regulas fidei quas nobis imi-
tandas prefixit sumopere amonuit nipluf sape quam
oportet. sed sape adsobrietatem. Vnde cum aliquid
mira nostre occurrit qd ipsa sui sublimitate atq̃; pba-
bilitate delectat. Habemus quadraturam xpiane doctrine qua intellectis cognitis iuxta ponere debemus.
& siquid demeditationib; nostris excesserit ad normam
illius festinato iudicio resecare. ita & dampnabilium er-
rorum pictionem deuitari. & philosophorum picturas quę taquam
superflua quędam inmisceas nostris studiis apta est: commo-
de salubriterq̃; potest famulari. Vt autem indissimulabi-
liter pnoscas quam pniciosum sit eorum imitari fidem quoy
ingenium admiramur. Aspice quid pretendat inp-
ma parte sui philosophicę confessionis asserto: quam
abeisdem suptam. macrobi libro suo apponendam
curauit his uerbis   ·VI·

Qui prima causa & est & uocatur unus omnium que
sunt quęq̃; uidentur ee. princeps & origo est. Hic
ds superhabundante maiestatis fecunditate dese
mentem creauit. Hec mens que noys uocatur qua patrem inspicit. plenam similitudinem seruat actoris.
animam uero dese ipsa creat posteriora respiciens. Rursus anima noys patrem qua intuetur induitur.
ac paulatim regrediente respectu infabricam corpo-
rum incorporea ipsa degenerat. Nonne si horum uer-

Editor's Foreword

The Dallas Medieval Texts and Translations series pursues an ambitious goal: to build a library of medieval Latin texts, with English translations, from the period roughly between 500 and 1500, that will represent the whole breadth and variety of medieval civilization. Thus, the series will be open to all subjects and genres, ranging from poetry through philosophy, theology, and rhetoric to treatises on natural science. It will include, as well, medieval Latin versions of Arabic and Hebrew works. In the future, the publication of vernacular texts is a possibility. Placing these texts side by side, rather than dividing them in terms of the boundaries of contemporary academic disciplines, will, we hope, contribute to a better understanding of the complex coherence and interrelatedness of the many facets of medieval written culture.

In consultation with our distinguished board of editorial advisers, we have established principles that will guide the progress of the series. The primary purpose of the Dallas Medieval Texts and Translations is to render medieval Latin texts accessible in authoritative modern English translations; at the same time the series will, however, strive to provide reliable texts in Latin where such are not yet available. The translations will therefore be established either on the basis of existing good critical editions (which we will not normally reprint) or, when necessary, on the basis of new editions. To enhance the accessibility of the texts to a large academic public, including graduate students, the critical apparatus of the editions will be limited to important variants. Each volume will comprise scholarly introductions, notes, and annotated bibliographies.

Works published in the Dallas Medieval Texts and Translations series will be unexcerpted and unabridged. In the case of a work too long to appear in a single volume, we will start with the beginning of the work or publish integral parts of it, rather than creating a selection of discontinuous texts.

It is an honor and a pleasure for us to open this new series with a volume prepared by a young and gifted scholar, Dr. Robert Ziomkowski of Cornell University. Dr. Ziomkowski's version of Manegold of Lautenbach's *Contra Wolfelmum* is the first translation into any modern language of this fascinating anti-philosophical treatise, which was written at a time when medieval Christian thought began to undergo a slow transformation into Scholasticism. Dr. Ziomkowski's book is a model of what our series attempts to achieve: it presents an elegant English translation together with an introduction that places Manegold's work within the cultural and intellectual context from which it emerged; its annotations help the reader identify references and make sense of difficult passages; and the bibliographical essay provides an account of the state of research on Manegold of Lautenbach. While representing an accessible and attractive introduction to an often neglected figure in the intellectual history of the Middle Ages, Dr. Ziomkowski's volume will at the same time serve as the standard point of reference on Manegold in future scholarship.

Sixteen medievalists are currently working on volumes for our series. The second one, Margaret Jennings's translation of Ranulph Higden's *Ars compondendi sermones*, will appear within the next few months. Volumes with texts by Anastasius the Librarian, Pseudo-Scottus, Henry of Ghent, Peter Lombard, Johannes Canonicus, Roger Bacon, Achard of St.-Victor, Robert Grosseteste, Hugh Metel, and Averroes, among others, are forthcoming. Proposals for other volumes prepared in the spirit of the series are welcome.

Thanks are due, in the first place, to the University of Dallas, whose financial support has made this series possible. Professor Glen Thurow, formerly Provost and Dean of Constantin College, believed in this project years before the first contributor submitted a manuscript. His successor, Dr. Thomas Lindsay, has continued the University's generous assistance. Emmanuel and Paul Peeters enthusiastically embraced the idea for the Dallas Medieval Texts and Translations when we first discussed it with them in 1998. We are very pleased that our new series is associated with a publisher of such great tradition and renown. Thanks are also due to the medievalists in the United States and abroad who have agreed to serve on our board of editorial advisers. Professor Jos Decorte, of the Katholieke Universiteit Leuven, is not able to see the publication of this first volume: in October, 2001 he died in a tragic accident while biking home from work, as he always did. A future volume, with the translation of Henry of Ghent that he was preparing for our series, will be dedicated to his memory.

For the Editorial Board:
    Philipp W. Rosemann
    Dallas, Texas
    May, 2002

Table of Contents

Abbreviations

CCCM   Corpus Christianorum, Continuatio Mediaevalis
CCSL   Corpus Christianorum, Series Latina
CSEL   Corpus Scriptorum Ecclesiasticorum Latinorum
MGH   Monumenta Germaniae Historica
MGH Ldl   Monumenta Germaniae Historica, Libelli de lite
PG   Patrologia Graeca
PL   Patrologia Latina

Acknowledgments

I am grateful for the institutional and personal support that has enabled the completion of this project. The draft was finished at the Pontifical Institute of Mediaeval Studies with the help of an Andrew W. Mellon Fellowship and refined under the auspices of the Society for the Humanities at Cornell University, where I enjoyed the use of the John M. Olin Library. The earlier stages could not have been achieved without the resources of the Pontifical Institute's Library, the John M. Kelly Library of St. Michael's College, the Thomas Fisher Rare Book Library, and the John P. Robarts Library of the University of Toronto; I thank the inter-library loan department for their efforts on my behalf. I am also grateful for the cooperation of the Getty Center Library, the Division des archives of the Université Laval, the Robbins Collection at the University of California, Berkeley (particular thanks to Lucia Diamond, Luminita Florea, and Max Withers), the Badische Landesbibliothek in Karlsruhe (particular thanks to Rainer Fuerst), and the Biblioteca Ambrosiana in Milan, which provided a microfilm of the manuscript that contains the *Liber contra Wolfelmum* and granted permission to reproduce a folio from the manuscript for the frontispiece.

My work has benefited from correspondence with Bruce Barker-Benfield, Frank Bezner, Irene Caiazzo, and Paul Dutton. I am grateful to Virginia Brown, Greti Dinkova-Bruun, and Ron B. Thomson at the Pontifical Institute of Mediaeval Studies for the attention they were able to spare from their own projects and responsibilities. I am especially pleased to extend my lasting thanks to Winthrop Wetherbee for comments on an early draft of the translation, to Elizabeth New for comments on a revised draft, to Laura Linke for assistance with revisions and proofreading, and to my students at the Society for the Humanities for a lively discussion of the text and for helpful suggestions. I am greatly indebted to Charles Burnett of the Warburg Institute for reading the complete manuscript and providing essential recommendations. The debt to my family, whose patience and encouragement has been vital throughout my studies, can never adequately be acknowledged. Finally, I offer my gratitude to Philipp Rosemann and the Dallas Medieval Texts and Translations for their exemplary support at every stage of the project.

Preface

In a book on the reception of the classical heritage, R.R. Bolgar examined the oft-repeated denunciation of ancient learning during the eleventh century, when the content of Greek philosophy was increasingly becoming an object of widespread attention and the study of logic was beginning to offer new methodological possibilities in theology. Among the individuals who denounced the classical tradition because of its alleged subversive influence on Christian thought and morals was Manegold of Lautenbach. Citing a passage from Manegold's *Liber contra Wolfelmum*, Bolgar concluded, "the whole treatise with its extensive attacks on ancient philosophy deserves to be read."[1] The present translation is intended to make this treatise accessible to a wider audience.

Although Manegold's condemnation of ancient philosophy is sometimes thought to represent a certain kind of "medieval" or "monastic" attitude toward secular studies, it should be emphasized that his statement was not one of obscurantism, for he did not condemn out of ignorance. Presenting specific doctrines of the ancient philosophers, Manegold explained why each in turn had to be rejected if one were to safeguard western culture from the errors of its past. At the root of those errors Manegold identified a relativist notion of truth which threatened to undermine the certainties and standards that the universal claims of the Christian message had afforded European society. His critique was not a general rejection of reason; he opposed, rather, what he regarded as reason overstepping its boundaries. He feared lest reason usurp the place of revelation and challenge the authority that gave Christian society its identity and unity. Manegold neither shunned the reading of the philosophers, nor encouraged others to neglect them, but urged a selective reception of the classical heritage. Moreover, his attack was not an idle statement against the folly of pre-Christian culture; it was concentrated against certain institutional structures of the Christian society in which he lived. By attacking the ancient philosophers, Manegold was attacking the schoolmen who taught philosophy. He saw in the activity of the cathedral schools the institutionalization of a

---

[1] R.R. Bolgar, *The Classical Heritage and its Beneficiaries: From the Carolingian Age to the End of the Renaissance* (1954; repr. New York, Evanston, and London: Harper & Row, 1964), p. 415. See also G. Paré, A. Brunet, and P. Tremblay, *La renaissance du XIIe siècle: Les écoles et l'enseignement*, Publications de l'Institut d'études médiévales d'Ottawa 3 (Paris and Ottawa: J. Vrin and Institut d'études médiévales, 1933), p. 187 n. 3: "Tout l'opuscule est à lire...."

contentious and relativistic attitude toward truth that neglected the good of the soul in the interests of worldly success. Thus, the Investiture Controversy that shook Latin Christendom late in the eleventh century represented, in Manegold's view, the projection of this "scholastic" attitude onto society at large, and he saw imperial opposition to papal authority as the unwholesome fruit of the errors that the schools had insidiously planted. The *Liber contra Wolfelmum* was both a recognition of the power of education and an appeal for its reform.

Manegold's portrayal of the troubles besetting the society in which he lived was not free of exaggeration or distortion, nor indeed of oversimplification. Nevertheless, his statement was not without its subtlety and insight. Manegold's text deserves to be considered in full and on its own terms.

Introduction

1. The Reading of the Philosophers during the Investiture Controversy

Without the increased prominence of the cathedral schools during the eleventh century, the so-called "Renaissance of the Twelfth Century" could not have borne fruit.[1] The shift in the focus of learning from monasteries to cathedral schools had begun in the tenth century and by the late eleventh presented a significant alternative to monastic education. An impelling force behind this development was a desire on the part of secular rulers for more efficient government. The cathedral schools could provide skilled administrators, and thus were more suited to serve political ends than were the monastic schools, whose educational aims focused on the otherworldly ideals at the heart of the Christian message. The German emperors patronized the cathedral schools, drew talented men to the court chapel, and eventually made them bishops.[2]

The indispensable basis for the humanistic education of the cathedral schools was the classical heritage, especially the writings of Cicero, Seneca, and Quintilian, through which secular administrators were inculcated with the required civic values; Christian literature, by comparison, did not provide the necessary models for the formation of statesmen dedicated to active life in the world.[3] The monasteries, of course, had saved the classical texts from oblivion, but the cathedral schools tended to endorse the ancient writings to a degree that went beyond monastic standards of propriety. At the heart of the antagonism between monastery and cathedral was the clash between two visions for the education of Christian society. The Benedictine monastery, as "a school for the Lord's service,"[4] was dedicated to the task of perfecting the individual soul by

---

[1] For a recent survey, see R.N. Swanson, *The Twelfth-Century Renaissance* (Manchester and New York: Manchester University Press, 1999). On the cathedral schools before the year 1100, and their importance for the cultural flowering of the twelfth century, see pp. 12–39.

[2] See C. Stephen Jaeger, *The Envy of Angels: Cathedral Schools and Social Ideals in Medieval Europe, 950–1200*, Middle Ages Series (Philadelphia, Penn.: University of Pennsylvania Press, 1994), pp. 42–52.

[3] Ibid., pp. 48–49.

[4] *RB 1980: The Rule of St. Benedict,* ed. Timothy Fry (Collegeville, Minn.: Liturgical Press, 1981), pp. 164–65 (Prologue 45).

means of creating an ideal space (the cloister) that would enable an elite to focus on the essentials with minimal distraction, whereas the schools that were attached to the cathedrals had the task of educating clerics to serve in the less than ideal circumstances of the world at large. Just as the monasteries were suited for producing leaders of the Church, with the result that popes were often drawn from the ranks of the monks, the cathedral schools produced administrators to assist rulers in governing Christian society. The German emperors integrated the cathedral schools into their method of government, known as the "imperial church system." By appointing men educated in the cathedral schools as loyal bishops with broad secular responsibilities, the emperors minimized their reliance upon the powerful and contentious landed nobility and increased the political stability of their realm.[5]

This dependence on churchmen for the smooth functioning of imperial government, which was established by the reform-minded Ottonian emperors, endured for over a century. Its fatal flaw, however, was that it compromised — or, in any event, was later perceived to compromise — the transcendent aims of church office for the sake of political expediency. When the monk Hildebrand, who guided the Latin Church as Pope Gregory VII (1073–1085), attacked the so-called imperial church system, he was undermining Henry IV's ability to govern his own realm.[6] By opposing the emperor's appointment of bishops in the German lands, Gregory sought to redress what he regarded as a menacing decline of Christian discipline and morals that threatened the Church's mission to save souls. Yet Gregory observed the call to righteousness at the price of political turmoil. The ensuing strife prompted Guibert of Ravenna (the antipope Clement III) to ask, "What Christian ever instituted so many wars or killed so many men?"[7] In the attempt to revive the Christian ideal, Gregory sacrificed the practical concerns of secular government, with bitter outcome.

It is within this environment that Manegold of Lautenbach wrote the *Liber contra Wolfelmum*, his twofold attack against the philosophers and against the enemies of Gregory VII. Since the work of Joseph A. Endres,[8] Manegold has traditionally been placed among the so-called "anti-dialecticians" — eleventh-century churchmen who denounced what they regarded as the excessive study of philosophy and dialectic

---

[5] For recent literature on the subject, see Jaeger, *The Envy of Angels*, pp. 43–44, 388 n. 15. A helpful summary is provided by H.E.J. Cowdrey, *Pope Gregory VII, 1073–1085* (Oxford: Clarendon Press, 1998), pp. 78–80.

[6] See I.S. Robinson, *Henry IV of Germany (1056–1106)* (Cambridge: Cambridge University Press, 1999), pp. 114–15, 184.

[7] Cited in Cowdrey, *Pope Gregory VII*, p. 311.

[8] See, for example, *Forschungen zur Geschichte der frühmittelalterlichen Philosophie*, Beiträge zur Geschichte der Philosophie des Mittelalters 17.2–3 (Münster: Aschendorff, 1915), pp. 87–113.

in their day. Among them are counted Peter Damian (1007–1072) and Otloh of St. Emmeram (ca. 1010–ca. 1070).[9] Damian ranted,

> I reject Plato, prying into the secrets of hidden nature, ascribing limits to the orbits of the planets, and calculating the movements of the stars. Pythagoras…I count for little. Nichomachus also…I denounce. I likewise turn aside from Euclid…. Finally, all the rhetors with their syllogisms and their sophisticated quibbles, I consider unworthy…. May the simplicity of Christ instruct me….[10]

Otloh, for his part, regretted his study of the philosophers earlier in life: "What then are Socrates, Plato, Aristotle, or even the rhetor Tully himself, the source of worldly teaching, to me? Tell me what use were they earlier to me, a wretch?"[11]

While these sentences strike a chord with passages in the *Liber contra Wolfelmum*, one must note certain features of Manegold's life and work that set him apart from the other "anti-dialecticians," and which, indeed, complicate the traditional image of Manegold as an obscurantist monk railing against secular learning. To begin with, Manegold was not, strictly speaking, a monk; he was a canon regular — a distinction of some importance at the time, for there was serious rivalry between the two orders, as each considered itself to be leading the ideal Christian life more faithfully than the other.[12] The movement of canons regular represented the attempt of the Gregorians to extend their reforming ideals to the secular clergy. By convincing clerics to live according to the rule of St. Augustine, the reformers hoped to bring them together to live in community rather than in private homes; this measure would help enforce priestly celibacy and the renunciation of personal property.[13] Manegold served in the vanguard

---

[9] See Étienne Gilson, *History of Christian Philosophy in the Middle Ages* (London: Sheed and Ward, 1955), pp. 615–16. More recently, see John Marenbon, *Early Medieval Philosophy (480–1150)*, rev. ed. (London and New York: Routledge, 1988), pp. 87–88, 90.

[10] See Irven M. Resnick, "Attitudes towards Philosophy and Dialectic during the Gregorian Reform," *The Journal of Religious History* 16 (1990), pp. 115–25, at 117. I have modified the translation presented by Resnick. For the Latin text, drawn from the *Liber qui appellatur Dominus vobiscum* 1 (PL 145: 232B–33A), see Bolgar, *The Classical Heritage and its Beneficiaries*, pp. 414–15.

[11] Cited in Resnick, "Attitudes towards Philosophy and Dialectic during the Gregorian Reform," p. 117. The text is drawn from Otloh's *De doctrina spirituali* 14 (PL 146: 279B).

[12] Consider, for example, the conflict between the canons regular of Rottenbuch and the Benedictine monks of Schaffhausen in 1096; see Appendix, Texts 7 and 8; see also Texts 16 and 18. For an introductory essay, see Grover A. Zinn, "The Regular Canons," *Christian Spirituality I: Origins to the Twelfth Century*, ed. Bernard McGinn and John Meyendorff with Jean Leclercq, World Spirituality 16 (New York: Crossroad, 1985), pp. 218–28.

[13] See *Augustine through the Ages: An Encyclopedia*, ed. Allan D. Fitzgerald (Grand Rapids, Mich.: William B. Eerdmans, 1999), p. 709; also Charles Dereine, "Chanoines," *Dictionnaire d'histoire et de géographie ecclésiastiques*, ed. Alfred Baudrillart et al., vol. 12 (Paris: Letouzey et Ané, 1953), cols. 353–405.

of this attempt to reform clerical morals. He is credited with co-authoring a supplement to the Augustinian rule that was widely used by canons regular in southern Germany,[14] and his service to the papacy incurred imprisonment at the hands of the emperor.[15]

Manegold is, in fact, further distinguished from the other "anti-dialecticians" by his involvement in the propaganda war that swirled around the Investiture Controversy. Peter Damian and Otloh of St. Emmeram died before Gregory VII was elected pope, and their writings may be regarded to some extent as literary exercises in a traditional genre inspired by patristic literature, rather than evidence of a "real conflict" with an "emerging humanism."[16] As Irven Resnick observes, "The fact that the polemicists attack the philosophers of antiquity rather than named contemporaries…leads one to wonder whether these polemics are more than a conventional literary device."[17] Yet such is clearly not the case with Manegold's *Contra Wolfelmum*; the very title contradicts the notion that he was writing a merely conventional denunciation without a specific, contemporary enemy in mind. In fact, Manegold enables us to identify five of his enemies: Wolfhelm of Cologne (d. 1091); Wenrich of Trier (d. after 1095); Theodoric, the bishop of Verdun (d. 1089); Wibert (or Guibert), the archbishop of Ravenna, who was the antipope Clement III (d. 1100); and Emperor Henry IV (d. 1106). All are denounced in the *Contra Wolfelmum*. The conflict in which Manegold was engaged was undoubtedly very real. It is true that his denunciation follows the form and employs the standard rhetorical strategies of the anti-philosophical genre, yet what Damian and Otloh may have written idly with a vague sense of malaise, Manegold wrote with deadly earnest in a very specific controversy.

A closer look at the circumstances of Manegold's denunciation of the philosophers and their contemporary adherents further calls into question the evaluation of the *Contra Wolfelmum* as an example of formulaic obscurantism. While the root of the Investiture Controversy was the incompatibility between two visions for the governance of Christian society that in a general way reflected the tension between the monasteries and the cathedral schools, there was actually no clear-cut dichotomy between the adversaries at the institutional level. The German emperor, Henry IV (1056–1106), was not without his monastic supporters. In fact, the target of Manegold's polemic, Wolfhelm of Cologne, was almost certainly the Benedictine abbot of

---

[14] See Joseph Siegwart, *Die Consuetudines des Augustiner-Chorherrenstiftes Marbach im Elsass (12. Jahrhundert)*, Spicilegium Friburgense 10 (Freiburg: Universitätsverlag Freiburg, 1965), pp. 18–31.
[15] See below, pp. 16–17.
[16] Resnick, "Attitudes towards Philosophy and Dialectic during the Gregorian Reform," p. 119.
[17] Ibid., p. 124.

Brauweiler (1065–1091).[18] When Manegold denounced Wolfhelm, a canon regular was denouncing a monk. Therefore, Manegold does not represent conservative monasticism airily questioning the value of humanistic studies; he represents a new variety of monasticism, which was committed to reform, questioning the integrity of the old monasticism.

Manegold thought he knew very well what had divided Wolfhelm's loyalties, and by attacking the reading of the philosophers, he was tracing the fault back to the cathedral schools where Wolfhelm had acquired his devotion to classical literature. Wolfhelm had once been a secular master at Cologne;[19] when he became abbot of Brauweiler, he abandoned neither the loyalty to secular government that the cathedral schools inculcated through the study of classical literature, nor the scholastic frame of mind. Manegold identified this scholastic way of thinking as one that was concerned with form rather than content, and with success in disputation rather than truth.[20] He accused the schoolmen of being overly interested in the classical authors and too little concerned with the orthodox interpretation of sacred Scripture.[21] He drew the conclusion, which to modern ears may sound fanciful, that it was precisely the reading of the ancient philosophers that induced Wolfhelm and his associates to oppose the sound teachings of the papacy and to lend their support to the emperor. As I.S. Robinson observes, "Manegold links together two totally different groups of opponents, intending that the reader should regard them as identical: both those who hold the doctrines of the *philosophi* and those who oppose Pope Gregory VII belong to the body of Satan."[22]

Was this linkage merely opportunistic, or did Manegold have some real insight into the political nature of education in the empire? By singling out the reading of the

---

[18] Wilfried Hartmann, "Manegold von Lautenbach und die Anfänge der Frühscholastik," *Deutsches Archiv für Erforschung des Mittelalters* 26 (1970), pp. 47–149, at 60–64. See also *Die deutsche Literatur des Mittelalters: Verfasserlexikon*, ed. Wolfgang Stammler et al., 2nd ed., vol. 10 (Berlin and New York: Walter de Gruyter, 1999), cols. 1367–70.

[19] See Goswin Frencken, "Die Kölner Domschule im Mittelalter," *Der Dom zu Köln: Festschrift zur Feier der 50. Wiederkehr des Tages seiner Vollendung am 15. Oktober 1880*, ed. Erich Kuphal, Veröffentlichungen des kölnischen Geschichtsvereins 5 (Cologne: Creutzer & Co., 1930), pp. 235–56, at 245–47, 256. See also Jaeger, *The Envy of Angels*, pp. 53–54.

[20] See *Contra Wolfelmum*, Chapter 24. See also Peter Godman, *The Silent Masters: Latin Literature and its Censors in the High Middle Ages* (Princeton, N.J.: Princeton University Press, 2000), p. 58.

[21] On the likely distortion inherent in Manegold's accusation of Wolfhelm's scriptural ignorance, see Resnick, "Attitudes towards Philosophy and Dialectic during the Gregorian Reform," pp. 119–21, 124.

[22] I.S. Robinson, "The Bible in the Investiture Contest: The South German Gregorian Circle," *The Bible in the Medieval World: Essays in Memory of Beryl Smalley*, ed. Katherine Walsh and Diana Wood, Studies in Church History, Subsidia 4 (Oxford: Basil Blackwell, 1985), pp. 61–84, at 76–77. Cited in Resnick, "Attitudes towards Philosophy and Dialectic during the Gregorian Reform," p. 122.

philosophers, as practiced "in the manner of the schoolmen," Manegold was attacking the cathedral schools that taught philosophy and produced imperial administrators whose loyalties were secular rather than spiritual. The alumni of the cathedral schools, when they converted to the monastic life, might then carry the habits of their education into the monasteries, corrupting the cloisters with secular values. For Manegold, Wolfhelm embodied this threat. While Manegold's decision to cast the ideologues of the emperor as followers of the misguided pagan philosophers, who did not know Christ, had the advantage of demonizing his enemies through a familiar literary convention, nevertheless his linkage of the philosophers with the enemies of Gregorian reform was not capricious, for it reflected the role that the cathedral schools played in the imperial church system. Thus, it is fair to say that Manegold's attack upon philosophy was "more political than theoretical, intended to stigmatize the political opponents of Gregory VII rather than to attack the arts themselves";[23] moreover, this rhetorical strategy was well grounded in the realities of education and ecclesiastical leadership within the empire.

Manegold's denunciation of the philosophers might be regarded as evidence of a growing and widespread interest in Plato's *Timaeus* (the only Platonic dialogue available in Latin at the time), which was to flower fully during the twelfth-century Renaissance. However, the paucity of sources for this period in the history of the cathedral schools prevents one from drawing any firm conclusions about the intensity with which Platonic texts were being studied.[24] Manegold's *Contra Wolfelmum* proves at least that Macrobius, a Platonist of late antiquity who cites the *Timaeus* at points in his commentary on Cicero's *Dream of Scipio*, was being read in the lands of the empire; how much one can extrapolate from such evidence is a difficult question.[25] It is worth

---

[23] Resnick, "Attitudes towards Philosophy and Dialectic during the Gregorian Reform," p. 116.

[24] See Swanson, *The Twelfth-Century Renaissance*, p. 14. As C. Stephen Jaeger observes in *The Envy of Angels*, p. 176: "The actual nature of *Timaeus* studies in the eleventh century is simply not known. There are many indications of intense interest in the subject but few indications of the results of its study. The discrepancy suggests that at present we do not know what was going on." For an overview of the manuscript evidence, which represents the results of *Timaeus* studies for the medieval period, see Paul Edward Dutton, "Material Remains of the Study of the *Timaeus* in the Later Middle Ages," *L'enseignement de la philosophie au XIIIe siècle: Autour du "Guide de l'étudiant" du ms. Ripoll 109*, ed. Claude Lafleur and Joanne Carrier, Studia artistarum 5 (Turnhout: Brepols, 1997), pp. 203–30. There is a recent, unpublished study that examines the early manuscript evidence: Anna Somfai, *The Transmission and Reception of Plato's Timaeus and Calcidius's Commentary during the Carolingian Renaissance*, Ph.D. thesis, University of Cambridge, 1998.

[25] For a recent study of the medieval reception of Macrobius, see Irene Caiazzo, "Le glosse a Macrobio del Codice Vaticano Lat. 3874: Un testimone delle *formae nativae* nel secolo XII," *Archives d'histoire doctrinale et littéraire du moyen âge* 64 (1997), pp. 213–34, especially p. 214 nn. 1–5 for bibliography. See also her forthcoming edition and study, *Lectures médiévales de Macrobe: Les "Glosae Colonienses super Macrobium"* (Paris: Vrin).

asking in this connection whether Manegold would ever have written a denunciation of the study of Macrobius had it not been for the Investiture Controversy, which provided a reason for him to draw attention to a feature of late eleventh-century education that would otherwise have probably gone unremarked. In all likelihood, the reading of the philosophers was not an uncommon feature of the late eleventh-century schools, and the mere fact of such reading in itself would probably not have precipitated Manegold's denunciation.[26] It was in the specific context of the Investiture Controversy that the reading of the philosophers took on alarming significance for Manegold and compelled him to publish a statement of censure.

According to Manegold's testimony in the opening lines of the *Contra Wolfelmum*, his stimulus to speak out against the study of the philosophers was an argument with Wolfhelm of Cologne in "the gardens of Lautenbach," where they were reading the *Commentary on the Dream of Scipio* by Macrobius, "in the manner of the schoolmen." What alarmed Manegold was Wolfhelm's contention that the philosophy of Macrobius did not contradict the Christian faith and that a Christian could endorse its doctrines in good conscience. Manegold did not object to the reading of Macrobius, but rather to the thesis that the Platonic philosophy found in Macrobius could be used to inform Christian theology. The *Contra Wolfelmum* is a detailed refutation of specific doctrines drawn from Macrobius that contradict the central tenets of the Christian religion; the fundamental error that Manegold denounces is the attempt to combine philosophy and theology in a vital union. He calls attention to the third-century theologian, Origen of Alexandria, whom he depicts as a tragic figure: Origen had written numerous texts to the glory of the Church but was eventually snared by the "mousetrap" of philosophy, which led him into heresy.[27] If a great theologian of antiquity had been ruined in the attempt to make Christian sense of pagan error, how could Wolfhelm think he might escape a similar fate?

It seems that Manegold made the connection between the reading of the philosophers and the struggle between pope and emperor only after his encounter with Wolfhelm. The circumstances of their meeting are regrettably unclear. It seems odd that Manegold should have had anything to do with Wolfhelm had he known that his interlocutor was a supporter of the emperor rather than the pope; perhaps it was during the discussion of Macrobius at Lautenbach that Manegold discovered Wolfhelm's political alignment. However and whenever Manegold made this discovery, it is clear

---

[26] Manegold allows that the philosophers are worth reading, since ignorance is not a virtue, but he insists that one must be careful not to accept doctrines that contradict Christian teaching. See *Contra Wolfelmum*, Chapters 1, 5, 8, 10, and 22.
[27] *Contra Wolfelmum*, Chapter 6.

that his enmity toward the philosophers was, in the larger scheme of his concerns, not the central feature of his thought. He had already been working on a massive statement in defense of Gregory VII, known as the *Liber ad Gebehardum*, in which the denunciation of the philosophers is not a significant theme; it is thought that Manegold's progress on the *Ad Gebehardum* was interrupted by the altercation with Wolfhelm.[28] Only at that juncture did it apparently dawn on Manegold that there was an insidious connection between the reading of the philosophers and the rejection of papal authority in the strife that had divided Christendom, and this flash of insight so startled him that he momentarily abandoned his work on the *Ad Gebehardum* in order to make others aware of his discovery.

Manegold's sudden awareness that the reading of the philosophers could have unfortunate spiritual consequences may have troubled him all the more because it appears that he himself had once lectured on the philosophers in the schools, before his conversion to the religious life. The evidence for this conclusion is not as unambiguous as one would hope, but the thesis is nevertheless extremely plausible. The style of the *Contra Wolfelmum* in itself suggests the manner of scholastic disputation that Manegold denounces,[29] and his familiarity with the doctrines of the ancient philosophers also suggests that he had once read them intensively; furthermore, he admits in the opening lines of the *Contra Wolfelmum* that he was skilled in reading the philosophers "in the manner of the schoolmen." A letter by Ivo of Chartres, which is addressed to a religious named Manegold and which probably refers to the Gregorian polemicist,[30] reveals that Manegold had entered the cloister after treading "many winding paths," and that during his earlier career he had "given birth to sons beneath the slavish yoke of philosophy."[31] Another source calls Manegold the "master of the modern masters."[32] There is additional evidence as well which identifies a renowned teacher named Manegold and which possibly applies to Manegold of Lautenbach.[33] Although Wilfried

---

[28] See below, p. 18.

[29] See Godman, *The Silent Masters*, p. 58; Wilfried Hartmann, "Rhetorik und Dialektik in der Streitschriftlichenliteratur des 11./12. Jahrhunderts," *Dialektik und Rhetorik im früheren und hohen Mittelalter: Rezeption, Überlieferung und gesellschaftliche Wirkung antiker Gelehrsamkeit vornehmlich im 9. und 12. Jahrhundert*, ed. Johannes Fried, Schriften des Historischen Kollegs, Kolloquien 27 (Munich: R. Oldenbourg, 1997), pp. 73–95, at 85. For the presence of scholastic methodology in Manegold's *Liber ad Gebehardum*, see Hartmann, "Manegold von Lautenbach und die Anfänge der Frühscholastik," pp. 123–38.

[30] The question at issue is whether all references to a famous teacher named Manegold who lived in the late eleventh century actually point to a single individual, or whether there might not have been two distinguished figures with this name. See below, pp. 24–25, 28–29.

[31] See Appendix, Text 5.

[32] See Appendix, Text 23.

[33] See below, pp. 23–27.

Hartmann, the most recent editor of the *Contra Wolfelmum*, does not think that certainty in this matter is possible, he is inclined to believe that Manegold had indeed been a teacher in the schools before he became a canon regular, and that the *Contra Wolfelmum* can be seen as a denunciation of his own former career.[34] More recently, this thesis has been accepted by Peter Godman, who writes, "The zeal of the convert lies behind Manegold's fulminations…. Attacking the excesses of the *philosophi* in their dealings with questions of the faith, this repentant teacher of philosophy drew on the example of Peter Damian to attack his former self."[35]

If this interpretation of the *Contra Wolfelmum* is correct, as seems likely, then Manegold was anxious to undo some of the harm he thought he may have inflicted upon his former students. The conflict between Manegold and Wolfhelm thus touches upon the question of the attitude that former schoolmen should have toward secular education after leaving the world for the cloister. The careers of Wolfhelm and Manegold contradict Peter Damian's complaint that the cloisters were emptying because monks were eager for disputation in the schools. There was clearly a movement in the opposite direction as well.[36] This retirement of secular masters into the monastic houses raised the problem that the character of monasticism would be transmuted by their influx. As the *Contra Wolfelmum* clearly indicates, Macrobius was being read not just in the schools, but in the cloisters as well; while the monasteries were not beholden to the cathedral schools for their knowledge of Macrobius, their reading of that author would have been influenced by monks who had formerly been schoolmen. Both Wolfhelm and Manegold were the heads of their respective communities, strongly influencing the character of life in the houses they governed. We know that Manegold continued to teach after he became a canon regular; what the content of his teaching was is not certain, but it is not unlikely that he continued to lecture on the classical texts as well as the Bible. Wolfhelm would presumably have done the same. The difference between them was, in Manegold's view, how each attended to the context in which the philosophers were read. Whereas Wolfhelm (according to Manegold's admittedly hostile testimony) recognized the ancient philosophers as authorities in their own right, Manegold insisted they could safely be read only if one continually recalled that they represented human reason's feeble attempts to understand truth before revelation made the truth manifest. Whenever

---

[34] See Hartmann, "Manegold von Lautenbach und die Anfänge der Frühscholastik," pp. 147–49.
[35] Peter Godman, *The Silent Masters*, p. 57. See also p. 348: "…Peter Damian, Manegold of Lautenbach, and John of Salisbury directed their most vehement abuse against their former selves…." Irven Resnick has likewise accepted the thesis that the *Contra Wolfelmum* constitutes an attack by the author on his earlier career; see "Attitudes towards Philosophy and Dialectic during the Gregorian Reform," p. 125.
[36] See Resnick, ibid., pp. 121–22.

philosophical speculation conflicted with Christian wisdom, it was necessary to reject the former.[37] In cases of uncertainty, one could look to the judgment of the pope, who was the highest authority in the Church and the final arbiter of orthodoxy. It was because Wolfhelm read the philosophers outside this context that he fell into error.

Where precisely Manegold taught over the course of his career is a debatable matter. It is certain that he gave instruction to the community of canons regular at the priory of Marbach, in Alsace, during the 1090s.[38] Teaching was presumably also among his responsibilities when he served as the dean of the canons regular at Rottenbuch, in Bavaria, during the 1080s.[39] Previous to this, Manegold's career is shrouded in obscurity. His status at Lautenbach is not known, nor can one surmise when he joined the community there. If the letter by Ivo of Chartres, noted above, applies to Manegold of Lautenbach, it is conceivable that he had once taught as far afield as northern France, where he would presumably have made Ivo's acquaintance. Modern scholarship has often associated Manegold with the school of Laon and with the school of St. Victor outside Paris, under the assumption that Manegold had been the teacher of Anselm of Laon and William of Champeaux; however, the evidence for this is too ambiguous to allow any firm conclusions.[40] Indeed, Manegold's reputation as a founding figure in the scholastic movement is based on ambiguous external evidence rather than on his own treatises, one of which denounces rather than approves the application of philosophy and dialectic to the study of theology. The fragmentary references regarded by some as evidence that Manegold had once been a wandering scholar in northern France, before he settled down to the life of the cloister in Alsace, is tantalizing but nothing more.[41] On the whole, one enjoys complete confidence only when situating Manegold on the borders of the German empire rather than in northern France, and in the Investiture Controversy rather than the scholastic movement.

---

[37] See *Contra Wolfelmum*, Chapter 5.
[38] See Appendix, Text 11.
[39] See Appendix, Text 16.
[40] See Appendix, Text 13; see also pp. 25–26, below. On Manegold's connection to the School of Laon, see Hartmann, "Manegold von Lautenbach und die Anfänge der Frühscholastik," pp. 85–110. On his reputation as the teacher of William of Champeaux, see ibid., pp. 48–49, 51. Hartmann concludes at the end of his study that Manegold was indeed a significant figure during the period of scholastic origins, but that his connection to the school of Laon is doubtful; see ibid., p. 149.
[41] See below, pp. 25–27.

2. MANEGOLD'S WORKS AND IDEAS

Only two of Manegold's works can be identified with certainty, both of which are polemical treatises written during the Investiture Controversy: the *Liber contra Wolfelmum* and the *Liber ad Gebehardum*.[42] The supplement to the Rule of Augustine known as the *Consuetudines Marbacenses*, or Marbach customal, is also thought to be inspired largely by Manegold, who was the first prior at Marbach; yet it is not certain how much of this guide for canons regular is Manegold's and how much is the work of his successor, Gerung. Several commentaries on biblical and classical texts have been attributed to Manegold. On the authority of a twelfth-century catalogue of ecclesiastical authors, Manegold is thought to have written brief glosses on Isaiah and full-length commentaries on the Psalms and the Gospel of Matthew.[43] While none of these texts has been identified with absolute certainty, there are reasons to believe that an extant commentary on the Psalms known under the name of "Pseudo-Bede" is in fact Manegold's. It is uncertain whether the commentary on the Apocalypse by a certain "Master Manegold" is the work of Manegold of Lautenbach. Marginal glosses in manuscripts that refer to the opinions of a certain "Manegold" have prompted some to conclude that the polemicist also wrote commentaries on the Pauline epistles. Similar stray references have been taken as evidence that Manegold commented on Ovid's *Metamorphoses*, Horace's *Ars poetica*, Priscian's *Institutiones grammaticae*, Cicero's *De inventione*, Boethius's *De consolatione philosophiae*, and Plato's *Timaeus*; yet there remains much uncertainty in these attributions.

With regard to the polemical works, we must consider the question of Manegold's audience. As with most polemical literature, the principal audience would not have been the enemy, whose intransigence could hardly be swayed with bitter words of denunciation, but rather the undecided bystanders and those who already shared the author's position, and who for purposes of morale could appreciate arguments backed up by authoritative sources that confirmed the rightness of their cause. This assumption is supported by the testimony of the canon regular Gerhoh of Reichersberg, writing in the year 1131, who identifies exiled bishops and canons regular at Rottenbuch among the most avid readers of the *Ad Gebehardum*.[44] Indeed, the prologue to the *Ad Gebehardum* is addressed to a stalwart ally — Gebhard, the archbishop of Salzburg (d. 1088) — rather than the enemies whose pamphlet provoked Manegold's response, namely, Wenrich of Trier and Theodoric, the bishop of Verdun. The *Contra Wolfelmum*,

---

[42] See the Bibliographical Essay for scholarship on all the works mentioned in this paragraph.

[43] See Appendix, Text 23.

[44] See Appendix, Text 16.

on the other hand, is consistently addressed to the enemy — usually to Wolfhelm of Cologne, but also at times to his fellow imperial supporters; yet the main purpose of the text was probably to alert "the less-informed" (*minus intelligentes*), who might be led astray by the specious reasoning of Wolfhelm and company.[45] It is true that Manegold claims to have written the text in the hope of persuading Wolfhelm to see the error of his ways, but it is doubtful that he sincerely thought Wolfhelm could still be persuaded; his invitation to Wolfhelm's repentence is likely to have been nothing more than a rhetorical ploy intended to win the favor of his wider audience by a display of magnanimous concern. Both the *Contra Wolfelmum* and the *Ad Gebehardum* do not seem to have been read very widely, or for very long after the controversy had been more or less settled at Worms in 1122.[46] They are extant in one manuscript apiece, each copied in the twelfth century. The *Ad Gebehardum* was copied at the Benedictine monastery of St. John in Blaubeuren.[47] The manuscript containing the *Contra Wolfelmum* was probably copied at the Augustinian priory of Saints Rufus and Andrew at Avignon.[48] It appears that Manegold's works were known not only by his allies, but also by his enemies, for a late eleventh-century poem hostile to Manegold echoes his ideas in derision,[49] and Gerhoh of Reichersberg draws attention to a secular cleric of the following generation who expressed the hope that the *Ad Gebehardum* had been buried along with its author.[50]

The *Contra Wolfelmum*, as it is preserved in its twelfth-century manuscript, consists of a prologue, table of contents, and twenty-four chapters. Thematically, the work can be divided into three main parts. The prologue and Chapters 1–10 constitute the main attack against the philosophers, with Chapter 22 as a reprise of this theme. Chapters 11–21 present an outline of salvation history, for the sake of correcting Wolfhelm's theological errors, which serves as a statement of Manegold's own cherished beliefs. Chapters 23–24 set the polemic within the context of the Investiture Controversy, as foreshadowed in the prologue and Chapter 1.

---

[45] See *Contra Wolfelmum*, Chapter 24.

[46] On the settlement at Worms, see Uta-Renate Blumenthal, *The Investiture Controversy: Church and Monarchy from the Ninth to the Twelfth Century*, Middle Ages Series (Philadelphia, Penn.: University of Pennsylvania Press, 1988), pp. 172–73.

[47] The manuscript is Karlsruhe, Badische Landesbibliothek, MS. Rastatt 27 (formerly Codex 93), fols. 1r–102v. For additional information, see the Bibliographical Essay.

[48] The manuscript is Milan, Biblioteca Ambrosiana, MS. N 118 sup., fols. 117r–134r. For additional information, see the Bibliographical Essay.

[49] See Appendix, Text 9.

[50] See Appendix, Text 16.

In the specifically anti-philosophical chapters, Manegold singles out several errors that all Christians must unequivocally reject: the transmigration of souls, which contradicts the resurrection of the dead (Chapters 1 and 22); the world-soul (Chapter 2); the idea that the human soul is a natural force rather than a supernatural entity that is destined for eternal life in the kingdom of heaven (Chapter 3); the existence of the Antipodes, which implies that there are inhabitants on the far side of the earth who cannot be saved because a torrid zone at the equator prevents missionaries from extending the message of salvation to them (Chapter 4); creation from eternal, preexistent matter rather than creation *ex nihilo* (Chapter 8); and the Neoplatonic schematization of the divine Trinity as a hierarchy of essences rather than one God in three equal and co-eternal persons (Chapters 6, 8, and 11).[51] Manegold judges that reliance on fallible human reason is the source of schism, for the devil takes advantage of human ignorance to delude people into thinking that they are pursuing wisdom even while they wander the paths of error. Hence, anyone who follows one's own reason will inevitably end up following the devil, the arch-deceiver who conceals his true identity under the mantle of reason and virtue (Chapter 9). Only the sure guidance of authority, which comes from God, can offer protection against the devil's superhuman wiles (Chapter 5).

Since Manegold objected that Wolfhelm either neglected Scripture or read it without understanding its meaning, he includes a long section, amounting to about half the work, as a synopsis of the Bible, with running commentary to reveal its inner meaning. This capsule of salvation history can be seen as an extended rhetorical insult to Wolfhelm, who in Manegold's conceit is so ignorant that he must be taught the basic tenets of the Christian faith; it also serves as Manegold's theological statement. Beginning with God and creation (Chapter 11), Manegold proceeds with the Christian interpretation of the Old Testament (Chapters 12–13), and dwells at length on the lessons of the New Testament (Chapters 14–21). The discussion is only infrequently punctuated by appeals to Wolfhelm, and by the occasional reminder of the dangers of philosophy.

The last thematic section is in two parts, and here Manegold addresses not only Wolfhelm, but the other enemies of Gregory VII as well. Chapter 23 reviews the history of the Investiture Controversy, and Chapter 24 draws attention to the propaganda war. It is in the last chapter that Manegold announces his intention to publish the *Ad Gebehardum* in the near future. While the last two chapters are valuable for setting the anti-philosophical polemic within the context of the Investiture Controversy, they do not reveal much of Manegold's political theory or other vital opinions pertaining to the central issues of the controversy. These are developed at length in the *Ad Gebehardum*.

---

[51] Cf. I.S. Robinson, "The Bible in the Investiture Contest," p. 76.

Manegold's central concern throughout the *Contra Wolfelmum* is the soul. In the prologue, Manegold depicts himself as a doctor of souls, and Wolfhelm as an ailing patient.
Chapters 1–3 review the philosophers' errors concerning the soul; Chapter 22 revisits
the theme, but from the perspective of the soul's counterpart, the body. The rejection of
the doctrine of the Antipodes in Chapter 4 is likewise motivated by his concern for the
salvation of souls. It should be noted that Manegold does not reject the cosmological
proposition that the earth is spherical, but only the idea that Christian missionaries
might not be able to reach inhabitants on the other side of the globe because the equa-
torial torrid zone, according to Macrobius, would prevent them. In addition to the
emphasis in the above-mentioned chapters, the concept of the soul in need of salvation
resonates throughout the treatise as its leitmotiv (see especially Chapter 16). The only
other concepts of comparable vitality are Manegold's abhorence of schism and his insistence on obedience to the apostolic authority of Rome.

Manegold singled out the philosophers' doctrines on the soul as the most objectionable of their errors because the soul was the very focus of the Church's mission in
the world. He attacked the various philosophical definitions of the soul and did not
attempt to define it himself.[52] For Manegold, the soul was not an entity to be
defined, but a mystery at the heart of the drama of salvation, the ineffable basis of
personal identity that would endure forever, in heaven or in hell. The closest Manegold came to defining the soul was in acknowledging that Plato was near the mark
when he defined it as "an essence that moves itself." Manegold presumably understood the Platonic definition in reference to freedom of will, since the soul is an
entity that makes its own moral choices. Thus, Manegold's views on the soul were
incommensurable with the philosophical mentality that the schools endorsed, for
whereas they attended to the soul's ontology, Manegold's concern was wholly deon-
tological — moral rather than scientific. As Manegold saw it, the schoolmen and the
monks who had not abandoned the scholastic mentality were content to define and
demystify the soul in the most idle fashion while failing to realize that it was on the
level of the soul that the struggle between empire and papacy was being waged. The
soul was either an indefinable mystery, or it was defined by the individual's moral
choices. As an Augustinian canon, Manegold had dedicated his life to the care of
souls, and his earnestness in this vocation impelled him to exercise his ministry
beyond the confines of the cloister by engaging in the war of words. The *Contra
Wolfelmum* represents the opening statement of the best-documented period of
Manegold's life, which remains for us to consider.

---

[52] *Contra Wolfelmum*, Chapter 3.

3. GREGORIAN POLEMICIST AND CANON REGULAR

Owing to the ambiguous and fragmentary character of most of the sources for Manegold's biography, much that has been written about him in modern scholarship is unreliable, as some historians have taken liberties in order to form a coherent picture that includes all possible evidence[53] and others have uncritically repeated them.[54] Attempts to correct the errors of earlier scholarship have not always been salutary.[55] Manegold remains "exasperatingly mysterious."[56] Given the uneven state of the scholarship, it will be worthwhile here to review the sources on which a reconstruction of Manegold's biography must be based and to evaluate their reliability. This endeavor will separate what is certain from what must remain conjectural. To facilitate the task, I have prepared a dossier of sources in translation, arranged and numbered in chronological order, in the Appendix. In the notes to the pages that follow, I shall refer to these texts as numbered in the dossier, where one will find full bibliographical references.

The dates of Manegold's birth and death are unknown; his career can be outlined for approximately eighteen years of his life — from about 1085 to 1103. The first of these limits is drawn from the internal evidence of the *Contra Wolfelmum*, wherein Manegold speaks of Pope Gregory VII as one deceased; it is known that Gregory died on 25 May 1085.[57] The other limit is based on a letter of Pope Paschal II, dated 2 August 1103, which identifies Manegold as the prior of a house of canons regular at Marbach, in Alsace;[58] it repeats the privilege of papal protection that had been extended to Marbach by Pope Urban II on 24 March 1096, when Manegold attended the council of Tours.[59] This privilege was later renewed by Pope Calixtus II (1119–1124), but in his letter of

---

[53] Numerous errors can be traced back to the Maurists; see *Histoire littéraire de la France* 9 (1750; repr. Paris: Victor Palmé, 1868), pp. 280–90. One must also exercise caution when consulting Philippe André Grandidier, *Œuvres historiques inédits*, ed. J. Liblin, vol. 2 (Colmar: Revue d'Alsace, 1865), pp. 256–86.

[54] A particularly uncritical recent study of Manegold's life is found in Charles Haaby, *Stift Lautenbach*, Alsatia Monastica: Forschungen herausgegeben von der Gesellschaft für Elsässische Kirchengeschichte zu Strassburg 2 (Kevelaer: Butzon & Bercker, 1958), pp. 22–38.

[55] A reasonably good critical study that is marred by unfortunate faults, such as assuming the conclusion it purports to prove and inadequately citing its sources, is François Châtillon, "Recherches critiques sur les différents personnages nommés Manegold," *Revue du moyen âge latin* 9 (1953), pp. 153–70. The best and most thorough recent study is Wilfried Hartmann, "Manegold von Lautenbach und die Anfänge der Frühscholastik" (see above, n. 18). For additional sources, see the Bibliographical Essay.

[56] Beryl Smalley, *The Study of the Bible in the Middle Ages* (Oxford: Basil Blackwell & Mott, 1952), p. 48.

[57] See *Contra Wolfelmum*, Chapters 23–24 (Text 3 in the Appendix).

[58] See Appendix, Text 12.

[59] See Appendix, Text 6; see also Text 7.

30 October 1119, Calixtus identifies the prior as Gerung, who was Manegold's successor; thus we can conclude that Manegold was no longer alive by that time.[60]

The chronicler Bernold of Constance (d. 16 September 1100), who also wrote polemical treatises in support of the Gregorian cause, and whose writings were in fact used by Manegold,[61] mentions that "Master Manegold of Lautenbach" joined the canons regular at Marbach in the year 1094.[62] His report was repeated in the *Annales Marbacenses* (the annals of Marbach, written ca. 1210),[63] which modified Bernold's account by noting that it was in the year 1094 that construction of the canons' cloister was begun, but that Manegold was already present at Marbach when its church was founded in 1090.[64] Although the *Annales Marbacenses* was written over a century after these events, it was based on sources written earlier; certainly much of the information on Manegold is drawn from Bernold's chronicle (or a source that drew upon Bernold's chronicle), since the two texts correspond at several points verbatim. However, the sources that supplemented Bernold's account are no longer extant.[65]

As these most reliable of sources for Manegold's biography show, the best-documented period of his life was dominated by his service to the papacy and his involvement in the movement of canons regular, which the Gregorians fostered for the purpose of reforming clerical morals.[66] Bernold's chronicle in fact focuses on Manegold's success in winning back Alsace to communion with the Roman Church in the year 1094. Bernold also reports that Manegold's devotion to the papal cause led to his imprisonment in 1098, when he fell into the hands of Henry IV. This report is repeated in the *Annales Marbacenses*, but the later source is no more explicit than Bernold in disclosing the circumstances that led to Manegold's captivity, nor does it relate how long Manegold was held prisoner. In fact, the *Annales Marbacenses* is less precise, for it telescopes the events of 1094 and 1098 (as reported by Bernold) into a single introductory entry for the year 1090. Since Bernold describes the imprisonment as a past event, rather than an ongoing one, when he presents it in his entry for the year

---

[60] See Appendix, Text 15.

[61] See Kuno Francke, MGH Ldl 1: 302; specific instances are noted in the source apparatus to the edition of the *Liber ad Gebehardum*, ibid., pp. 308–430.

[62] See Appendix, Text 11.

[63] See Appendix, Text 24.

[64] Another source, the *Codex Guta-Sintram*, provides evidence that the community at Marbach was actually founded in 1089. See Appendix, p. 132 n. 170.

[65] Note that the *Annales Argentinenses* (annals of Strasbourg), which was once considered to be a source for the *Annales Marbacenses*, is now recognized as an eighteenth-century forgery; see Appendix, Text 31. Another late source that is supposedly based on earlier texts no longer available is a report of the founding of Marbach by Heinrich Elten, prior of Marbach from 1508 to 1518; see Appendix, Text 30.

[66] See *Augustine through the Ages*, ed. Allan D. Fitzgerald, p. 709.

1098, it would be fair to suppose that "a long time" was a matter of several months, and that Manegold was free by the end of the year. A poem by an author styling himself "Hugh the Orthodox" taunts Manegold for having hurt himself with his own sword when he set his pen in defense of Gregory VII. The poem seems to have been occasioned by Manegold's imprisonment, since Hugh chides Manegold for complaining against the loving embrace of his "mother," who wants to save him from the delusions of the heresiarch Hildebrand (that is, Gregory VII). The "mother" is presumably the German Church that remained faithful to Henry IV, and the loving embrace is presumably Manegold's detention by the emperor; yet the poem is fraught with ambiguity, and the date of its composition is unknown.[67] A report by the canon regular Arno of Reichersberg ca. 1146 also mentions Manegold's imprisonment without dating the event.[68] In any case, Manegold was free by 2 August 1103, since Pope Paschal II's letter of that date locates him at Marbach.

A drawback of the foregoing evidence is that none of it mentions Manegold's *Liber contra Wolfelmum*, nor its companion, the *Liber ad Gebehardum*. These two texts are certainly the work of Manegold of Lautenbach, for the manuscript of the *Ad Gebehardum* identifies the author by his full name,[69] and the opening sentence of the *Contra Wolfelmum* associates its author with Lautenbach, even though the title identifies him simply as "Master Manegold."[70] Moreover, the two texts are linked to one another by internal evidence. In the last chapter of the *Contra Wolfelmum*, Manegold denounces the anti-Gregorian pamphlet written by Wenrich of Trier[71] and asserts that he has resolved to publish a reply. Manegold's reply was in fact the *Ad Gebehardum*, as its prologue makes clear.[72]

While the *Contra Wolfelmum* itself serves as the earliest certain evidence for Manegold's biography,[73] and the *Ad Gebehardum* also furnishes some historical information, Manegold's autobiographical remarks actually do very little to clarify where he wrote

---

[67] See Appendix, Text 9.

[68] See Appendix, Text 18.

[69] "Liber Manegoldi de Lutinbach." See Francke, MGH Ldl 1: 302.

[70] The full title of the text is "Liber Magistri Manegaldi contra Wolfelmum Coloniensem." See Manegold von Lautenbach, *Liber contra Wolfelmum*, ed. Wilfried Hartmann, MGH Quellen zur Geistesgeschichte 8 (Weimar: Hermann Böhlaus Nachfolger, 1972), p. 39.

[71] Wenrich's pamphlet is printed in MGH Ldl 1: 280–99. It is believed to have been written in the latter half of 1080 or the earlier half of 1081; see Francke, MGH Ldl 1: 284, 302; see also *Die deutsche Literatur des Mittelalters: Verfasserlexikon*, 2nd ed., vol. 10 (1998), cols. 1219–24, at 1221–22.

[72] Compare Texts 3 and 4 in the Appendix.

[73] A letter by Bernold of Constance which mentions a "brother Manegold" may be earlier, but the letter cannot be dated precisely, and it is not certain that the figure in question is Manegold of Lautenbach. See Appendix, Text 2.

the texts or what he was doing previous to his life at Marbach. Furthermore, the historical evidence provided by the two texts is not without its problems. For example, it would be a simple matter to conclude that the *Ad Gebehardum* was written after the *Contra Wolfelmum*, but for the fact that a few passages in the *Ad Gebehardum* clearly indicate that Gregory VII is still alive,[74] whereas the *Contra Wolfelmum* indicates that he is dead.[75] Furthermore, Manegold's stated intention in the *Contra Wolfelmum* of replying to the anti-Gregorian pamphlet "more quickly" (*velocius*) suggests that he had previously been working on a reply, but had not yet completed it. The best explanation for the seeming contradiction, then, is to suppose that Manegold had been working for some time on the massive *Ad Gebehardum*, that he was then interrupted soon after the middle of 1085 by the need to write the *Contra Wolfelmum*, and that he finally returned to finish the *Ad Gebehardum* with more haste than before.[76]

Unfortunately, Manegold intimates none of these details in his prologue to the *Ad Gebehardum*, where he mentions Gregory only once by name and alludes to him as the "apostolic bishop" in his summary of Wenrich's pamphlet.[77] Neither instance, however, indicates whether Gregory was still alive. In many ways this prologue is a singularly unsatisfying and troublesome text. It seems likely that it was the last portion of the *Ad Gebehardum* to be composed (since Manegold provides in it an overview of the book's contents, written in the past tense) and would therefore postdate the *Contra Wolfelmum*.[78] However, Manegold does not mention Wolfhelm here, nor does he specifically state that his composition of the *Ad Gebehardum* was interrupted, although his complaints about the adverse conditions under which the book was written are in accord with this hypothesis. Apart from the crucial references to "Wenrich, master at the school of Trier," and "the bishop of Verdun," who commissioned Wenrich's pamphlet,

[74] The best example is *Liber ad Gebehardum* 44, MGH Ldl 1, p. 387, line 33, to p. 388, line 6. For additional passages, see Francke's introduction, MGH Ldl 1: 301 n. 5.

[75] See *Contra Wolfelmum*, Chapter 23 (ed. Hartmann, p. 102, lines 14–19), and especially Chapter 24 (ibid., p. 107, line 20, to p. 108, line 16).

[76] This hypothesis was first made by Paul Ewald, "Chronologie der Schriften Manegolds von Lautenbach," *Forschungen zur deutschen Geschichte* 16 (1876), pp. 383–85. It has since won general acceptance. See Francke, MGH Ldl 1: 301–02; *Contra Wolfelmum*, ed. Hartmann, p. 13; Horst Fuhrmann, "'Volkssouveranität' und 'Herrschaftsvertrag' bei Manegold von Lautenbach," *Festschrift für Hermann Krause*, ed. Sten Gagnér, Hans Schlosser, and Wolfgang Wiegand (Cologne and Vienna: Böhlau, 1975), pp. 21–42, at 28 n. 15. Francke suggests that the original ending of the *Ad Gebehardum*, which may have mentioned Gregory's death, has been lost (see MGH Ldl 1: 302 n. 2); certainly the *Ad Gebehardum* ends rather abruptly, without a peroration comparable to the one in the *Contra Wolfelmum*.

[77] See Appendix, Text 4. Note, however, that I have not translated the portion of the prologue in which Manegold refers to "our Gregory."

[78] See *Contra Wolfelmum*, ed. Hartmann, p. 13.

the prologue is a model exercise in ambiguity — and also in rhetorical excess. Manegold's belabored self-abasement is taken to such lengths that it verges on self-parody.
He likewise protests overmuch when he explains that it was only at the instigation of
his prior and his brothers that he undertook the writing at all. In his hands this common literary conceit takes on a bizarre form: Manegold depicts himself as raising such
a scene in his attempt to avoid the task enjoined upon him that he and his brothers
were all forcibly ejected from the monastery where they were staying as guests.
Throughout the prologue, Manegold insists that he is wholly unequal to the task. Yet
in all of this, his rhetorical strategy is transparent: "it would…be more glorious for the
Church and more humbling for her adversaries if a youth, and one who is almost
entirely ignorant, should put their vain assertions to rout."[79] Even a young ignoramus
could refute the arguments of the anti-Gregorians.

The entire prologue is calculated to convince readers that it is not Manegold who
speaks, but the apostolic tradition that speaks through him. Indeed, the *Ad Gebehardum* is largely a collection of source-material.[80] Argument from authority is central
to its design, and much of the text simply reproduces the authoritative sources at
length. Nevertheless, Manegold's insistence upon the negligibility of his authorial con-
tribution is excessive. His self-accusation of dire ignorance is contradicted by the
rhetorical sophistication of the prologue and by the seventy-seven chapters of the *Ad
Gebehardum* that follow, and also by the evidence of the historical record external to
the text. For, as Bernold of Constance indicates in his chronicle, Manegold was teaching the canons at Marbach in less than ten years' time; and before that he was already
the dean at Rottenbuch, where his duties presumably involved teaching.[81] What then
are we to make of Manegold's assertion of his youth? Was he in fact a young man in
the 1080s when he wrote the *Ad Gebehardum*, as he avers, or did he lie about his age
for rhetorical effect?

This question has been an important one in biographical studies of Manegold, for
how one interprets Manegold's remarks about his youth will determine how one interprets the ambiguous sources for his early career. It is worth noting that Manegold's
Contra Wolfelmum says nothing about his age and entirely lacks the egregious self-dep-
recation that pervades the prologue to the *Ad Gebehardum*. The *Contra Wolfelmum*
gives the impression that Manegold is a free agent, unbeholden to any officious prior
and cohort of fellow religious who would impel his actions; he exudes the confident
bearing of a master who has taken upon himself the refutation of an erring colleague

---

[79] See Appendix, Text 4, p. 110.
[80] Hartmann, "Manegold von Lautenbach und die Anfänge der Frühscholastik," p. 57.
[81] See pp. 10, 23.

and who, without external compulsion, has determined to respond to the propaganda circulated by the enemy. The disparity in tone, then, seems to be the result of rhetorical distortion. It is not entirely clear why Manegold would have followed such different strategies in two works that were written so closely together, yet it may have been a question of the different audiences that he anticipated. The *Ad Gebehardum* appeals to a dignitary who represents the sensibilities of a fairly broad audience, one that could appreciate argument from authority in matters of church governance.[82] For such readers, it was appropriate that Manegold should minimize his own authoritative voice and assume the persona of an ignorant youth who could barely read or write — yet one who could read well enough to grasp the lessons of authority and write well enough to transcribe those lessons in order to pass them on to others. The *Contra Wolfelmum*, however, was aimed at a narrower audience of intellectuals, men who were accustomed to dispute about abstract concepts, who were sensitive to the problematic nature of argument from authority, who indeed even claimed to regard Macrobius as an authority greater than the Bible in certain matters. For such an audience it would be useless to adopt a self-abasing attitude and the persona of callow youth when it was the authoritative voice of a learned master, indeed a colleague, that alone could demand attention and respect.

It remains for us to determine when and where Manegold wrote the two texts. Although we cannot be certain how long after Gregory VII's death the *Contra Wolfelmum* was written, an argument from silence on this question is admissible. Manegold does not indicate the identity of the rightful pope, even though he twice names the antipope, Wibert of Ravenna.[83] One reasonably assumes that Manegold would not have kept silent about the true apostolic successor, had he known his identity. The fact of the matter is that, apart from Wibert's claim to the leadership of the Church as Clement III, the papacy was vacant for a period of twelve months after Gregory's death; it was only on 24 May 1086 that Desiderius, the abbot of Monte Cassino, was elected pope and took the name Victor III. In all likelihood, then, the *Contra Wolfelmum* was written during this period of vacancy (allowances being made for the travel of news). Since it is a brief text, it could have been composed fairly quickly.[84]

The same cannot be said of the *Ad Gebehardum*. This lengthy text, which relies heavily on the citation of canonical sources, required a well-stocked library for its

---

[82] See above, pp. 11–12.

[83] *Contra Wolfelmum* 23, ed. Hartmann, p. 99, line 21, and p. 102, line 13.

[84] See Wilhelm von Giesebrecht, "Ueber Magister Manegold von Lautenbach und seine Schrift gegen den Scholasticus Wenrich," *Sitzungsberichte der königlich-bayerischen Akademie der Wissenschaften zu München*, Jahrgang 1868, Band 2 (Munich: Akademische Buchdruckerei von F. Straub), pp. 297–330, at 304 n. 10.

production. Manegold asserts that he would gladly have adduced far more examples from authoritative sources if only he could have gained access to libraries located in cities that were barred to the Gregorian party by the emperor's forces. Manegold must have written the *Ad Gebehardum* within an eight-year period, between the composition of Wenrich's pamphlet in 1080/1081 and the death of the text's namesake, Gebhard, the archbishop of Salzburg, in 1088.[85]

The question of where Manegold was at the time he composed these two texts is more difficult to answer, and it is complicated by the question of where the disputation with Wolfhelm of Cologne took place. In the opening sentence of the *Contra Wolfelmum*, Manegold refers to "the gardens of Lautenbach" as the setting of the confrontation, but this reference raises problems that cannot be resolved. It is generally accepted that Manegold's adversary must have been a certain Benedictine abbot named Wolfhelm (d. 1091), who was once a master at the cathedral school of Cologne, before his appointment in 1065 to a monastery not far from the city, at Brauweiler. There is little reason to doubt the accuracy of this identification, for Wolfhelm of Brauweiler is known to have sympathized with the imperial party and, as a former teacher from Cologne, he would have been familiar with the writings of the philosophers. However, if Wolfhelm met Manegold at Lautenbach, one must wonder why the aged Benedictine abbot was traveling in Alsace, some 250 miles from home. Furthermore, since he had sided with the imperial faction, one must wonder why he was being entertained by Gregorian sympathizers, passing the time by reading the ancient philosopher Macrobius. A *Life of Wolfhelm*, written some twenty or thirty years later by a monk of Brauweiler, unfortunately does not provide answers. The text delicately avoids the subject of Wolfhelm's political affiliation and instead dwells on his reputation for sanctity, for it is a hagiography in praise of a former abbot of the monastery; it certainly does not mention an altercation with Manegold at Lautenbach nor any travels in the vicinity that could be dated to 1085.[86] These difficulties raise a suspicion that casts

---

[85] The *Ad Gebehardum* does not specify that its recipient was the archbishop of Salzburg, but Manegold mentions this figure in the *Contra Wolfelmum* (Chapter 23) as an important person among the Gregorians. The south German Gregorians were led sometime afterwards by another Gebhard, the bishop of Constance (1084–1110), who according to the *Annales Marbacenses* visited Marbach in 1105; see Text 24. However, despite an argument for the identification of this younger Gebhard with the recipient of Manegold's text that was made by Pietro De Leo, scholarly consensus maintains the identification with the archbishop of Salzburg. See Pietro De Leo, "Ricerche sul *Liber ad Gebehardum* di Manegoldo di Lautenbach," *Rivista di storia e letteratura religiosa* 10 (1974), pp. 112–53; and the response by Wilfried Hartmann, *Deutsches Archiv für Erforschung des Mittelalters* 32 (1976), pp. 260–61.

[86] On the author, Conrad of Brauweiler, see *Die deutsche Literatur des Mittelalters: Verfasserlexikon*, 2nd ed., vol. 5 (1985), cols. 146–47. The text is printed in the *Acta Sanctorum: Aprilis*, ed. Godefridus Henschenius and Daniel van Papenbroeck, vol. 3 (Paris and Rome: Victor Palmé, 1866), pp. 77–89. A somewhat abridged version is available in MGH SS 12: 180–95.

doubt upon the value of Manegold's prologue as a source of historical information. Could it be that Manegold and Wolfhelm did not actually meet in the gardens of Lautenbach, but that Manegold was merely employing the topos of the idyllic setting in order to establish the dramatic mood for his literary production, as the stylized quality of the prologue might imply?[87] This possibility must be seriously considered, yet one must also wonder why Manegold would have mentioned Lautenbach specifically if the garden setting itself were fictional.

Although Manegold does not actually state where he was dwelling at the time of the disputation or where he wrote his response to the event, his name is associated with Lautenbach in several sources.[88] It would be fair to suppose that Manegold was at Lautenbach when he wrote the *Contra Wolfelmum*, but on this point the prologue of the *Ad Gebehardum* once again muddies the waters. Manegold complains therein that his "little monastery" (*monasteriolum*) has been destroyed by his enemies, but he does not identify its location.[89] It has often been supposed that the little monastery in question was the priory at Lautenbach; but if so, Manegold could not have completed the *Ad Gebehardum* there.[90] Furthermore, he could hardly have failed to mention Lautenbach's destruction when writing the prologue to the *Contra Wolfelmum*, had the event already taken place by then. The disparity suggests that the *Contra Wolfelmum* was written at

---

[87] See *Contra Wolfelmum*, ed. Hartmann, p. 13.

[88] The manuscript in which the *Contra Wolfelmum* is preserved identifies its author simply as "Master Manegold," but the manuscript of the *Ad Gebehardum* appends the toponym "of Lautenbach"; see above, p. 17. In addition to his own works, the following sources in the Appendix link Manegold to Lautenbach: Texts 11, 18, 24, 25, 28 (debatable), 30, 31. It should be noted that only the first two of these were written prior to the thirteenth century.

[89] MGH Ldl 1: 311, line 16.

[90] The affiliation of the house at Lautenbach is not certain for this period. The cloister had been founded as a Benedictine monastery in the ninth century, but it adopted the Augustinian rule at some point during the eleventh; see *Lexikon für Theologie und Kirche*, ed. Walter Kasper et al., 3rd ed., vol. 6 (Freiburg et al.: Herder, 1997), cols. 690–91; L.H. Cottineau, *Répertoire topo-bibliographique des abbayes et prieurés*, vol. 1 (Mâcon: Protat Frères, 1935), col. 1570. It seems the foundation at Lautenbach — if it was in fact the *monasteriolum* to which Manegold refers — was already an Augustinian priory when Manegold was there because the prior Harmann, who supposedly gave Manegold the task of writing the *Ad Gebehardum*, does not seem to have had a superior. The superior of a house of canons regular used the title "prior" (*praepositus*), which in the Benedictine rule is the title of an office below that of the superior, the abbot. See *RB 1980: The Rule of St. Benedict*, ed. Timothy Fry, pp. 284–85 (Chapter 65); and Charles Dereine, "Chanoines," *Dictionnaire d'histoire et de géographie ecclésiastiques*, vol. 12, col. 399. Charles Haaby, the author of the most extensive study of the foundation at Lautenbach, was unable to determine when this conversion from the Benedictine to the Augustinian rule occurred. Haaby supposes that Manegold began his career as a Benedictine monk at Lautenbach ca. 1080 and then played a key role in the conversion of the monastery to the Augustinian rule, but there is no evidence to substantiate such a claim. See Charles Haaby, *Stift Lautenbach*, pp. 25, 39.

the cloister of Lautenbach shortly before its inhabitants were put to flight, and that the *Ad Gebehardum* was written partly at Lautenbach but finished elsewhere — probably at Rottenbuch, which was a haven for Gregorian refugees.[91] Rottenbuch suggests itself as the probable location on the testimony of Gerhoh of Reichersberg, whose *Epistola ad Innocentiam papam*, written in 1131, asserts that a certain Manegold who was once the dean of Rottenbuch wrote a book in defense of Gregory VII. Although Gerhoh does not mention the title of the work, there can be no doubt that the book he describes is the *Liber ad Gebehardum*.[92] This in turn would imply that Manegold was serving as the dean of Rottenbuch by 1086.[93] He appears to have held that office for some four to eight years, since by 1094, and probably already by 1089/1090, he had returned to Alsace and was dwelling at Marbach, some ten miles from Lautenbach.[94]

4. MASTER OF THE MODERN MASTERS

The foregoing analysis of the *Contra Wolfelmum* and the *Ad Gebehardum* illustrates the extremely limited usefulness of Manegold's autobiographical statements. His remarks are simply too ambiguous to shed more than the dimmest light on his own historical situation. The remaining sources that must be considered likewise offer nothing more than shadowy images. Among these sources, one that has been singled out as particularly important is the work of a writer formerly known as "Anonymous of Melk" (*Anonymus Mellicensis*), who is now identified with Wolfger of Prüfening. In his inventory of ecclesiastical authors and their works (written ca. 1165), Wolfger includes "Manegold the priest," and gives him the remarkable appellation, "master of

---

[91] See Jakob Mois, *Das Stift Rottenbuch in der Kirchenreformation des XI.–XII. Jahrhunderts: Ein Beitrag zur Ordens-Geschichte der Augustiner-Chorherren*, Beiträge zur altbayerischen Kirchengeschichte 19 (Munich: Verlag des Erzbischöflichen Ordinariats München und Freising, 1953), p. 98.

[92] See Appendix, Text 16.

[93] Manegold's ambiguous remark about the forcible ejection from a monastery at which he and his brothers were guests (see Appendix, Text 4) presumably does not refer to Rottenbuch.

[94] A letter by Pope Urban II to the monks of Rottenbuch, dated 7 August 1096, identifies the dean simply with the initial "M." (see Text 8). Some scholars have assumed this "M." refers to Manegold. Yet Manegold was the prior of Marbach at the time; he had in fact met Urban II five months earlier at Tours, where he received papal protection for his priory (see Text 6). Since this situation would require Manegold to have been the superior at one house and a subordinate at another simultaneously, in locations some 200 miles apart, one concludes most reasonably that the "M." who was the dean of Rottenbuch in 1096 was not Manegold of Lautenbach. See Horst Fuhrmann, "Papst Urban II. und der Stand der Regularkanoniker," *Sitzungsberichte der Bayerische Akademie der Wissenschaften, philosophisch-historische Klasse*, Jahrgang 1984, Heft 2, pp. 35–36 n. 82.

the modern masters."[95] The ensuing biographical description clearly identifies this Manegold as the Gregorian defender who suffered imprisonment at the hands of Henry IV. However, when Wolfger lists the works that Manegold had written, he mentions only commentaries and glosses on biblical texts; the *Contra Wolfelmum* and the *Ad Gebehardum* are notably absent.

Opinions are divided on the value of Wolfger's testimony. Some scholars have accepted it as evidence that Manegold played a key role in the early stages of the scholastic movement.[96] Others have dismissed it as a conflation of two different Mane-golds: that is, the biographical portion describes Manegold of Lautenbach, but the works attributed to him belong to a different Manegold, the one who was the "master of the modern masters."[97] Each side has something to commend it. On the one hand, there is no reason to suppose that Manegold of Lautenbach did not write works besides his two polemical treatises — certainly his role as a teacher of canons regular would have entailed commentary on biblical texts — and it is not unreasonable to suppose that Wolfger omitted the polemical treatises from his record simply because he was unaware of them; after all, his enumeration of the works of the other ecclesiastical authors in the catalogue is not comprehensive. Thus, as a renowned teacher, Manegold could have had a wide-ranging influence on early scholastic culture. On the other hand, it must be admitted that Wolfger of Prüfening was guilty of conflating two distinct individuals in another one of his entries.[98] Moreover, given what we know of Manegold's career — especially his vehement attack on philosophy in the *Contra Wolfelmum* — he would have been an unlikely herald of scholasticism, which sought precisely what Manegold condemned, namely, the use of philosophical authorities in the study of theology. Furthermore, one must also realize that "Manegold" was not an uncommon name in Germany during the Middle Ages.[99] In the remainder of this

---

[95] See Appendix, Text 23.

[96] Hartmann examines this thesis and provides bibliographical references in his study, "Manegold von Lautenbach und die Anfänge der Frühscholastik," pp. 50–54.

[97] See Giesebrecht, "Ueber Magister Manegold von Lautenbach und seine Schrift gegen den Scholasticus Wenrich," p. 312; N. Paulus, "Études nouvelles sur Manegold de Lautenbach," *Revue catholique d'Alsace* (1886), pp. 219–20; Châtillon, "Recherches critiques sur les différents personnages nommés Manegold," p. 158 n. 9.

[98] For example, Guitmund of Aversa and Christian of Stavelot; see *Dictionnaire de théologie catholique*, ed. A. Vacant and E. Mangenot, vol. 6/2 (Paris: Letouzey et Ané, 1920), cols. 1989–92, at 1990. See also Francis Roy Swietek, *Wolfger of Prüfening's De scriptoribus ecclesiasticis: A Critical Edition and Historical Evaluation*, Ph.D. thesis, University of Illinois at Urbana-Champaign, 1978, pp. 68–69, 292, 300.

[99] A glance at any number of German necrologies easily bears this out. See Appendix, Texts 19, 22, 25, and 28. It should be noted that there was a canon named Manegold who taught in Germany, at Paderborn, in the middle of the twelfth century. See *Monumenta Corbeiensia*, ed. Philipp Jaffé, Bibliotheca

biographical introduction, our investigation will be overshadowed by the question of whether the sources refer to one or more Manegolds.

Wolfger of Prüfening mentions a letter by Ivo of Chartres addressed to Manegold, which is still extant.[100] Features of this letter suggest its recipient could very likely have been Manegold of Lautenbach: it was written between 1090 and 1115 (the years that Ivo was bishop of Chartres), and it clearly situates Manegold as a person of some authority at a religious house where he was engaged in teaching. When Ivo looks back nostalgically at his own life as a simple canon regular before he was elevated to the see of Chartres, his pious envy of Manegold's present state of life seems to imply that Manegold himself had become a canon regular (rather than a Benedictine monk).[101] From Ivo's testimony we learn additionally that Manegold adopted the religious life after first treading "many winding paths," and that he was a famous teacher of philosophy when he still lived in the world. Could this be evidence that Manegold had been a wandering scholar, and that his itinerant teaching had taken him to northern France, where he befriended Ivo?

Another letter originating in northern France again speaks of Manegold as a renowned teacher, and once again in a context that implies the milieu of the canons regular.[102] Both sender and recipient of this letter are unknown; the former indicates that he is studying at Paris, and he identifies the latter as his "prior" (presumably the head of a house of canons rather than a Benedictine monk of intermediate status). We learn that the student at Paris has been living in exile for some time; the location of the prior is not indicated, but a German setting is suggested when the bishop of Worms is mentioned toward the end of the letter.[103] The student reports that he has been attending the school of William of Champeaux, recently founded at St. Victor. Since William began to teach at St. Victor ca. 1108 and was elevated to the see of Châlons-sur-Marne in 1113, the letter would have been written between 1109 and 1112. The student praises William for

---

rerum germanicarum 1 (Berlin: Weidmann, 1864), pp. 275–88, nos. 166–67; and Wilhelm Hemmen, "Der Brief des Magisters Manegold an Abt Wibald v. Corvey (1149)," ed. Klemens Honselmann, *Von der Domschule zum Gymnasium Theodorianum in Paderborn* (Paderborn: Verein für Geschichte und Altertumskunde Westfalens, 1962), pp. 79–105.

[100] See Appendix, Text 5.

[101] The letter addresses Manegold as "brother." Since Ivo was himself a canon regular before he became bishop of Chartres, it is tempting to think that "brother" (*frater*) implies that the two men belonged to the same order. However, this was not necessarily the case. For example, we find that Bernold of Constance, a Benedictine, addressed the canons regular of Rottenbuch as "brothers." See *Libellus* 11, MGH Ldl 2: 142.

[102] See Appendix, Text 13.

[103] I have not translated the entire letter in the Appendix. For the reference to the bishop of Worms, see *Monumenta Bambergensia*, ed. Philipp Jaffé, Bibliotheca rerum germanicarum 5 (Berlin: Weidmann, 1869), p. 287, no. 160.

teaching "in the manner of Master Manegold of blessed memory." As in the case of Ivo's letter, the circumstances of this one conform to what is known about Manegold of Lautenbach and do not contradict that record. If the letter does indeed refer to the former prior of Marbach, it situates his death sometime before 1109/1112.

This letter, along with Ivo of Chartres's missive and Wolfger of Prüfening's report of Manegold as "the master of the modern masters," has been taken as evidence that Manegold taught in northern France early in his career and that he had even been the teacher of William of Champeaux, who enjoyed the reputation among the early scholastics as a "modern master."[104] However, the letter by the anonymous student at St. Victor does not actually link Manegold to northern France or to William of Champeaux. It does not actually say that William of Champeaux was ever taught by *anyone* named Manegold. It reports only that William, *like* Manegold, "devotedly and kindly taught anyone who came to him, free of charge and only for the sake of God." Thus, Manegold is mentioned primarily for the sake of comparison; the implication is that the recipient of the letter was familiar with Manegold's reputation and could recognize William of Champeaux's scholarly merit by regarding him as a teacher of the same caliber. This by itself may suggest only that Manegold was well known in the region where the recipient was located (presumably Germany), not that Manegold had acquired an international reputation. However, the letter is too ambiguous to shed clear light on the question of where Manegold had made his reputation as a teacher.

Other sources that mention a renowned teacher named Manegold are similarly vague. A poem by Baudri of Bourgueil identifies a certain Manegold as the teacher of Gerard of Loudun, but where Gerard studied with this person is not intimated.[105] An anonymous chronicle of Frankish history from Fleury mentions "Manegold the German," along with Lanfranc of Bec, Guido the Lombard, and Bruno of Rheims, as an illustrious master who flourished around the time that William the Conqueror died.[106] Otto of Freising mentions a certain Manegold along with Berengar (of Tours) and Anselm (probably of Laon rather than Canterbury) as an illustrious teacher in the furthest west, that is, in "the regions of Gaul and Spain."[107] These reports imply only in ambiguous terms that Manegold (whoever he was) taught in France. Surely we cannot take Otto's remark as evidence that Manegold had visited Spain. Given, then, the geographical imprecision of the statement, might not "Gaul" have included Alsace in Otto's imagination?

---

[104] See Hartmann, "Manegold von Lautenbach und die Anfänge der Frühscholastik," p. 51.
[105] See Appendix, Text 10.
[106] See Appendix, Text 14.
[107] See Appendix, Text 17.

Other sources locate Manegold the teacher in Germany. One of these is an early twelfth-century biography of Theoger, the abbot of St. George in the Black Forest, who was also for a short time the bishop of Metz (1118–1120). The *Vita Theogerii*, which was written ca. 1138–1146, probably by Wolfger of Prüfening (the source for the appellation "master of the modern masters"), apparently mentioned a famous master in Alsace named Manegold. Unfortunately, the evidence on this point is compromised, for we cannot rely on the *Vita Theogerii* itself, whose sole manuscript has been mutilated, but must turn to the use of the complete text that was made by Johannes Trithemius in the sixteenth century. Thus, the modern editor of the *Vita Theogerii* has supplemented the lost beginning of the text with the summary found in Trithemius's entry for the year 1087 in the *Annales Hirsaugienses* (written 1509–1511). There Trithemius reports that Theoger was educated by "a certain Manegold, prefect of the schools in the province of Alsace."[108] The *Annales Sancti Georgii* (from the monastery where Theoger was abbot) also mentions "a certain Manegold" for the year 1094, by whom "the simoniac heresy was bitterly denounced."[109] A chronicle written soon after the middle of the twelfth century by Richard of Poitiers (a monk of Cluny) also places "Manegold the philosopher" firmly in Germany rather than France.[110]

5. HUSBAND AND FATHER?

The chronicle by Richard of Poitiers is arguably the most remarkable of sources for Manegold's biography. Richard observes that Manegold "was learned beyond all his contemporaries in letters divine and secular," and then unexpectedly adds, "His wife and daughters also flourished in the religious life, having an impressive knowledge of the Scriptures; and his aforesaid daughters taught their own students." This surprising reference to a family has been a key passage for scholars who oppose the assumption that all allusions to a famous master named Manegold point to the same man. Those who defend this assumption, however, have nevertheless accommodated Richard's curious report with the career of the Gregorian polemicist who, in the *Ad Gebehardum*, railed against the horror of married priests; they have easily assumed that Manegold did not become a priest until after his wife died.[111] Richard's report has been worked into a quaint portrait of Manegold with wife and daughters, touring France and delivering

---

[108] See Appendix, Text 29.
[109] See Appendix, Text 20.
[110] See Appendix, Text 21.
[111] See *Histoire littéraire de la France*, vol. 9, pp. 281, 283; Haaby, *Stift Lautenbach*, pp. 22–23.

public lectures as a family. This portrait may owe less to Richard's account and more to the version presented by Ptolemy of Lucca in the fourteenth century, for Ptolemy asserts that "wife and daughters were most greatly learned in philosophy,"[112] whereas Richard says simply that in practicing the religious life, they had an impressive knowledge of the Scriptures (*religione florentes multam in scripturis habuere notitiam*). As suggested by Hastings Rashdall, the phrase *religione florentes* should probably be taken to signify that Manegold's wife and daughters were nuns, not merely that they were good Christians.[113] Hence, when Manegold's daughters taught their own students, they could have done so in the cloister, independently of their father, and not as his itinerant teaching assistants. Moreover, if Rashdall's interpretation of the phrase *religione florentes* is correct, then there is no need to assume that Manegold's wife had died before he himself became a canon; spouses could of course separate in order to pursue the religious life, as in the example of Peter Abelard's parents, and indeed of Abelard and Heloise as well.[114] Clearly Richard of Poitiers has left some important details out of his brief report.[115]

Scholars who have rejected the identification of the married philosopher with the Lautenbach polemicist have argued that the evidence actually implies the existence of two Manegolds who were born one generation apart; these scholars have argued that the polemicist was born ca. 1060, whereas the philosopher was born ca. 1030 or so.[116] The date for the polemicist's birth is based on a literal reading of his own assertion that he was a young man (*iuvenis, etate immaturus*) when he composed the *Ad Gebehardum*.[117] Thus, if it is assumed that the polemicist was about twenty-five years old in 1085, he must have been born ca. 1060; and as a young canon regular, he could not have been a husband and a father. Furthermore, Richard of Poitiers mentions the married philosopher in his account of the reign of King Henry I of France (1031–1060); hence, this Manegold must have been someone else, born in the preceding generation. However, there are serious problems with this interpretation of the evidence. On the one hand, a literal reading of Manegold's statement about his age may not be warranted; he may

[112] See Appendix, Text 27.

[113] Hastings Rashdall, *The Universities of Europe in the Middle Ages* 3: *English Universities, Student Life*, ed. F.M. Powicke and A.B. Emden (Oxford: Oxford University Press, 1936), p. 396 n. 3.

[114] See M.T. Clanchy, *Abelard: A Medieval Life* (Oxford and Cambridge, Mass.: Blackwell, 1997), p. 196.

[115] There is an eleventh-century poem that complains about women studying philosophy, which has recently been suggested as evidence in support of Richard's report. However, its connection to Manegold is not at all obvious. In all likelihood, the poem is entirely irrelevant, but I have included it in the Appendix to let readers judge for themselves; see Text 1.

[116] See Giesebrecht, "Ueber Magister Manegold von Lautenbach und seine Schrift gegen den Scholasticus Wenrich," pp. 311–18; Paulus, "Études nouvelles sur Manegold de Lautenbach," p. 215–19.

[117] MGH Ldl 1: 311, lines 19, 26.

have pretended to be far younger than he really was, as part of his polemical strategy.[118] On the other hand, Richard of Poitiers is often imprecise in his dates,[119] and his organization of reports according to regnal periods is by no means rigid. Thus, Richard mentions the married philosopher after reporting that Hugh of Semur began to govern Cluny as its abbot — yet Hugh's abbacy spanned fifty years (1049–1109) and reached beyond the reign of Henry I's successor, Philip I (1060–1108). Moreover, Richard asserts that "during this time Manegold the philosopher *began* to flourish in the German land." This lack of precision allows the possibility that Manegold began to teach in the year 1060, and that his career may have lasted as long as Hugh of Cluny's abbacy. In this connection it is worth noting that the thirteenth-century chronicle of Alberic of Trois Fontaines mentions a certain Manegold in the report for the year 1060, along with Berengar, Lanfranc, and Anselm (men who lived until the years 1088, 1089, and 1109, respectively).[120] Consequently, the married philosopher in Richard's account could conceivably have educated his children and then joined the canons regular by 1085, when he would have written the *Ad Gebehardum*; if so, his claim of being young would have been a deliberate distortion, true only in the figurative sense that he was a newcomer to the religious life. Clearly one cannot rely on the incidental reports of the chroniclers to resolve chronological problems, and Manegold's own report in the rhetorically charged atmosphere of his polemical treatise is likewise intrinsically too suspect to settle the problem. Since the evidence provided by Manegold and Richard of Poitiers is severely compromised by ambiguity on either side, there is not enough reliable data to determine whether their testimony is incompatible. Moreover, if one may justifiably hesitate to accord Manegold's own words the status of unadulterated truth, one may also be justified in doubting the accuracy of Richard's report, as the following paragraph will elaborate.

It is impossible either to confirm or to dismiss the thesis that Manegold of Lautenbach had raised a family before he became a canon regular. The arrangement would have been unusual, but it poses no insuperable contradictions.[121] Moreover, it appears that Richard's report about a wife and children may not actually be a unique witness, for in

---

[118] See above, pp. 19–20, as well as Endres, *Forschungen zur Geschichte der frühmittelalterlichen Philosophie*, p. 92.

[119] For example, the chronicle asserts that Henry II was the German emperor during the reign of the French king, Henry I, but Emperor Henry II died in 1024 and King Henry I of France did not begin to rule until 1031.

[120] See Appendix, Text 26.

[121] A similar problem has recently been noted in the biographical evidence for Robert Grosseteste, bishop of Lincoln (d. 1253). See N.M. Schulman, "Husband, Father, Bishop? Grosseteste in Paris," *Speculum* 72 (1997), pp. 330–46.

fact there is one other piece of evidence that scholars seem to have overlooked. It is the necrology of Rottenbuch. This necrology contains an entry reminding the canons that every 15th of July they are to pray for the souls of "Manegold of Lautenbach and his wife Irmelgart, and Peter the subdeacon and Conrad, both sons of theirs."[122] While Manegold's association with Rottenbuch is certain,[123] there are problems with the evidence provided by the necrology. First, the Latin place-name, *Liutenpach*, could also be translated "Luttenbach" — a hamlet in the vicinity of Rottenbuch. The alternative reading would suggest that the Manegold in question was a local Bavarian nobleman (otherwise unknown), not the famous Alsatian teacher. Secondly, the necrology mentions sons, not daughters. It is worth noting that in the Latin of this period the words for "sons" and "daughters" differed by only a single letter — *filii* and *filie*, respectively. Might Richard of Poitiers, writing half a century after Manegold's death, have received an inaccurate report? Might a scribal error have crept into the manuscript tradition at some early stage, substituting *filie* for *filii*?[124] If we may suppose that "daughters" was really a mistake for "sons," then another point is worth considering as well: one of Manegold's sons is identified as a subdeacon, and one of the functions of a subdeacon was teaching — as, for example, in the case of Bernard of Chartres, who lectured on Plato's *Timaeus* in the early years of the twelfth century.[125] This detail, then, would accord with Richard's statement that Manegold's children flourished in the religious life and that they taught students of their own. The third problem with the necrology of Rottenbuch is that the manuscript which preserves the text was transcribed in 1490. Even though this late fifteenth-century transcription of an earlier exemplar (no longer extant) includes entries that date back to Rottenbuch's foundation in the eleventh century,[126] there is no way of knowing when in this span of five centuries the entry for Manegold and his family was added.

---

[122] See Appendix, Text 28. *Necrologium Raitenbuchense*, ed. Franz Ludwig Baumann, MGH Necrologia Germaniae 3, p. 113: "Manegoldus de Liutenpach et uxor eius Irmelgart et Petrus subdyac[onus] et Cuonradus, ambo filii eorum."

[123] See above, pp. 10, 11, 23.

[124] Consider the edition of Richard's chronicle by Muratori, which initially presents "sons" and subsequently "daughters," thus: "Uxor quoque & filii ejus religione florentes…, & discipulos proprios filiae ejus predictae docebant." See *Antiquitates italicae medii aevi*, ed. Lodovico Antonio Muratori (1738–1742; repr. Bologna: A. Forni, 1965), vol. 4, cols. 1075–1114, at 1085C. On the manuscripts, see Élie Berger, "Richard le Poitevin, moine de Cluny, historien et poète," *Bibliothèque des écoles françaises d'Athènes et de Rome* 6 (Paris: Ernest Thorin, 1879), pp. 43–138, at 56–72; G. Waitz, *Ex Richardi Pictaviensis Chronica*, MGH SS 26 (Hannover: Impensis bibliopoli Hahniani, 1882), pp. 74–84, at 74–76; August Potthast, *Wegweiser durch die Geschichtswerke des europäischen Mittelalters bis 1500* (Berlin: W. Weber, 1896), vol. 2, p. 969.

[125] See Paul Edward Dutton, *The Glosae super Platonem of Bernard of Chartres*, Studies and Texts 107 (Toronto: Pontifical Institute of Mediaeval Studies, 1991), p. 28.

[126] See MGH Necrologia Germaniae 3, pp. 109, 110 (5 March).

In the final analysis, then, the problems associated with the necrology of Rottenbuch vitiate its utility, yet they do not entirely invalidate it as a potentially relevant source. Although the evidence may not apply to Manegold of Lautenbach at all, I have presented it here at some length because it has not, to the best of my knowledge, been noticed in the existing scholarship. Moreover, it poses an uncanny array of coincidences: a man named Manegold from a place that could legitimately be translated "Lautenbach," who was closely enough associated with Rottenbuch to be entered into its necrology, had a wife and children, one of whom (at least) was dedicated to the religious life and could conceivably have had students of his own.

A study of other necrologies does not clarify this matter, but does yield some information. Two in particular are worthy of attention: the one produced at Marbach[127] and another produced at the convent of Schwarzenthann, a daughter-house of Marbach.[128] Of the two, the older is the one produced at Schwarzenthann. It was begun in the year 1154, whereas the Marbach necrology was begun in 1241. Both necrologies include entries for individuals who are known to have died before 1154, but neither of them presents any Manegold for 15 July or mentions a wife and children. Of the numerous Manegolds who appear in the necrology of Schwarzenthann, Manegold of Lautenbach is thought to be the one who alone is identified as both "priest" and "master." This entry in the Schwarzenthann necrology for 24 May corresponds to an entry in the text of Marbach. It must be noted that Marbach also offers an explicit entry for "Manegold of Lautenbach" on 2 January; however, it is written in a seventeenth-century hand and has no corresponding entry in the necrology of Schwarzenthann. It follows that the entry of 2 January in the necrology of Marbach indicates a late revision for purposes of liturgical observance rather than evidence for the day on which Manegold died. Likewise, one may conclude that the entry in the necrology of Rottenbuch need not indicate that the Manegold to whom it refers died on 15 July, only that the canons of Rottenbuch decided to remember him on that day; certainly one need not assume that Manegold's wife and two sons also perished on 15 July. Therefore, the evidence supplied by Marbach and Schwarzenthann does not actually contradict the evidence provided by Rottenbuch. One may also conclude from the corresponding entries in the two most trustworthy necrologies that Manegold died on 24 May. There is no evidence, however, for the year of his death.

---

127 See Appendix, Text 25.
128 See Appendix, Text 22. A third necrology — that of Zwiefalten — has sometimes been cited in biographical studies of Manegold (see Text 19), but it is irrelevant. Zwiefalten was a Benedictine monastery, and there is no evidence that Manegold of Lautenbach had any connection with it. Any correspondences with the necrologies of Marbach and Schwarzenthann that it exhibits are, in all likelihood, merely coincidental. See Giesebrecht, "Ueber Magister Manegold von Lautenbach und seine Schrift gegen den Scholasticus Wenrich," p. 317 n. 42; Endres, *Forschungen zur Geschichte der frühmittelalterlichen Philosophie*, p. 93 n. 4.

Remarks on the Translation and Notes

The translation is based on the edition by Wilfried Hartmann and the unique manuscript that preserves the text; the latter I have consulted on microfilm provided by the Biblioteca Ambrosiana. For details, see the Bibliographical Essay. Hartmann's edition is very reliable and greatly enhanced by his copious source apparatus. Readers who are interested in conducting further research on the *Liber contra Wolfelmum* are highly encouraged to consult it. One should be aware, however, that Hartmann's punctuation is at times misleading; I have signaled the more significant instances in my notes. While my own notes are deeply indebted to Hartmann's observations, I have drawn from his apparatus selectively; and yet I have in many places gone beyond the guidance he offers, particularly in explaining passages where Manegold's oblique style makes him exceedingly obscure. I have, furthermore, supplied updated references to scholarly treatments of the themes that Manegold discusses. While focusing as much as possible on scholarship available in English, I have not neglected studies in other languages.

I have rigorously traced Manegold's numerous biblical citations and allusions, since the importance of intimate familiarity with the Bible was at the very heart of his message. Like other medieval authors, Manegold at times wrote in a collage of biblical phrases. In order to help the reader separate Manegold's own prose from the citations that he seamlessly weaves into his text, and to facilitate a study of Manegold's use of Scripture, I have set biblical quotations in italics, followed by references to chapter and verse within square brackets (or, when a quotation can refer to several locations in the Bible, the multiple references have been placed in the notes). Quotation marks enclose direct citations from sources other than the Bible, as well as definitions, dialogue, logical propositions, and rephrased biblical words or passages.

Scriptural references are keyed to the Latin Vulgate, which was the version of the Bible that Manegold knew, and thus correspond to the Douay translation, whose chapter and verse numbers differ in places from those of other translations. This discrepancy is especially pronounced in the case of the Psalms. Thus, references to the Psalms correspond to the numbering of the Septuagint system that the Vulgate follows, rather than the Hebrew system that the Authorized Version follows. When the titles of the books in the Vulgate differ significantly enough from modern titles to raise the possibility of confusion (especially in the case of 1–4 Kings), I have reminded the reader of the discrepancy in the notes by presenting the modern title in parentheses following the Vulgate title. While I have consulted the Douay Bible in preparing my translation,

I have often translated the Vulgate passages afresh in order to eliminate needless archaism and to maintain a sense of integration with the style of Manegold's prose. Personal pronouns that refer to God have been capitalized, for the sake of clarifying Manegold's meaning in passages where he does not indicate a change of subject clearly.

Stylistically, I have done my best to preserve the elevated, sometimes bombastic, tone of the Latin original, to the extent that modern English will accommodate it. However, it has been necessary to depart at times from Manegold's choice of grammatical constructions, particularly with regard to some of his long periodic sentences. These I have broken up into shorter units, according to current English practice. The obliquity of Manegold's prose, mentioned above, can make his meaning frustratingly obscure, and the reader may need to rely on the notes occasionally to complete the sense. While Manegold cultivated such obliquity for rhetorical effect, there are a few difficult passages of unclear prose in the Latin that seem to suffer from lack of polish rather than rhetorical over-sophistication. These unrefined passages may reflect the haste with which Manegold must have written his polemical text. I have endeavored to provide a readable translation in these instances, drawing attention to the substandard quality of the original only in the notes.

The Book of Master Manegold
against Wolfhelm of Cologne[1]

When recently we met in the gardens of Lautenbach and in the manner of the school-men discussed the writings which we then held in our hands, you and I fell into a serious disagreement. As our speech rushed on, we stumbled upon a kind of knot, as it were, and by tugging at the rope of contention, made it tighter. You asserted that there was little the philosophers had said with which you did not agree, and especially Macrobius in his *Commentary on the Dream of Scipio*,[2] which we were then discussing. I, to the contrary, maintained that I had found in their writings much that opposed the Faith and endangered our salvation. As the torrent of our words overflowed, it became patently clear either that you were too little learned in the divine letters by some innate wildness and eagerness for contradiction (since you seemed to know nothing of their content, nor did you show any willingness to defend them), or if you did know Scripture, as you claimed, then you had obviously turned aside from the principles of sound faith.

It is ever the case that some attend to the noise of the words and the superficial meaning of a narration, but do not consider its deeper sense and the intention of its author — like those who gnaw a radish but cannot taste or smell it, for having lost their senses, they do not discern the strength of a taste or a smell[3] — while others pry into the meanings hidden beneath the sound of the words and, being able to tell the difference between what is bland and what is spicy, they divide the good from the bad and spurn the latter all the more vigorously that they are delighted by the good. Since I perceived there was something wrong with your senses, I drew near to examine you and to diagnose your malady. Calling to witness specific doctrines of the philosophers, I sought to discover whether you clearly understood and endorsed them, in order to be certain that you did not find them pernicious to believers.[4] You responded rashly enough to submit that you were unaware of anything in them that was seriously objectionable. Exasperated by your many insults, I left while you ranted and raved. I now propose to reach out to you on the matter in writing, so that you may recognize the heretical perversity that is contained in the doctrines of those books whose error you pretend not to see.

At the same time I have also deemed it worthwhile to append a statement concerning the Lord Pope Gregory, whom you slander with unclean mouth, so that you may realize how one sin is often the cause of a more serious sin.[5]

HEADINGS FOR THE CHAPTERS THAT FOLLOW[6]

I. That not all the opinions of the philosophers are to be rejected, but only those in which they are deceived and by which they deceive others. And concerning the opinion of Pythagoras on the soul, which should be firmly rejected.

II. On Plato and his mythological metaphors, by which he describes the composition of the Soul which permeates all bodies without exception.[7]

III. On the various opinions of the philosophers concerning the soul.

IV. That they err in measuring the sun and the moon, and in their opinions about the habitable spots of the earth. And if anyone believes Macrobius on these matters, he unquestionably imperils his faith.

V. That according to the Apostle such things must be tested and reduced to the sobriety of Christian standards.

VI. On the unsound confession of the philosophers. And on the fall of Origen, who was exceedingly fond of their doctrines.

VII. On the Holy Spirit and the sound and balanced teaching He inspires. That He forsakes the proud and permits the unclean spirit to tear them apart.

VIII. That the philosophers, deprived of the blessings of the patriarchs, did not merit to acquire the slightest understanding of the mystery of the Trinity.

IX. That such errors arise from the malign spirit. And the author of disunity has disguised the sin of idolatry with various artifices.

X. That the pagan authors are the Egyptians who must be despoiled. And that they have gathered up the treasures and ornaments of eloquence for our benefit.

XI. On God, who is the subject of our discussion. And on the correct confession of faith. And on the creation of angels; and of men, for whom the sentence of the Lord was mercifully tempered on account of the Fall.

XII. On the precepts that had to be obeyed so that a man who had disregarded the Law could be rehabilitated. This reparation for sin was noted in numerous examples among the ancient fathers, whose grievous sins were pardoned in order to reveal the greatness of God's grace — particularly in the case of David, from whose lineage the Agent of forgiveness was born.

XIII. On the prophets who foresaw the two Comings with great yearning.

XIV. That God was born of a Virgin in order to fulfill the prophecies. And the consequent refutation of the philosophers.

XV. The purpose for which He was born.

XVI. That with His birth the full truth of Scripture was made plain by Him. And on the resuscitation of souls, and the lesson of humility.

XVII. On the simplicity of Peter the apostle and the merit of his faith.

XVIII. On the sacraments of rebirth and refreshment, both of which were instituted before the Passion at the Last Supper.

XIX. That in the cross of Jesus Christ is the remission of sins and the redemption of all people, including the saints of the Old Testament.

XX. On the glory of the Resurrection. And that the disciples were called to announce eternal life, not to philosophize.

XXI. On the coming of the Spirit, and what He accomplished through the apostles. And that in the present we do not enjoy the fullness of beatitude, but only its inception.

XXII. That one must briefly say something about the philosophers, so that it may be shown how great a peril there is in assenting to their writings, since they knew nothing about the resurrection of bodies. And that their definition [of man] must be refuted. And a spirit enslaved by the flesh has lost its ability to perceive their error.

XXIII. That certain Germans have fallen away from obedience to and unity with the Roman Church, saying they have no pope but Caesar.

XXIV. Concerning the letter that they have written against the saintly Pope Gregory, and that by the grace of God one must reply to this letter.

I.

<That not all the opinions of the philosophers are to be rejected, but only those in which they are deceived and by which they deceive others. And concerning the opinion of Pythagoras on the soul, which should be firmly rejected.>[8]

First we wish our readers to know that we do not in the least consider all the teachings of the philosophers to be damnable: on the one hand, we have scarcely been able to penetrate their meaning on certain subjects, owing to the great subtlety of their ideas; on the other, we are not unaware that some of their teachings have been accepted by saintly men.[9] We wish, rather, to suppress your temerity, for you commend their subtleties without paying heed to the manifold errors implicit in their vain imaginings. To be sure, the gift of reason bestowed upon them by nature had not been so severely corrupted by the sin of the first parent that they were wholly unable to attain certain knowledge in some subjects through diligent reasoning, as far as human limitations allowed. However, because they lacked *the Spirit* of Him who *teaches all truth* [John 16.13] and whose Wisdom *reaches from one end of the world to another mightily and disposes all things perfectly* [Wis. 8.1], it was inevitable that they should from time to time exceed the bounds of truth, being only human, and therefore liars.[10] And once they began to defend falsehood, they were carried away by various deceptive arguments.[11]

Pythagoras was among the early leaders of this tradition and made certain useful discoveries which he transmitted to posterity.[12] Yet when he applied his mortal powers of reason to the inner nature of the rational animal[13] and strove to comprehend matters that could hardly be known without the help of the author of nature, his ingenuity was taxed so greatly beyond its strength that he fell into gross error: he concluded erroneously that the human soul, which is endowed with everlasting reason,[14] could at some point become irrational. In other words, he thought that the soul was enticed away from its bliss as a pure spirit by the desire of inhabiting a body, and as a result fell to the depths in which it presently finds itself.[15] Furthermore, he believed that if this soul should live wickedly while in its first body (whether in the present age or at some time in future ages, of which he posited an infinite series),[16] it would receive an inferior body; and thenceforth with the accumulated weight of sinful deeds, it would ultimately come to such a pass that what had once been a man would be thrust down to live within the vilest of bodies, as in some horrible prison.[17] Behold the outcome to which that sublime meditation brought him![18] Incited by the folly of his heart, he was not afraid to draw such a reprehensible conclusion about the creature that was made after *the image and likeness* [Gen. 1.26] of the creator of all things.[19]

Tell me, I implore you, whether you do not dissent from that opinion. What honest hope do you envision for yourself? Tell me what you expect to share of the beatitude enjoyed by those who in the complete resurrection of body and soul will receive a twofold robe.[20] For their hope is founded upon the words, *eye cannot see, ear cannot hear* [Is. 64.4; 1 Cor. 2.9], all that God, in *the abundance of grace* [Rom. 5.17] and for the sake of His glory, is preparing *for those who love Him* [1 Cor. 2.9]. But according to the philosophy embraced by you and your compatriots entrenched in the German kingdom — where you[21] have been able to defy the Apostolic See and the jurisdiction of the saintly Pope Gregory, disregarding the sentence of damnation incurred by your innumerable offenses — it will happen that when you are separated from the present body, you will some day in a future age descend into a more disgraceful body; and when once more you will have polluted it with the contagion of wild beasts, you will inhabit an innumerable series of bodies in a ruinous descent, until at last you will reach an end in the bowels of the earth; and there, lodged in squalid places, you will forever lack eternal salvation.[22]

II.

<On Plato and his mythological metaphors, by which he describes the composition of the Soul which permeates all bodies without exception.>[23]

Yet that crude belief was not approved even at that time by the philosophers who succeeded him and who maintained beliefs more worthy of themselves. Follies less severe tarnished their opinions. Among them Plato was more perspicacious than the rest.[24] Yet in his study of the origins of things, he ponderously described the composition of the Soul[25] with mythological metaphors,[26] through which he asserted that it consists of an essence that is indivisible and divisible according to the nature of the Same and the Different.[27] Thus he observed that celestial and terrestrial bodies are vivified by the Soul, so that the vigor of perpetual fire that it imparts, of its own power, would counter the natural deterioration of the bodies to which it gives life.[28] Macrobius attests that Cicero, Virgil, and other Latin students of philosophy believed this doctrine, which one can easily learn for oneself if one cares to peruse his treatise on *The Dream of Scipio*.[29] This is what Plato relates through the words of his pupil Timaeus, whom he introduces in order to demonstrate in a rather abstruse discussion about numbers that a single Soul penetrates and vivifies every animated body without exception.[30] When he speaks about God fashioning the Soul,[31] he calls the mixture of the aforesaid essences "yeast."[32] Thus he says: "First He took one part of the whole body of yeast: from it He extracted another part which was twice as great as the first, then a third which was one-and-a-half times as great as the second,"[33] and so on in words that we cannot in the least recall, since the sheer obscurity of his gibberish stupefies the mind of the reader. If anyone should desire to read the passage for himself in the words of Plato, or of Macrobius who undertook the task of finding a way to cast some light upon this darkness,[34] let him attend to these matters as best he can. Yet it will be a wonder if he does not feel contempt for what he reads.

III.

<On the various opinions of the philosophers concerning the soul.>

In that same source[35] you will find assembled Pythagoras, Plato, Xenocrates, Aristotle, Posidonius, Hippocrates, Heraclitus,[36] Zeno, Democritus, another Heraclitus, Critolaus,[37] Hipparchus,[38] Anaximenes, Empedocles, Parmenides, Xenophon,[39] Boethos, and Epicurus. Many of them were *puffed up by the sense of* their *flesh* [Col. 2.18] and led astray by diverse *spirits of error* [1 Tim. 4.1], scattered by their dissension as they put forth dissonant and disputed opinions against one another, each according to the judgment of his soul.[40] Among them, Plato is seen to have come close enough to the truth[41] when he defined the soul as an essence that moves itself.[42] Another[43] defined it as a number that moves itself. Another[44] called it "entelechy," which is translated "form of the body."[45] Others offered these definitions: harmony,[46] idea,[47] the exercise of the five senses,[48] a subtle spirit,[49] light,[50] a spark of stellar essence,[51] a spirit compounded with a body,[52] a spirit mingled with atoms,[53] the fifth essence,[54] fire,[55] air,[56] blood,[57] a mixture of earth and fire,[58] a mixture of earth and water,[59] a mixture of air and fire and spirit.[60] Consider then, in light of such a divergence of opinion, whether you may claim with sound mind that you agree with each and every one of these definitions.[61] And if you can consent to the idea that your soul is correctly identified with your blood,[62] tell me, I ask you, what share do you expect in the kingdom of heaven? For if you remain in your present condition as *blood and flesh,* you *cannot possess the kindgom of God* [1 Cor. 15.50].

IV.

> <That they err in measuring the sun and the moon, and in their opinions about the hab-
> itable spots of the earth. And if anyone believes Macrobius on these matters, he unques-
> tionably imperils his faith.>⁶³

You scarcely seemed to hear me when I warned you of the great peril involved in speaking of certain other subjects: the sphere and the orbs[64] and celestial harmony,[65] the misguided calculation of the sizes of the sun and the moon and the orb of the earth,[66] but especially the disposition of the four habitable spots arranged in the circuit of this terrestrial point.[67] According to the faith you place in your Macrobius, the regions he calls "Antipodes" and "Antoeci" are disposed in such a way that travel between them is impossible.[68] And once you accept that there are four regions inhabited by men, and that no travel whatsoever between them is possible on account of the barriers erected by nature, you must explain — tell me, I beg you! — how the confession of the holy and apostolic Church is true and can reasonably be fulfilled: that the Savior came for the salvation of the entire human race — as foretold by the first fathers when this world was still, as it were, in its swaddling clothes, and later by the patriarchs and prophets who announced His Coming *variously* and *in many* evident *ways* [Heb. 1.1], and at last *in the fullness of time* [Gal. 4.4] when it was made resplendently known by the ineffable works of His humility and charity. But how might this be if three races of men, as the aforesaid Macrobius argues, can exist apart, beyond this habitable region in which the temperate climate of the zones of heaven and earth permit us to dwell — three races to whom the news of our salvation cannot reach?[69] Why is it that the faithful one,[70] whom the Lord found to be *a man according to His own heart* [Acts 13.22], exclaimed in the spirit of truth — God *has revealed His justice in the sight of the peoples* [Ps. 97.2], and in the same place, *all the ends of the earth shall see the salvation of our God* [Ps. 97.3][71] — if some ends of the earth are inhabited by men who have not heard the words of our prophets and apostles, since they were thwarted by nature, unable to traverse the insuperable expanses of water, cold, and heat?

V.

> <That according to the Apostle such things must be tested and reduced to the sobriety of
> Christian standards.>

Surely enough I read all this with you and, as I recall, I said time and again that things such as the spheres should be considered, but merely in order to be aware of them, not to believe that they have the strength of truth. For according to the precept of the Apostle, *all things must be tested* [1 Thess. 5.21] and searched thoroughly with the mind's clear vision. And just as in regard to things that are perceived by the senses, so too in matters intellectual, indeed especially in the sciences, there are so many and varied modes of apprehension that unless *the spirit of godliness* [Is. 11.2] is present to direct us by His rule, *the perverse and unsearchable heart of man* [Jer. 17.9] will tend to be seduced by specious reasoning. Hence, unless intelligence is reined in by a certain degree of sobriety, it will swell up and sooner or later collapse under its own weight. Then indeed, having been led far astray and dragged down into the depths, it will be submerged in the murkiness of folly. The mind of the Apostle, illuminated by the grace of the Holy Spirit, foresaw this; hence, among the rules of faith which he set out for us to obey, he above all admonished: *do not seek to be wiser than is necessary, but be wise with a sense of sobriety* [Rom. 12.3].

Consequently, when something comes to mind that is seductive by virtue of its probability or magnificence, we ought to set our notions and conceptions against the perfect measure of Christian doctrine that we already possess,[72] so that if something in our meditations is found to exceed this standard, we should cut it down to length without hesitation. In this way it is possible to avoid the peril of damnable errors and to retain what is fitting and beneficial in the teaching of the philosophers, leaving aside the superfluous enormity that we have observed in their conflicting theories. However, in order that you may recognize with a clarity that brooks no doubt how pernicious it is to imitate the "faith" of those whose thought astonishes us, pay heed to what Macrobius puts forth in the statement, found in the first part of his philosophical confession, which he drew from the same sources and presented in his book, borrowing these words:[73]

VI.

<On the unsound confession of the philosophers. And on the fall of Origen, who was exceedingly fond of their doctrines.>[74]

"God, who both is and is called the First Cause, is the sole lord and origin of all things that are and that seem to be.[75] This God created a Mind from Himself by the overflowing fecundity of His majesty. This Mind, which is called *Nous*, preserves the complete likeness of the creator as long as it looks upon the Father; but as it looks upon lesser things, it creates a Soul from itself. The Soul, in turn, as long as it looks upon *Nous* [and] the Father, assumes [their] place;[76] but by gradually removing its gaze, it degenerates into the fabric of bodies, though in itself it is incorporeal."[77]

Do you not think that if you took those words to heart, you would once again bring to life many errors that were identified and suppressed by the vigilant skill of the fathers in the early days of the Church? Among those errors, Arius introduced an inequality of persons into the formulation of the divine simplicity,[78] and Manichaeus wrongly taught that the unworthy devil shares in divinity by asserting that he is the creator of wicked creatures.[79] No one who has read about the history of the Church will be unaware of the terrible havoc that the Faith suffered and of the extent of the ensuing evil that was born of such nefarious perversity. Origen,[80] that great man of the Church and a wondrous commentator on the divine utterances, by the terrible judgment of God did not merit to escape the snare of this philosophical mouse-trap.[81] For after he had written numerous useful and excellent treatises which he published to the glory of the Holy Church, he finally undertook to expound the Song of Songs and asserted that the Father is not seen by the Son, and that the Son is not seen by the Holy Spirit.[82] Blessed Jerome makes note of this in his letters and deeply bewails the fall of so great a teacher, where he says: "After Origen had made fools of his rivals on various subjects, he made a fool of himself when commenting on the Song of Songs."[83] As long as his praiseworthy genius was enflamed with the guidance of love and did not recede from the light of apostolic teaching, he proceeded along a straight path and shared with others the depth *of spiritual understanding* [Col. 1.9]. When, however, he tried to combine the incomprehensible profundity *of the wisdom and knowledge of God* [Rom. 11.33] (which a man, who is inherently foolish, cannot attain through his own efforts, but through holiness) with the profane doctrines of the Greeks (of which, perhaps, he had previously become too fond) he fell most grievously, as one fallen from the loftiest height. For example, when treating of the resurrection, he denied that the bodies rising up again would be solid, and thereby he rejected the truth of the doctrine altogether.[84] Weighed down by the woeful condition of human frailty, this extraordinary man of sublime intellect was made an example for posterity, demonstrating how great must be the reverence and fear of one who seeks the loftiness of the divine plan and the profundity of the mysteries of God, so that it might be clear to everyone that the faster the motion of one's soul, the more inclined it is to a fall, unless one moves with caution and heavenly protection. The Savior declares this to His disciples when He encourages them to stand firm in making their confession of faith before the powers of the world, which might easily frighten or seduce them to fall away from His own Spirit: *Do not think about how you will speak or what you will say, for it is not you who speak, but the Spirit of your Father who speaks in you* [Matt. 10.17–20].

VII.

<On the Holy Spirit and the sound and balanced teaching He inspires. That He forsakes the proud and permits the unclean spirit to tear them apart.>

Such is His *Spirit of discipline, who flees deceit* [Wis. 1.5], whom *a body subject to sin* [Wis. 1.4] cannot merit, who departs whence He wishes and, transcending time and place, effortlessly reaches wheresoever He wishes, bearing away with Him the sign of His coming. Whatever He supplies is right and godly, whatever He utters is *firm and sound* [Job 21.23], whatever *He brings forth is pleasing* [Ecclus. 24.23] and delightful. For *in Him is the grace of truth, in* Him is our *hope of life and of virtue* [Ecclus. 24.25]. When He enters the home of those who cannot speak, He renders them eloquent,[85] and when He comes upon those who are cold and dark of heart, He transforms the seat of their vices into a tribunal of integrity. In His presence nothing can be vain or fruitless. He esteems nothing that is disorderly or dissonant, loves naught that is immoderate. He is the very standard, the measure without measure. Each of His gifts suffices — for even if what I merit may seem too little according to my desire, I am nevertheless not confounded by any shortcoming, but possess everything, as long as I remain in communion with the entire body of the Church, which God Himself vivifies. And because He, who is ever one and the same, detests schism and dissension, He multiplies the gifts of His graces and distributes them in such a way that He creates one harmonious body of enduring love.[86] So when this Spirit, who is a lover of humility, looks upon a mind that presumes too much of itself, He despises the place where pride holds sway. Consequently, *the unclean spirit* [Matt. 12.43; Luke 11.24] takes possession of the soul that is prone to disunity and, filling that soul with its own qualities and proclivities, hideously tears it apart, scatters it among various errors, and drags it down in the end to wrack and ruin.

VIII.

<That the philosophers, deprived of the blessings of the patriarchs, did not merit to acquire the slightest understanding of the mystery of the Trinity.>[87]

This is what happened to those whom we are discussing, those whom the earlier age of the Gentiles called "philosophers," whose fathers proceeded from the clan of the patriarchs of the Israelite people, but who were deprived of the hereditary blessings and thereby lacked a true knowledge of the Lord our God throughout the time that God was known in Judea. And they bequeathed their detrimental ignorance to their sons until the blessed seed[88] arrived, the one who was to have *the Gentiles for* His *inheritance* [Ps. 2.8]. In the meantime, they began to be tormented by a natural hunger and, like those who seek bread among rocks, or gold among flints, or the sun *in the caves of the earth* [Job 30.6; Heb. 11.38], in a similar manner some of them occupied themselves in the study of the nature of things, contemplating the universal substance that makes up the fabric of the world[89] and the harmonized discord of the elements,[90] while others strove to discern the causes of future events, which they believed to be signaled through the conjunction of the planets and the stars,[91] in accordance with the impelling force of fate.[92] Dispersed along these winding paths, as it were, they wandered in circles around the highest good,[93] vainly consumed in many studies.

If, however, there were among them some whom a purer and freer inspiration drew onward, they should have pressed on to something that was older and better than the creature itself,[94] a being whose power surrounds the whole of creation, whose Providence holds together all the transient, impermanent things that exist according to certain ratios of *weight and number* [Wis. 11.21]. Yet when they came to that *inaccessible light* [1 Tim. 6.16] which transcends the entire firmament and the height of heaven, they did not in the least merit to attain an awareness of the ineffable Trinity's simplicity, which must be venerated and adored, nor of the threefold mystery of its single majesty.[95] Instead, they posited three principles — a craftsman, forms, and matter[96] — and they located an intelligible world[97] in the mind of God which is the exemplar of this sensory world,[98] and which according to the principle of number intelligibly contains in itself all things destined to fall under the perception of the senses. They dishonored God's omnipotence by believing in these principles and by espousing the premise that "nothing comes from nothing."[99]

Such are the doctrines which you boast to have studied with great effort, and which I myself have read along with you; but having read them, I have applied myself for the most part in refuting them. They have in them much that poses difficulty, little that is of use, and nothing that offers salvation. Thus, when I pursued them by way of trial to see whither they would lead, I marveled at the place to which they brought me: a vast expanse, as it were, in which I was surrounded by something like orbs of smoke;[100] and I despaired of finding a way out that might lead forth to the truth.

IX.

<That such errors arise from the malign spirit. And the author of disunity has disguised
the sin of idolatry with various artifices.>

Such, indeed, are the seeds sown by the one who in his pride styled himself equal to his God.[101] Once he had taken possession of the minds of the Gentiles, as had been permitted him,[102] he promised them the sublime, he raised them up on high — he prepared them for a fall. The hearts of mortals could not escape his deceptions and his "thousand arts of injury."[103] Indeed, he sometimes leads them into blasphemy while making them think they are on their way to sanctity: he relaxes the laws of his own dominion so that his adherents might raise themselves up to a certain level of virtue, but at the same time he holds them back so that they might remain subjected to his own state of degradation.[104] And so, through his own depravity he taints their goodness, and while he most deplorably abuses another's treasure, he thoroughly conceals the wretchedness of his own disordered condition.[105] No place is narrow enough, no time is remote enough, to escape the reach of his clutches, since the secrets of nature are for him ready at hand. He fears only to enter the citadel where the Spirit who loves holiness presides.[106] Yet the rebellious one was powerful enough that when he cast his gaze upon the dejected masses of the aforementioned nations, he was able to lead them into ruin with a bacchanalian fury.

Accordingly, since he is the author of schism, he divided the human race among various doctrines and contrary sects. That is why the Socratics, the Pythagoreans, the Platonists, and members of the countless other schools of philosophy have wandered along various paths and, with their subtle arguments, have encouraged others to follow their errors. The throng of poets has followed closely, also drawing profit and strength from the devil's nursery.[107] Flocking together like jesters at the wedding of idolatry, they have delighted the souls of those who pursue vain things by reciting their fantasies and their extravagant panegyrics. For the sake of profit, they were equally prepared to condemn or to praise, and even to deify wicked princes and bloodthirsty robbers. By ringing out bombastic phrases and festooning their sentences without any regard for preserving the truth, they have rendered their services in immortalizing what is better forgotten and in exalting what is base;[108] indeed, with mythological metaphors they have adorned all that is disgraceful and obscene.[109] As natural inclination prompted them, some wrote comedies, others lyrics or satires or tragedies, and they seduced the souls of sinners with various whimsical images. Even those who were relatively innocent were blinded in the deep night of ignorance and failed to understand the dignity of their innate character, so that they became like — or rather, more debased than — the beasts, bowing down to worship stones and images unspeakably perverse.[110]

X.

<That the pagan authors are the Egyptians who must be despoiled. And that they have gathered up the treasures and ornaments of eloquence for our benefit.>

These are the Egyptians, whom God's dispensation subjected to plundering by the holy Church.[111] With the spoils taken from them we adorn the face of the Lord's temple. The gift of nature,[112] which they *with pride and abuse* [Ps. 30.19] kept for themselves

to the effect of incurring their own damnation, has devolved upon the lovers of humility, who have turned it to its destined uses, presuming nothing of their own powers,
ascribing naught to themselves, not even seeking *the things that are their own* [Phil.
2.21], but rather announcing the glory of the eternal kingdom — being prudently simple and simply prudent, they have transformed the armor of perfidy into the robe of
faith. Thus, by the spirit of charity they have revived the knowledge that was dead and
bloated. These are the people of whom we have been told: *Others have labored, and you
have inherited the fruits of their labor* [John 4.38]. All their wisdom was swallowed up
by the deep wells of the questions they posed, in which they searched for, but could not
find, *the fountain of water leaping up unto life eternal* [John 4.14]. Instead, the abundant
wealth of words and the treasuries of eloquence were, most fittingly, prepared for us, to
whom the knowledge of salvation was given for *the remission of sins* [Matt. 26.28] by
the heart of the mercy of God [Col. 3.12]. And so they wove snares for the enticement
of fools, *wasting away like a spider* [Ps. 38.12][113] by emptying out their own innards in
the deranged effort to festoon the false joys of the senses.[114] Yet we have broken
through their diabolic net.[115] We have left behind the bare carcass of idolatry and have
offered to the Savior and liberator of our souls the embellishment of eloquence and fine
rhetoric, in which *the vessels for common use* [2 Tim. 2.20] had for a long time hidden
their carrion.[116]

XI.

<On God, who is the subject of our discussion. And on the correct confession of faith.
And on the creation of angels; and of men, for whom the sentence of the Lord was mercifully tempered on account of the Fall.>[117]

Now the matter upon which we expend the ornament of words is that about which
enough can never be said by us, to wit, the Wisdom of God the Father,[118] consubstantial and coeternal to Him with the Holy Spirit, One God, immortal and unseen,
whose honor and glory alone all things *in heaven, on earth, and under the earth* serve
[Phil. 2.10], whether willingly or unwillingly. When He who *did whatever He willed
in heaven and on earth, in the sea, and in all the deeps* [Ps. 134.6] looked upon the mis-
erable human race, He eased the justice of His will with merciful prudence and tempered the strength of His might with love. Contrary to the absurd confession of the
philosophers, He does not in any way degenerate in any part of His being; He never
diminishes nor receives any additional essence, whereby He would begin to exist and
at some earlier point He would not have existed.[119] He is complete everywhere, and
not divided up into separate locations. He always exists; indeed, He is the creator of
time, the one who perfectly balances all *numbers and weights* [Wis. 11.21]. The man

of reason perceives rightly of Him when he recognizes His terrible greatness, which is beyond our ability to worship fittingly. By His Wisdom and Providence, He effects not only the division of the elements from a state of primordial chaos, but also tirelessly and without error links the things composed of the elements in a wondrous sequence of causal relationships.

This is our God [Ps. 47.15], and *there is no other besides Him* [Mark 12.32],[120] who being perfect in Himself does not suffer from the need of another's support or approval. According to the pleasure of His will, the Lord of all created from nothing *heaven and earth and all things that are contained by the vault of heaven* [Esther 13.10]. Among these things He created beings who are not His equals, though similar to Himself by virtue of their reason — angels and men — so that eternal praise should be paid to the unseen God by innumerable ranks of attendant spirits in the heavens,[121] and the actions of grace should be acclaimed in a transitory fashion by man on the earth. In the latter case, the display of praise, motivated by the affection of those rendering the praise, would be pleasing to the Lord receiving the praise only if the reward of eternal life were forthcoming to benefit the ones praising Him.

The first to forsake this constant homage was the one who was made more sublime than all the others. Not under any duress from the creator, but by his own willful abuse of his endowments, and in swelling pride, he seduced himself[122] and conceived a lust for seizing limitless plunder: equality with God.[123] Since by the peerless verdict of the creator his fall was rendered irredeemable, he began to circle about the whole of creation, seeking to add another to his own ruin.[124] He forsook the angelic legions, whose steadfastness he could not hope to sway;[125] he took no heed of the creatures lacking reason, whose end he perceived to come too swiftly. Against the human race alone, which he saw propagated for eternal life whether it would stand or fall, he turned the full force of his malice, straining with all his might to abolish in man *the image* of his maker [Gen. 1.26], so that man would become like himself, punished with the sentence of irrevocable damnation. And so he persuaded and was heeded, he fought and he conquered. And even though the holy Lord had imposed the warning of the Prohibition[126] as a special measure — in addition to the freedom of will by which man was able not to sin — nevertheless, knowing that the deceivable *mud*[127] had accepted the counsel of pride from a source outside itself, He thus tempered the severity of the deceived wretch's sentence so that by His command the inevitability of death would be repealed.[128] Hence, even under the debt of death, the means of rising again could be acquired through the merit of obedience, which in the meantime would provide for the soul; afterwards, once the duration of the present life should come to an end, body and soul alike would be restored.

XII.

> <On the precepts that had to be obeyed so that a man who had disregarded the Law
> could be rehabilitated. This reparation for sin was noted in numerous examples among
> the ancient fathers, whose grievous sins were pardoned in order to reveal the greatness of
> God's grace — particularly in the case of David, from whose lineage the Agent of for-
> giveness was born.>

And thus He set forth certain lessons concerning obedience among the early fathers,
before providing the Law. In order to cover the grand narrative in a few brief words, we
may say that He preordained sacrifice through Melchizedek,[129] circumcision and
immolation through Abraham,[130] and the erection of the memorial stone through
Jacob as a figure of the high priesthood and of the true sacrifice,[131] which were to be
revealed to the Church at the appropriate time through His Son. Later, through Moses
His servant, He weighed down a carnal people with precepts and legal customs,
employing mysteries of great profundity, so that in all those things the Wisdom of God
the Father would prefigure *by manifold means* [Heb. 1.1] the sacraments of human salvation and of His own Coming, and the actions of that people would establish by
means of mystical intimation the truth of deeds to be done in later times. Thus, the
lengthy description of the ark and of holocausts and of the cult of the Lord's temple[132]
pursues no end other than to outline the state of the Church, both present and future.
Moreover, God took great care to rouse man toward an awareness and understanding
of the sacrament of his own salvation, not to pry into the secrets of lowly creatures nor
to weary the mind with sterile meditation.

It is worthwhile to look even at the lapses of the men of the earlier people, among
whom David erred most greatly. Our saints, when considering his sin from a better van-
tage-point, judged that it contained a great harbinger of the grace to be revealed. They did
not think that it was done without its reason or without value for the Faith, which shone
gloriously among the patriarchs.[133] For afterwards, his crime of adultery,[134] to which no
remission was due according to the letter of the Law, served as an example of mercy.
Surely it was fitting that the Lord, who does not cause evil but brings order out of it,
should have provided for the salvation of the human race in such a way that the one who
had been raised up from the depths to the heights of kingship by the merit of faith was
the one who would be expelled from the heights to the depths by the guilt of lust. Likewise, the Lord's chosen one,[135] His favored preacher of the grace to come, would demonstrate in his own person how much wretched man needs the help of a merciful God. For
the one whose sin was of the flesh, endured as his persecutor the fruit of his flesh, namely,
Absalom.[136] Likewise, he who ultimately triumphed by obeying God,[137] first had to expi-
ate the impudence of his arrogant flesh by undergoing disgrace. Thus, pelted with the
stones of his servants and branded with curses,[138] he fled into exile and lost his royal

office. Yet after he turned away in humility from the deep hell to which he had drawn near, he raised his mortified eyes to the fountain of mercy, from which he had often drunk before, and *cried from the depths* [Ps. 129.1] of his heart to *the greatness of* God's *pity* [Ps. 50.3], having no hope for himself according to the indulgence of the Law. Then he was made the standard-bearer of the coming Savior, and he promised to bring the drink of grace to sinners, saying: *I shall teach the unjust your ways and the wicked shall turn to you* [Ps. 50.15]. Because of his repentence, the guilty man[139] would become more ardent about the prophecy of the Lord's Coming and, having been redeemed from the severity of the Law, he would be deprived neither of his reign as a criminal nor of his life as an adulterer. Rather, the humble king was crowned with the privilege of so great a favor, that *by a wonderful miracle* [Is. 29.14] of divine indulgence, the human race would be justified with an abundance of faith and by the grace of the Holy Spirit — upon whom the same prophet called with pure intent to *renew* his *entrails and* his *heart* [Ps. 50.12].

Upon purification[140] he would become worthy to serve the virginal creature[141] who would be acclaimed by the rod of Aaron,[142] of the same tribe as he, so that through a remarkable miracle she would flower and bear fruit without earthly assistance. Likewise Isaiah would soon foresee with a clear eye, by the ineffable working of the Spirit, that she would conceive the fountain of all propitiation[143] and would be of service in bringing grace to all, so that from the seed of the penitent[144] the Agent of forgiveness[145] would be born. The harper,[146] who had escaped the penalty of the Law, foretold this good news, this holy work, this *new song* [Ps. 39.4 et al.],[147] with a spiritual shout of joy, just as though he were already joined to the people yet to be born, and were dancing[148] before the bridal chamber of the one who would always be a virgin, singing: *We have received your mercy, O God, in the midst of your temple* [Ps. 47.10] — and many other songs that seem to indicate the full joy of one who is in attendance rather than the mood of one who still waits.

XIII.

<On the prophets who foresaw the two Comings with great yearning.>

Nor were the holy prophets content to herald so great a time of remission but, turning their faithful eyes to the two Comings of the Son of God,[149] they announce one after the other: one of humility,[150] the other of sublimity,[151] the first of gentleness, the second of power. And because human pride tends to hold in contempt what is humble, they show how great must be the reverence with which the preceding one should be received by emphasizing the grandeur of the one to follow. As a consequence, there will be no injustice against the man who merits the terrible sentence on *the day of wrath* [Apoc. 6.17] for having disdained the time of indulgence.[152] This is what Isaiah portends when he evangelizes[153] and Jeremiah when he laments,[154] after the calling of the Gentiles and the building up of the walls into one *cornerstone* [Is. 28.16]. And deploring the hardships of the wholesale captivity following the destruction of the people and city of Jerusalem, *they seek the city that lasts* [Heb. 13.14], in which the Lord of majesty already enthroned is beheld by us, who are still in the flesh.

This is *the promised land* [Heb. 11.9] and *the land of the living* [Ps. 114.9], not the kingdom in which many thousands fell time and again and in which the people help-lessly gazed upon their sons and grandsons who were slain by the violence of kings, by famine, by the sword, and by other means of death. This is, rather, the land about which David, among others, expressed wonder as he prophesied the clear truth, saying: *How lovely your dwelling, O Lord of hosts* [Ps. 83.2]. And: *Blessed are they who dwell in your house, O Lord; they shall praise you forever and ever* [Ps. 83.5]. He exhorts his own soul to turn to this land, anticipating the Lord's blessing by which he would soon be *delivered from death*, his *feet freed from stumbling* and his *eyes freed from tears* [Ps. 114.8].

They caught a glimpse, I say, and after this glimpse they sighed with supreme desire. For when they saw that this desert of a world filled with bitterness was but *a valley* sprinkled *with tears* [Ps. 83.7], they clamored for a mightier and better Moses, even though they were placed in *the promised land* [Heb. 11.9] of this world, and cried with fervent groans: *Come, O Lord,* and do not tarry, *rouse your might, O Lord God of hosts* [Ps. 79.3, 5]. And the venerable order of those fathers did not hush the outcry until the moment of the Nativity of Jesus the great leader, when the assembly would exult with ardent cries of joy, and say: *Behold, the Lord God of hosts has come with kingdom, power, and sovereignty in his hand.*[155]

With these and other words of this kind, the heralds of truth prepared the carnal-minded for accepting the humble birth of the Savior, and with certain signs and indi-cations of His might, they announced the greatness of the one to be born for the sal-vation of all, lest the unfaithful Jew[156] and the vain Gentile feign ignorance and pretend not to see the one who had been shown to them by so many foreshadowings.

If you should have cared to taste the writings of these prophets according to their inner sense, you would have realized at once that it would be the height of madness to insist upon the study of worldly knowledge to the extent of neglecting and not delight-ing in the saving profundity of the mystical sense of the Scriptures.[157]

XIV.

<That God was born of a Virgin in order to fulfill the prophecies. And the consequent refutation of the philosophers.>[158]

Therefore, when all the things that were necessary for announcing the birth of *the new man* [Eph. 4.24; Col. 3.10] had been ordained and fulfilled figuratively according to the predestination established by the intention of the merciful Lord before all ages, *God sent His Son into the world in the fullness of time, born of a woman, born under the Law* — yet not merely *to redeem those who were under the Law* [Gal. 4.4–5], for He decided to exclude no one from salvation, since He willed that no one *should perish* [2 Pet. 3.9].[159] Now, when you hear "God sent," do not suppose that the one sending is greater than the one sent, or that the one sent undergoes any change, for divinity does not experience alteration.[160] Rather, consider that the phrase implies the good will of the Father and the pious obedience of the Son, as well as the cooperation of the consubstantial Spirit.

Should you ask how the miracle of this Incarnation was accomplished, I do not know how better to reply than to draw your attention to the question that the Virgin asked and the answer that the Archangel supplied: divinity is united with the virginal flesh by the Spirit coming upon and overshadowing her through the power of the Most High.[161] Such was the efficacy of this sacred union that the Son of God, begotten before all time, God from God,[162] was born of the Virgin in time, ineffably yet truly made flesh, without confusion of nature, one person who is both God and Man.[163]

Thus teaches the vessel of grace,[164] after *the scales* of perfidy *had fallen from* his *eyes* [Acts 9.18], *when he was seized in ecstasy to the third heaven*, and *he heard* even *the secret words that man is not permitted to utter* [2 Cor. 12.2–4]. And he says: *Since He was in the form of God, He did not judge that equality with God was something to be grasped* [Phil. 2.6]. Thus, in order to indicate that the most perfect union of the Father and the Son belongs to their inherent nature, he called the Son the "form" of the Father. In this case, the notion of "grasping" something does not apply, since they were already equal by virtue of sharing the same majesty. Nor should you take "form" to mean a word which signifies, as it does in human experience, something that is different from the object that is formed, with the implication that its substance is divided into parts.[165] The preacher of truth[166] reaches out to us, and he conveys an understanding of mortal things by using a word that describes what the senses perceive, in order to help us comprehend the ineffable Word. In this way, things that humans cannot describe with a word might be grasped by faith. And in order that he might disclose the mystery of the Incarnation for the salvation of believers, he subsequently added, *He emptied Himself* [Phil. 2.7]; and in order that you may understand that the word for "emptying" does not signify a word that diminishes the immutable Deity, but one that signifies His honor, note carefully that he added, *accepting the form of a slave* [Phil. 2.7].[167]

Therefore each of the two nativities is wondrous; the arguments of human invention fail in either case.[168] The first, on account of the unity of the Trinity, reaches beyond the understanding of angels and men; the second, on account of the unusual manner of His birth, is outside the realm of philosophical reasoning altogether. For they proposed, according to an invariable consequence, "If she gave birth, she must have had intercourse with a man."[169] However, *a strong boy was born* [Is. 9.6], angelic in wisdom, a philosopher of chastity, who canceled the aforementioned logical proposition by means of His honorable birth from one who was always a virgin, since He was born from a mother who did *not know man* [Luke 1.34] and who, therefore, could by no means be said to have had intercourse with a man.[170]

XV.

<The purpose for which He was born.>[171]

In order to understand the purpose for which that wonder took place on the earth, let us return to the teacher of the Gentiles,[172] who shows the outcome of this Nativity with the words: *The grace of God our Savior appeared to all men, instructing us to renounce ungodliness and worldly desires, to live soberly and justly in this age, and to await the blessed hope and the coming of the glory of the great God* [Titus 2.11–13]. Therefore let us be raised in the birth of *the new man* [Eph. 4.24; Col. 3.10], that we may renounce *the desirable things of the world* [Titus 2.12], which cannot be loved while preserving one's godliness. And just as the holy fathers of the earlier people sighed with desire for the First Coming, so too may we, for whom the Truth has already been born into the world, groan with expectation for the Second, patiently abiding until the blessed glory arrives.

Before the coming of grace, the human race was capable only of vanity and pride, and was unable to live secure in virtue, apart from a few Israelites to whom it had been *granted* to be present before *the mystery of the reign of God* [Mark 4.11].[173] But after the humble king's appearance, we are obligated to follow His gentleness with great solicitude and to embrace His charity, so that we may continually fix upon His cross our members, which formerly served uncleanness under *the old man* [Rom. 6.6; Col. 3.9]; let us keep them in propriety for the sake of sanctification and set up the sign of God's humiliation[174] as the standard of victory against all pride. This sign is opposed by Gentile folly and by Jewish lack of faith;[175] since they were unaware of God's inestimable goodness, by which God humbled Himself so profoundly for their sake, they could only be ungrateful. We, however, who heed what the Apostle amongst us says, raise up the tree of life[176] against pride, responding to the Jew with the words of Paul, who himself was chosen from among the Jews: Christ became for our sake *obedient even unto death on a cross* [Phil. 2.8]; and to the Gentile who boasts of his empty knowledge: *We consider ourselves to know nothing in comparison to you, except Jesus who was crucified* [1 Cor. 2.2], since *for this reason God exalted Him, and gave Him the name that is above every other name, so that at His name, every knee must bend* [Phil. 2.9–10] — for the end of the humble man is exaltation, just as the end of the proud man is a fall.

XVI.

<That with His birth the full truth of Scripture was made plain by Him. And on the resuscitation of souls, and the lesson of humility.>[177]

Thus, the King of the Jews and Gentiles was submissive, in a manner befitting a God who was born of a virgin, and He demonstrated at the outset whether He was the one who had been heralded through *the Law and the prophets* [Matt. 11.13; Luke 16.16] by undergoing circumcision,[178] as the Law demanded according to the requirement of a singular operation, so that it might be proven that He was not the destroyer of the former covenant, but the one who would fulfill it.[179] Thus He intended that the Jews, who would put Him to death by performing an outward observance of *the letter that kills* [2 Cor. 3.6], would be drawn into an inner life for the sake of their salvation.

Therefore, He upheld what was written so that He might explain its meaning. He fulfilled the letter, He enlarged its spirit, He removed the figure, He disclosed the truth. In this way God, the omnipotent Wisdom, the true and just Man, by His teaching and action would stand firm against the subjection of the Law. And by virtue of the two natures that were combined in the Mediator, He fulfilled the sure plan whereby He freed men and snatched them *from the darkness to the light* [1 Pet. 2.9].[180] Thus, the Law is fulfilled so that grace might enter, and the dead are restored to life through the exercise of a most powerful act so that the souls of the living might be heartened.

Three distinct episodes of raising the dead demonstrate the resuscitation of souls, for the soul of any sinner that has been given up for dead is still within its body and might readily be recalled to life — whether it has just crossed the threshold of death (as in the case of the synagogue leader's daughter),[181] or has left the gates of consciousness for some time (and is carried off for burial by the assembled crowds),[182] or has endured an even longer period of death (and is already fetid after being confined in the tomb, sealed beneath a heavy stone).[183] Thus, at the arrival of the omnipotent physician: the girl's hand is grasped and she arises; the bier of the young man is touched, and although he had been declared dead, he revives; the compassionate one sheds tears, and the one who had been entombed is called and comes forth.[184] There is no ill within the soul of the dying that exceeds the power of the healing Savior, for He is the one *who forgives all your iniquities, who heals all your infirmities, who even redeems your life from death* [Ps. 102.3–4].

For as the Lord wills, He forgives, as shown when He used His power in raising the dead. Since you see what He did for the entire human being, you should not despair that He can do the same for a part.[185] Therefore, you should hasten to exert yourself even in slight matters before you are buried.[186] And let not the wretched man be apprehensive about his unworthiness or his infirmity, for no one who approaches God is deemed unworthy of being healed by Him, for He deigned to become a poor man precisely so that all might have access to Him.

This is the will of the Father, this is the obedience of the Son, that in assuming flesh He would appear as the essential teacher of humility, the true and voluntary practice of which He would demonstrate, and would bring back to Himself the proud man, drunk with the vain things of the world and delirious among the corrupting influences of carnal desires. He accomplished this by being born of a poor and humble virgin in a cramped stable,[187] by the observance of circumcision and of the offering required by the Law,[188] by the acceptance of baptism from His herald,[189] by His encounter with the malignant spirit and by the sanctifying power of fasting,[190] and finally by the election of His disciples,[191] whom He chose solely from considerations of humility and charity, so that every occasion for pride might be completely banished from His discipleship, since He elected precisely those who could not at all boast of having left behind offices or wealth that they had once possessed.[192] Certainly this was done with great foresight, lest anyone judge others in the company of grace to be unworthy on account of poverty in earthly things — for they were found to possess nothing in terms of human glory that could be regarded as a reason for which they merited to be chosen.

XVII.

<On the simplicity of Peter the apostle and the merit of his faith.>

Thus, *Simon Bar Jonah* [Matt. 16.17] is received as the leader of the gentle company, chosen foremost for his simplicity and love, being a man who was encouraged *not by flesh and blood* [Matt. 16.17], but *by revelation from the Father of lights* [James 1.17], as noted when he answered Christ's imposing question[193] with the words: *You are the Christ, the Son of the living God, who have come into this world* [Matt. 16.16]. He responded swiftly while his colleagues hesitated, and provided a clear confession of faith regarding the Savior, for the instruction of all the faithful. Therefore, such firmness of perspicacious faith was made the foundation of the Church by the Son of God Himself, upon which the structure of the entire edifice would surge upwards. And Peter himself, made blessed by divine authority, became the key-bearer of the kingdom of heaven, receiving such plenitude of power that whatever he binds, truly is bound, whatever he looses, truly is loosed, both in heaven and on earth.[194]

Wherefore, since God the Father made this revelation through Peter by the Holy Spirit, the power and authority which descended upon him from the merit of his confession must be considered very carefully according to its inner meaning; this cannot be attempted except by one who applies the eye of faith. And yet, all can plainly see that the punishment of binding[195] has sometimes erupted with such power that it has resulted even in bodily destruction, as in the case of Ananias and Sapphira.[196] Whence, if you believe with *a pure heart*,[197] you shall be absolved, and *if you confess with your mouth, you shall be saved; for by virtue of the heart one is credited with justice, and confession with the mouth leads to salvation* [Rom. 10.9–10]. Built up in this manner, you shall be justified upon the foundation of the apostolic confession and, having been justified by faith, you shall live.[198] Certainly the prince of apostles leads the way in this justification by faith, for an abundance of faith conferred upon him primacy among the other elect in heaven and on earth.

Such is the excellence of his office that one who does not pay obedience to this faithful key-bearer is altogether unworthy of obtaining the Lord's grace. Thus, one is not permitted to enter the kingdom of heaven[199] if the key of Peter does not grant entry, since anyone whose sin he does not forgive, is not forgiven, and whomever he forgives, is forgiven.[200] Although this heavenly gift and spiritual power was granted by the generous Savior to all the apostles,[201] nevertheless it was clearly preeminent in the one who was questioned more often than they were about the depth of his love, as when he was asked whether he loved Him more than the others and was singled out to feed the sheep.[202]

XVIII.

<On the sacraments of rebirth and refreshment,[203] both of which were instituted before the Passion at the Last Supper.>[204]

And so the disciples were chosen as sons adopted into the Kingdom, and miraculous signs were abundantly displayed, which a mere man could never have performed and which proved by the fact of their occurrence (since they could not have been feigned) that divinity was the operative force, located bodily within the Son of Man. At last, when He had reached *the hour in which He would depart from this world and return to the Father* [John 13.1], fulfilling the plan of humility and love that He had undertaken in order to leave His co-heirs the sure hope of an inheritance,[205] He established by His own authority a *new covenant* [Heb. 9.15], in which *the old man* [Rom. 6.6; Col. 3.9] would be cleansed through *the baptism of new birth* [Titus 3.5] and transformed into *a new creation* [2 Cor. 5.17]; and afterwards he would be refreshed with the body of Christ, since there was no food other than His own body, which had been received from a virgin, that was suitable enough for such refreshment.

This body — truly immortal and incorruptible, even before the Resurrection, by virtue of its divine power — is offered up[206] so that when you hear that the Lord ascended bodily into the heavens,[207] you may not suppose that His faithful ones were defrauded of so great a gift; for although He is firmly seated at the right hand of the Father,[208] nevertheless by the same power He even now grants on the altar of faith that same body which He at that time gave to His disciples when He still appeared mortal among them. For just as *in baptism you are buried with Christ, taking part in His death* [Rom. 6.4], and the hands of the one administering baptism work like certain instruments outwardly, nevertheless it is He who stands in the midst,[209] as is written: *This is the one who baptizes* [John 1.33] — the one whom the faithful sees, the unfaithful does not acknowledge, the one who works the effect of salvation. So too at the table you are refreshed not with a merely figurative body, but with the true body of the same Christ. It is by means of faith that the bread which you see is accurately recognized for what it is, since that unseen priest is present, changing the created substance by raising it up with the ineffable working of sanctification.[210] Thus, when the priest utters the Lord's words,[211] which are living and sanctifying, one must take heed and, as blessed Ambrose witnesses, one must receive "not that which nature has formed, but that which the blessing has consecrated."[212]

XIX.

> <That in the cross of Jesus Christ is the remission of sins and the redemption of all people, including the saints of the Old Testament.>[213]

After celebrating and establishing this sacrament with His disciples, He gave a sermon concerning the mysteries of love and of unity in head and members, which was of surpassing sweetness, as the narrative by Saint John the Evangelist relates.[214] He was eager to employ the power by which He had taken up His soul, in order to lay it down, so that He could take it up again.[215] Then he proceeded to the cross, *willing in spirit, though weak in the flesh* [Matt. 26.41], so that by the spilling of His blood, the one establishing the covenant would make it firm.[216]

Concerning the effusion of His blood, one might ask what saving power it contains, or what merit it provides for the redemption of those for whom it was poured out. One must accept this premise: that any action a human being can offer is insufficient for atonement. Thus, it is the fervent attitude of the Christian that he cherishes in lasting memory the vital death that was *the price of* his *redemption* [Ps. 48.9] and inwardly praises the Lord his God, embracing so great a blessing with the unshaken firmness of faith, recalling that He died for him and arose by the power of God and sits at the right hand of the Father[217] — the God whom every rational creature adores. He is humbled before the cross of his Lord, mortifying his flesh in fear of Him, and if perchance he is weighed down by a multitude of crimes or by the dire circumstances of the age, he raises his eyes to the one whom the world hung upon the cross as a criminal. For that blood ever *washes us of our sins* [Apoc. 1.5], and having been shed for us, it never fails to exert its effect of salvation. When He was under the penalty of condemnation, indeed at the moment of death, He absolved iniquities committed a long time before.[218] And this one, for whom the present life ended ignominiously, opened the door to eternal rest by means of the meritorious confession of faith.[219]

Christ sanctified even His own torment, so that the cross, which had earlier been the disgrace of the condemned — among whom were counted those with horrible, unclean, blaspheming crimes on their conscience — became by His action the terror of unclean spirits and the Savior's glory. Anyone who desires to follow Jesus will bear this cross and deny oneself.[220] Bearing it, we shall set out unto life, and we shall be strengthened for the fight against the perils of the world. We shall single out and trample upon pride, so that by the cross on which the Master has been offered up, the disciple shall be made firm. This sign of His deliverance was recognized by the vessels of faith,[221] that is, by the saints of antiquity, when the Lord descended into hell in order to free His own,[222] bursting asunder *the gates of death* [Ps. 9.15][223] and defeating in battle the Prince of Darkness. For a long time they sat *in darkness and in the shadow of death* [Ps. 106.10],[224] waiting until *the way of peace* [Luke 1.79], which had been closed off by the death that Adam incurred, should be restored by the giver of life.[225] Certainly they knew about this inheritance, inasmuch as nothing was lacking in their faith — an inheritance of which we are certain because it was fulfilled in the past, and one which was certain for them, though its fulfillment lay in the future, by virtue of their unerring hope.

Thus, the destined people of Israel, who first had been set *beneath the rule of the pedagogue* [Gal. 3.24–25], weighed down and *locked beneath sin* [Gal. 3.22] by the servile yoke of the Law, were estranged from the Kingdom until the true Lamb was raised upon the cross; but by His blood they were freed, and in this manner those whom the Son had freed would be restored to eternal freedom.[226] Under the rule of the Son, who was the most powerful king of all, the same opportunity and grace of resurrection would be granted to the older and the younger peoples alike.[227] That which had already taken place among some of the earlier people[228] was confirmed by the testimony of the Gospel, when it describes how created things gave evidence of the dying Savior's power: *the sun was darkened, and the curtains were torn* [Luke 23.45], *and tombs were opened from which the bodies of many of the saints who had been asleep emerged and came into the holy city of Jerusalem and appeared to many* [Matt. 27.52–53].

XX.

<On the glory of the Resurrection. And that the disciples were called to announce eternal life,[229] not to philosophize.>

When the disgrace of the dead one was transformed into glory by His Resurrection, then at last He began to fulfill what He had announced before He had undergone the Passion: *When I shall have been exalted, I shall draw all to myself* [John 12.32]. For it was not only the ancient fathers (about whose desire for the First Coming we have spoken)[230] who were called out of darkness, but also the Gentiles, who lay prostrate *in the pit of misery* [Ps. 39.3] and in the depths of their vices; yet soon after the coming of the Spirit, they received the light of faith. Thus, when the apostles announced the powerful deeds of the one who had displayed most evidently by means of His risen body what the bodies of the faithful would become, they confidently hoped that they would also experience what had occurred to His bodily nature. For God, who is *the Word* [John 1.1], assumed a body and a soul like our own for no other reason than to raise both up, each in its own time. Therefore, although the sentence of the primordial curse is still visited upon man,[231] who remains mortal and must pay his debt with the price of death, nevertheless the mercy of God brooks no delay in the resurrection of the human soul, which on account of its dignity deserved to be treated more swiftly.[232] And thus God most clemently revived the souls of the elect, both those who lived before the Law and those who lived under the Law, through faith in Jesus Christ, who is life.[233] Even though the flesh of believers may be destroyed, for those revived no harm will be suffered — since there shall undoubtedly be *a resurrection of the dead* [Rom. 1.4] at the end of the ages, as He has predestined.

The Son of God prepared us for the certain truth of this resurrection well in advance, when He revealed to His disciples a body that was incorruptible yet palpable, contrary to the nature of things that are incorruptible.[234] He appeared twice for the sake of those who doubted whether or not He was truly seen,[235] so that while the earlier appearance might allay their doubts in order to build up their faith, the later appearance might provide inspiration so that they would strive after the life wherein they would, with eyes enhanced, forever enjoy the most joyous vision of the Lord's body — since here they could not, with their mortal eyes, continually look upon that which was blessed with immortality.[236] During His manifestation, He did not shrink from the touch of the saintly women;[237] and whether touching or sharing a meal, *until the day on which He ascended* [Acts 1.2], the Lord in His humble manner incited the minds of His friends to seek the kingdom of God by talking about that fatherland,[238] a place in which each of them, whether *man or woman* [Gal. 3.28], would be transformed with respect to sin but preserved with respect to their true nature, and would thereby *attain the measure of* His *full stature* [Eph. 4.13].

Of His kingdom we have here the beginning in Christ Himself, in whom they[239] were made *the first fruits* [1 Cor. 15.20] of those who will rise again. His kingdom will eventually be made perfect in us, when it becomes the crown of the saints. However, when the disciples, who had not yet been enlightened, listened to Him as He spoke about the baptism of the Spirit, they were preoccupied with His display of power, and they thought that He would restore the temporal kingdom of Israel. Thus, they asked: *Lord, will you now restore the kingdom of Israel? To which He replied, It is not yours to know the time or the moment, which the Father has reserved for Himself. But you will receive the power of the Holy Spirit coming down upon you, and you will be my witnesses in Jerusalem and in all of Judea and Samaria and unto the ends of the earth* [Acts 1.6–8].

Thus, the creator of time did not call them to speculate about the size of the celestial regions and the conjunctions of the planets,[240] nor to discern the motions of the stars;[241] neither did He call the lovers of everlasting life to the study of worldly philosophy, which requires one to expend almost the whole of one's attention on things that will perish. Rather, He said, *You will receive the Spirit coming down, in order to give witness* to my name [Acts 1.8]. It is just as if He said to *the poor in spirit* [Matt. 5.3] and to those who disdain the world:[242] "Do not inquire about the circuit of the sun[243] or the straying of the moon,[244] which the worldly philosophers have studied too eagerly while remaining ignorant of that which is most useful for you to seek and love. *Await the promise of the Father, which you have heard me utter* [Acts 1.4], and *remain here until you are clothed with power from on high* [Luke 24.49]. *For when the Spirit of truth has come, He shall teach you all truth, and He shall announce to you what is to come* [John 16.13]."

XXI.

<On the coming of the Spirit, and what He accomplished through the apostles. And that in the present we do not enjoy the fullness of beatitude, but only its inception.>

Christ ascended into the heavens as they looked on, and took His place at the right hand of the Father, enthroned above every height; and they received His promise after the days of Pentecost were completed, when suddenly a sound came from heaven like a rushing wind, which became manifest to them in the form of tongues of fire.[245] Our faintheartedness prevents us from speaking of what He accomplished in them — but we implore Him to be present to us now, to teach us in our infant-like ignorance, so that we may be able to perceive and announce what is worthy of Him. For who, unless *streams of living water flow from his belly* [John 7.38], is able to conceive how the Holy Spirit came and baptized them? And when the rust of iniquity had been completely scoured away, He filled them with the gift of all the virtues, so that from the abundance of His holiness, the timid suddenly became brave, the foolish became wise, the lukewarm became fervent, and they shared *one heart and one soul* [Acts 4.32], since the love of God was unstintingly suffused in their hearts by the divine power of the same Spirit who had come upon them.

Then at last when the work of God had been confirmed in them, and they had received the gift of true freedom, they offered to Christ the Lord the voluntary gifts of faithful hearts. Thus, they who earlier had been stricken with slavish fear were able, after the Spirit had enlivened them and they had received instruction in God's great plan, to give witness to the Resurrection, as had been enjoined upon them, with invincible strength in the hearing of the malevolent council.[246] Then truly *the heavens proclaimed the glory of God*, the apostolic *firmament announced the work* of the Spirit [Ps. 18.2],[247] and *the voice of majesty shook the desert as it thundered out in power* and *magnificence* [Ps. 28].[248] And although the Gentiles did not understand their words, the diversity of languages did not prevent *their message from going forth to every land* [Ps. 18.5] by virtue of the scintillating blaze of the divine fire;[249] and under the tutelage of *the Spirit who contains all things and fills the whole world* [Wis. 1.7], the knowledge of the Word was delivered to many nations. *Dividing* His gifts *as He willed, the Spirit* bestowed *upon some the ability to speak in tongues, upon others the grace of healing*, upon yet others *discernment of spirits* [1 Cor. 12.9–11], upon all believing in the Savior the remission of sins and that which is more excellent than all these things: an unfailing love of God and neighbor.[250] He enflamed the tongues of those who preached, and softened the hardness of those who listened. He made perfect the mouths of the ones speaking, and prepared the hearts of the learners for receiving the word of life, so that the teaching would proceed without delay and the learning without difficulty, a true and joyous perception of the salvific doctrine. Then the outpouring which the Lord God had once announced through Joel began to be fulfilled, namely: *I shall pour out my Spirit upon all flesh* [Joel 2.28], especially upon the sons of the Jews, that is, the holy apostles who prophesied the life to come. On the one side, the synagogue relinquished the bloodshed of animal sacrifices; on the other, the Gentiles relinquished the worship of idols. For the Spirit, who had made known His coming through the lips of the prophets, was sent forth from the Father and the Son,[251] and when the curtain of the Law was torn asunder,[252] He proceeded onwards to the whole human race, so that through the act of a new creation *He renewed the face of the earth* [Ps. 103.30]. And with the removal of the stains of idolatry, He joined together the separate walls into one house of the Lord,[253] making them *a holy nation, a people set apart, a chosen race, a royal priesthood*, all of them *called together into the wondrous light* [1 Pet. 2.9] of the Lord Jesus Christ.

Entirely at the prompting of the Paraclete,[254] who worked through the apostolic imposition of hands,[255] the sacred institution of holy orders was established, as well as the pious gathering of the reverend council.[256] Later fathers would imitate its form (since they were illuminated by the same Spirit) in order to avoid the lurking heresies, and they would ordain rules for the usage of their times and places through the gentle exercise of their authority. Animated by this Spirit, the apostles, as well as the apostolic men,[257] steadfastly overcame the torments imposed by ill-fated kings.[258] They even disdained the burning of their bodies, on account of the more intense heat of love,[259] glorifying God by the example of their faith, words, and deeds, patiently maintaining possession of their holy souls even unto their departure from this life, preserving the crown of martyrdom, *the treasure* of faith *in earthen vessels* [2 Cor. 4.7]. His is the inspiration, for that which the orthodox confession everywhere observes and that which all priests have uttered with sound understanding about the incarnate Word, whether for the education of others or for their own consolation, they have drawn from a source none other than Him. For *no one* loves *the Lord Jesus except in the Holy Spirit* [1 Cor. 12.3], who upon His arrival fires the hearts of the elect with love of the Word coeternal to Himself; and *with groanings that cannot be described* [Rom. 8.26], He makes them sigh and utter demands with the Psalmist: *Make known to me, O Lord, my end, and what is the number of my days, that I may know what* promise *I lack* [Ps. 38.5][260] as I sojourn here still, on this side of death.

Whenever the Spirit of piety makes us leap across to this infinite number of remaining days,[261] He also supplies us with *His anointing*, by which *He teaches about all things* [1 John 2.27],[262] since we *do not consider* ourselves *to have attained* everything [Phil. 3.13].[263] But having been initiated with the present sacraments, we *reach forth* with the Apostle toward the things to come, *toward the prize to which God calls* us [Phil. 3.13–14].[264] Mindful of that inheritance by which *we are delivered from the hand* of all *enemies* seen or unseen, *we shall serve at every* moment *in holiness and justice the one* [Luke 1.74–75] who will be bodily present.[265] For just as the earlier things pointed to these that are present,[266] so too these are effective for salvation, but merely as a foretaste of the things to come — *for by hope we have been saved* [Rom. 8.24], and *now we see through a glass, but then* we shall see *face to face* [1 Cor. 13.12], when *Christ* our life *will appear* and it will at last be seen *what we shall be* [1 John 3.2].

XXII.

<That one must briefly say something about the philosophers, so that it may be shown how great a peril there is in assenting to their writings, since they knew nothing about the resurrection of bodies. And that their definition [of man] must be refuted. And a spirit enslaved by the flesh has lost its ability to perceive their error.>

We have briefly touched upon the long sequence of God's works and have outlined for your consideration the character of the Church, so that you may have some basis from which to judge how contrary at many points and dissonant are the heavenly institution and the delusions of human imagination.[267] Granted, in matters of moral discretion that are not directly concerned with the sanctifying effect of faith, there is no discrepancy between philosophical reasoning and the understanding of orthodox opinion, as seen in many cases — such as in their description of the virtues, which they call political, purgatorial, and purified[268] — and in many other matters. Hence, the guides of the Church and the governors of the divine republic have borrowed certain things from them. Nevertheless, when it comes to a discussion of our bodies, they have proven to be deplorably obtuse, setting before themselves pernicious theories that run counter to the mystery of the resurrection, with which *the riches of* God's *goodness* [Rom. 2.4] and humility are especially concerned, and which, of course, they have merited neither to infer with nature as their guide nor to recognize with God as their inspiration. For indeed, judging that the body is composed of the elements, they were of the opinion that the heavy part of it would return to the earth by an inevitable necessity,[269] so that when the spirit would return to its companion star,[270] the individual components that had comprised the composite body would be unwoven into the essences from which they were born[271] — whence they deemed that the body is nothing but a prison and a tomb of the sorrowing soul.[272] From this it follows that anyone who has accepted as truth what is found in their writings, which contend that the restoration of bodies to eternal life is impossible,[273] and anyone who even regards the doctrine that "all heavy bodies shall be dragged into the earth by their own inclination"[274] as being worthier of assent precisely because it is sanctioned by the pagans, such a person without a doubt is an enemy to himself. He is, moreover, offensive to the creator of the elements, who *did whatever He willed* [Ps. 134.6], and who most certainly finds it as easy to place an element above its natural position[275] as He found it easy at the first moment of creation[276] to stabilize the jostling chaos by separating the elements.[277]

    And in this, I should think, you will agree with me: that God can do all that He wills. But perhaps you shall reply: although He may do whatever He wills, and does not do one thing while willing another, but certainly wills that which He does, since no one compels His will, nevertheless, to the one who practices philosophy it remains doubtful whether He really willed what the blessed simplicity of the faithful believes Him to have willed and done.[278] This knotty question is as difficult for the unbeliever as it is easy for the believer, and inasmuch as it is, as I deem, insoluble for man, it is solved if one employs *the key of David, which closes and no one opens, opens and no one closes* [Apoc. 3.7].[279] For us, then, this problem is solved in the example of faithful Abraham, among whose descendants[280] even the philosopher who believes becomes blessed. As seen in the column of cloud and fire at the time of Moses,[281] in the parting of the Red Sea,[282] and in the rest of the examples that we have briefly summarized above, the usual course of nature has been overcome so many times that by now even nature can hardly have any confidence in herself![283] And as the ultimate example, God is born as a man — from a woman who remains a virgin; and the same man, having been buried, comes back to life for all eternity in His true body, having earlier in all truth raised the rotting corpse of Lazarus to mortal life as proof of His power.[284]

Therefore, the philosopher is in error when he announces that "man is a rational, mortal animal,"[285] since *Christ, having risen from the dead, no longer dies; death shall no longer have any power over him* [Rom. 6.9]. And so in this case a certain man was made an immortal animal, one who imparts to His imitators the salvific doctrine. He helps them in disputation[286] to the extent that they, bravely resisting the devil who is the destroyer of faith, and his minions, believe in Him and urgently call upon Him to be present in order to remove the mortality by which wretched mankind had been sundered from God; and He grants their request by virtue of the immortality that had been conferred upon His humanity, and by which He, as God, had differed from mankind.[287] And thus through the wisdom and grace of Christ, the beings whom[288] the mortal philosopher in his fatuous sagacity divided with a transitory quality[289] come together in a single definition.

One cannot grasp this truth after he has subjected his spirit to the flesh, for since *the flesh lusts against the spirit* [Gal. 5.17],[290] the spirit shall waste away under the dominion of the flesh if it has denied itself its own fruits — which are, according to the Apostle in his exhortation to the Galatians: *charity, joy, peace, faith, continence, chastity* [Gal. 5.22–23] and other such virtues which are not subject to the force of the Law. When the spirit has become a disgraced servant oppressed by the command of a lascivious master, and has become accustomed to bear the yoke of sensuality, it immediately loses the patience to await the good things that will endure, and it is embroiled and confounded *in the works of the flesh — which are fornication, impurity, the avarice that is the worship of idols* (one should also include the transgression of disobedience as a form of *idolatry*), and finally *contention* and *dissension*[291] — in which you who are the servants of the flesh have most eagerly busied yourselves all this time.[292] *Those who do such things shall not inherit the kingdom of God* [Gal. 5.21]!

And thus one deprived of *the grace of God*, which is *eternal life*, works for *the wages of sin*, which are the unceasing torments of perpetual *death* [Rom. 6.23].[293] For although the spirit was meant to train and assist the flesh by the tutelage of the virtues and the exercise of saintly morals in order to seize the robe of immortality, the result, instead, is that the flesh drags down the spirit, blinded and suffocated, to receive the rewards of hell. And thus perishes *the faith that works through love* [Gal. 5.6], which is the most firm assurance of the good things that are to come, and is succeeded by faithlessness, which creates despair. And when the eyes of reason, by which one is able to discern what is true and honorable, as well as what is pure and beneficial, have been extinguished, one lives in the servitude of the senses, so that one desires what is dishonorable and hideous, and loves what is worthy only of condemnation. Thus a man who has been created to honor God is reduced in bestial disgrace to the likeness of the

uncomprehending brutes. The result is that he passes from vice to vice without inter-
ruption, since one sin becomes the cause of another sin.[294] At that point a tenacious
delight in sinning forcibly drags *the man with depraved sense* [Rom. 1.28] into the
uttermost depths of sin, until at last it seems there can be no remission of one's
offenses. Then that which is *better than sacrifice*, the good of *obedience*,[295] is despised;
for of course when the fear of God has expired, one obeys only one's overmastering
lust.

XXIII.

<That certain Germans have fallen away from obedience to and unity with the Roman
Church, saying they have no pope but Caesar.>

Certain persons have clearly prepared an abyss of great confusion for you and for themselves — unless the greater mercy of God should deign to save you from your perdi-
tion.[296] And these persons, moreover, are not inconsequential commoners but those
whom you address as bishops and archbishops.[297] Their fury in its abounding iniquity
is so great that it has made them lose their senses; hence, they have not hesitated to
despise the wholesome admonitions and canonical decrees of that holy man, the bishop
of the see of Rome, Gregory VII,[298] and to break themselves off from vital union with
the apostolic Church, the mother of all the faithful.[299] For when by the same Gregory
they were pressed with canonical arguments to give an account of their crimes, they
who were under the gaze of the wary and intensely dedicated man, and were either
condemned or under threat of condemnation, decided that no avenue by which they
might evade the consequences of their impiety should be overlooked: so they
embroiled their own king, Henry, in the same condemnation, adducing him as the
author of their heresy, and at the same time looking to him as their defender.[300] The
madness of the German kingdom swelled beyond measure, and in your unbridled sin
you imitated the Judaic perfidy — for in rejecting those who belonged to the Catholic
party, you wrongly opposed the teacher of the whole Church, the bishop of the highest see.[301] Neglecting the reverence that is due in divine worship, you audaciously
shouted again and again: *We have no* pope *but Caesar!*[302]

And with the intention that the body of Satan should remain whole in head and members,[303] *you demanded that a murderer be handed over to you* [Acts 3.14],[304] to wit, Wibert
the ex-archbishop of Ravenna,[305] whom the Roman Church had already condemned for
well-established crimes against the people, in a plenary synod at which the same Gregory
presided.[306] By your nefarious entreaties and actions you demanded with all your
strength that the disciple of Jesus, who spent himself completely in this matter so that the
holy Church would be restored to its due honor and state of required freedom, should be

taken out and crucified.[307] But because *the Lord knows those who are His own* [2 Tim. 2.19], and has elected *from every nation men acceptable to Him who fear Him and do justice* [Acts 10.35], there were yet present at that time great *men* who were *devout* [Acts 2.5] and who did not find such iniquity agreeable. And today there remain in the same kingdom some considerable number who by God's grace *have not yet bent their knees before Baal* [Rom. 11.4],[308] and who have refused to consider distinguished offices as something more precious than their own salvation;[309] to the contrary, regarding all things as *rubbish so that Christ may be* their *wealth* [Phil. 3.8], they have given their allegiance to the prince of the apostles and to his successor, Gregory, for the defense of the Faith. How wickedly, even by the standards of worldly laws, has he been treated in the course of this whole affair, in which for ten years and more during his tenure in the sacred office as pope he labored for the holy Church while it tottered[310] — as is manifestly known from the historical account attributed to the archbishop of Salzburg,[311] a man illustrious in those regions for his intense efforts to observe justice in this matter.

For this reason it is all the more amazing to behold your impudence and that of the others who wage war with numerous yet empty words against the cause of the Church, contrary to the rules of faith, not at all knowing what you are saying or what it is that you are declaring. For if the sacred Scriptures, which your hardness of heart makes you unworthy to understand, could not satisfy you (in spite of the Savior's words testifying that *the disciple is not greater than the master*[312]), then neither could the authority of the Holy Spirit — by which the supreme pontiff has been appointed to be judged by no one[313] — nor the concordance of the decretals[314] wrench the sword of judgment, by which you intended to slay the patriarch of Christianity, from your impious hands, or in any way subdue your obstinacy by the yoke of obedience. At the very least, you should have been brought to your senses by the discreet men among you who are learned in the law of the Lord, by the legitimate princes who honor God, and finally by the monks, hermits, and religious of every station who impugn your schism with an open display of disapproval. The fact that you oppose one set of canons with another set of canons demonstrates your senseless ignorance,[315] especially when the affair is not so complicated by ambiguity that it might not be made plain through careful thought, if only you were willing. To the contrary, your desire to use force, when the verdict is so clear, is the ploy of violent men who despair of justice.

Indeed, to this very day the two cities, of which one belongs to Christ, the other to the devil, have remained distinct from the beginning of this affair by the character of their citizens.[316] There is scarcely a single city in all the Latin world that does not have partisans of either side in this dispute, so that some with the bloodthirsty Cain offer beards of grain with ears of grain as a provocation before God, while others with the just Abel offer as a simple lamb the innocence of truth.[317] So it is that when you appeal to divine clemency in your sacrifices, and defend Wibert as the father and pontiff of your souls, you actually anger the Most High and increase your profanation. We execrate the same man as the most damnable of heretics, who tried to usurp and pollute the most sacred see of the apostles while our father and lord was alive,[318] through the bloody hand of a flagitious and excommunicated king,[319] obliging one another in sin.[320] In this matter there is no middle ground: either you, if we speak truly, are like those who most perniciously worship the devil instead of Christ and are in the grip of a condemnation that cannot be dissembled; or we, if we are mistaken, are misled by a prejudicial presumption against the innocent that is intolerable and exceedingly odious. Therefore, when our accusation has been proven, it remains to be seen whether *the wrath and indignation* [Jer. 36.7] of God shall seize you as you persist, or whether His mercy shall have compassion on the repentant.

But, as we expect, not one of your number (even though you have taken up your own defense) will be so impudent that he will dare to deny what is being said about the invasion,[321] for virtually the entire Roman world regards these men as villains whom general opinion has already convicted. Since, therefore, you perceive that your insolence in this matter has put you in the most dire straits, you take recourse to another subterfuge, just like thieves who have been caught and who deny whatever they expect shall prove them guilty and fabricate whatever they think shall acquit them. So now you pretend that Gregory never was pope,[322] even though the universal mother Church chose this man, who was given a pious and holy upbringing since boyhood in the bosom of the same Church,[323] to be her guide and the governor of all those reborn in Christ, by means of a solemn election of all those who at that moment in time were required and able to be present.[324] It was then necessary to accept his leadership when he became *a man filled with faith and the Holy Spirit* [Acts 11.24] and took upon himself the revival of the canons *in a time of need* [Ecclus. 8.12], when abuses had become rampant. He was acknowledged not only by the Gallican Church, but also by the Teutonic and Hispanic, and finally by the Greek and Latin, without objection and with due veneration. To this very day, when they recall having had such a pope, they do not fail to give thanks. The canons have taught them such things.[325] The Spirit who proceeds from the Father commanded this man tirelessly to serve His dove,[326] which He desires to be *without stain or wrinkle* [Eph. 5.27], so that the successors of the one whom the Lord called *Bar Jonah*,[327] that is, "the son of the dove,"[328] should be considered supreme pontiffs, since the power that was once received by this apostle has been transferred to them in succession. In this way the honor of the Church's highest office and the momentous concerns of its lofty affairs have been handed down. And in pronouncing judgments, the apostolic privilege is not abrogated even when the moral life of the one who holds the office is of low quality, since the merits of Peter his predecessor and the grace of the Holy Spirit are both active in him by virtue of legitimate ordination.[329]

As to whether you yourselves had ever accepted the same man as supreme pontiff, it is proven by the satisfaction that your king made in Italy after his first excommunication, when under the compulsion of desperate circumstances you realized that there was no escape from your ruin, apart from imploring his absolution.[330] Even if your intentions were treacherous, nevertheless at that moment you recognized him as your pastor and lord. We shall not write more concerning this subject, since all these events have been set out fully and clearly in the history written by the man whom we mentioned earlier.[331]

XXIV.

<Concerning the letter that they have written against the saintly Pope Gregory, and that by the grace of God one must reply to this letter.>

Yet surely we must not for any reason fail to mention a certain letter written against the same saintly Gregory, which your malignity contrived for the sake of corrupting the less-informed, for swaying the minds of the simple and adding them to your wicked cause — to fool them into thinking that what you do proceeds from zeal for justice, rather than from deception fueled by hatred.[332] This letter has been circulated throughout the various lands of the realm by unwitting men who assist you in your designs because they have been shaken by the horror of the lies that you spread. They fail to consider, however, whether the matter is truly as you report; they believe it is so because you have set your version down in writing. Hence, they think that your unheard-of cruelty is justified.

Yet it is clear to one who knows the truth of the matter that *you have the devil for your father*, and that *the father of lies* [John 8.44] has spoken through your mouth as if out of his own. He *stood not in the truth* [John 8.44] but compelled you to say and write dreadful things about *the Lord's anointed*[333] and the successor of the blessed apostles, things that one could hardly consider plausible even in a man of low status. However, as we have heard, a council for oppressing the just man was held in Trier,[334] and among all those in the *company of evildoers* [Ps. 63.3] who *sat in the chairs of pestilence* [Ps. 1.1], not one of them was found capable of composing a statement that would rebuke an innocent man, mock justice, and disparage the words of truth in a convincing manner. So the care of this business (it is said) was entrusted to a certain grammarian by the name of Wenrich, a master at Trier,[335] who used the bishop of Verdun[336] in the role of Eliphaz the Temanite[337] to utter fraudulent words and a deceitful series of questions that would increase the sorrow of saintly Job *as he sat on the dunghill* of worldly tribulation, *scraping* the *swarming worms* of the vices from the body of the Church with the hand of compassion and the *potsherd* of truth.[338]

Yet that grammarian, chosen from the horde of Philistines to reproach the living God,[339] lightly undertook the work in the manner of the schoolmen who teach rhetoric,[340] for in treating a given theme, they do not consider what has or has not been done, but sharpen their tongues in fictive cases and strive to outdo one another in leveling and responding to insult.[341] He wrote a letter overflowing with invective against the holy Church, to which we resolve to reply more quickly.[342] Our help in this refutation shall be the preeminent grace of the one by whose gift we are able to distinguish between pride and obedience, depravity and chastity, truth and falsehood, and even to determine how *an angel* differs *from Satan* when *he transforms himself into an angel of light* [2 Cor. 11.14]. For indeed in such a manner does the above-mentioned bishop feign, in the words of the letter, that he is a friend, so that in the guise of one who merely inquires, he pours out all the poison of the enemies.[343] If he really were a friend, he would not suffer the blasphemies of the sacrilegious to be published under his name, since it would be easy for him, if he cared, to refute the slander of the accusers. But this best of friends decided to repeat the false accusations against his *lord and master* [John 13.13–14] rather than offend the assembly of the impious! Were he to display any loyalty, however, he would burn up with due flames of indignation rather than condone the abuse as something that should be circulated!

And indeed, the aforementioned servant of the Lord, Gregory, who is *hidden in the shelter of the face* of God *from* your *plotting* and *protected in His dwelling from the strife of tongues* [Ps. 30.21],[344] enjoys *the beauty of the house* of God [Ps. 25.8], whose honor and freedom he loved, preached, and taught *with the word of truth and the power of God* [2 Cor. 6.7]. Like his predecessor, blessed Paul, he came before men *armed with justice — slandered, but praiseworthy; called a deceiver, but truthful; dying, but behold* he lives; *sorrowful* for a time, *yet now always rejoicing* [2 Cor. 6.7–10]. And having attained *the place where dwells the glory* of God [Ps. 25.8], *he is inebriated with the richness* of His grace *and* drinks from *the torrent of* eternal *pleasure* [Ps. 35.9], experiencing with David the faithful one *how great is the abundance of your sweetness, O Lord, which you have hidden away for those who fear you* [Ps. 30.20].

And so, while you *sharpen* your *tongues* among the *serpents* [Ps. 139.4] as you remain on the earth, he blesses the Lord who *showed wondrous mercy* to him, and resides *in a fortified city* [Ps. 30.22], namely, the heavenly Jerusalem, which your folly cannot attain and your curses cannot reach, for there presides the Truth of the Father, who from His holy place destroys *all those who speak falsehood* [Ps. 5.7]. Since He has *overcome the world* [John 16.33], He doubtlessly animates His champions of justice and defenders of Christianity so that they may *take courage* [John 16.33]. For even though He delays, He does not forsake, but shares the ever-present help of His omnipotence with those to whom He says: *Behold, I am with you, even until the end of the world* [Matt. 28.20]!

NOTES

All quotations in English that accompany references to Latin editions are newly translated, unless otherwise noted.

[1] In the manuscript (Milan, Biblioteca Ambrosiana, MS. N 118 sup., fol. 117r), the title appears as "The Book against Wolfhelm of Cologne." The attribution, "of Master Manegold," is written above the line, and a hairline indicates that the author's name should be inserted after the word "Liber" (which is itself abbreviated "L" with a bar through the stem).

[2] See Hartmann, "Manegold von Lautenbach und die Anfänge der Frühscholastik," pp. 57–60. On the medieval reception of Macrobius, see the following studies: Matthaeus Schedler, *Die Philosophie des Macrobius und ihr Einfluß auf die Wissenschaft des christlichen Mittelalters*, Beiträge zur Geschichte der Philosophie des Mittelalters 13.1 (Münster: Aschendorff, 1916); Pierre Duhem, *Le système du monde: Histoire des doctrines cosmologiques de Platon à Copernic* 3: *L'astronomie latine au moyen âge* (1919; repr. Paris: Librairie scientifique Hermann et Cie, 1954), pp. 62–71; Pierre Courcelle, "La postérité chrétienne du Songe de Scipion," *Revue des études latines* 36 (1958), pp. 205–34; William Harris Stahl, *Commentary on the Dream of Scipio by Macrobius*, Records of Western Civilization (New York: Columbia University Press, 1952), pp. 39–55; H. Silvestre, "Notes sur la survie de Macrobe au moyen âge," *Classica et Mediaevalia* 24 (1963), pp. 170–80; Birger Munk Olsen, "Quelques aspects de la diffusion du *Somnium Scipionis* de Cicéron au moyen âge," *Studia Romana in honorem Petri Krarup septuagenarii*, ed. Karen Ascani et al. (Odense: Odense University Press, 1976), pp. 146–53; Alison White, *Glosses composed before the Twelfth Century in Manuscripts of Macrobius' Commentary on Cicero's Somnium Scipionis*, D.Phil. thesis, Oxford University, 1981; Tony Hunt, "Chrestien and Macrobius," *Classica et Mediaevalia* 33 (1981–1982), pp. 211–27; Albrecht Hüttig, *Macrobius im Mittelalter: Ein Beitrag zur Rezeptionsgeschichte der Commentarii in Somnium Scipionis*, Freiburger Beiträge zur mittelalterlichen Geschichte 2 (Frankfurt am Main and New York: P. Lang, 1990). For additional bibliography, see Irene Caiazzo, "Le glosse a Macrobio del Codice Vaticano Lat. 3874: Un testimone delle *formae nativae* nel secolo XII," *Archives d'histoire doctrinale et littéraire du moyen âge* 64 (1997), pp. 213–34, at 214 nn. 1–5, as well as her forthcoming edition and study, *Lectures médiévales de Macrobe: Les "Glosae Colonienses super Macrobium"* (Paris: Vrin). For an overview of Macrobius, see Stephen Gersh, *Middle Platonism and Neoplatonism: The Latin Tradition* 2, Publications in Medieval Studies 23/2 (Notre Dame, Ind.: University of Notre Dame Press, 1986), pp. 493–595.

[3] Manegold is engaging in word-play on the meanings of *sensus* (sensation, reason, meaning) and *sapor* (taste, flavor — from *sapio*, to taste, to have sense, to know, to be wise).

[4] As a canon regular, Manegold was committed to the *cura animarum*, the "cure" or "care of souls." Here he depicts himself as a doctor of the spiritually ill and Wolfhelm as a patient in need of attention. The imagery is reminiscent of the opening book of Boethius's *De consolatione philosophiae*, in which Lady Philosophy poses a series of questions to the unhappy Boethius; see especially *De consolatione philosophiae* 1 pr. 6 (CCSL 94: 14–16), where the cause of the patient's malaise is diagnosed as forgetfulness of his own soul. Manegold's self-perception as a healer of souls motivated the writing of the *Contra Wolfelmum* and explains why his philosophical critique focuses on errors concerning the soul. See especially Chapters 1–3, 16, and 22.

[5] See Chapter 22 for Manegold's development of the idea that one sin leads to another. The phrase echoes Gregory the Great's *Moralia* 25.9 (PL 76: 334B–C) and *Homiliae in Ezechielem* 1.11.24 (PL 76: 915C). See also Manegold's *Liber ad Gebehardum* 42 (MGH Ldl 1: 384).

[6] Manegold may not be the author of the headings; the table of contents could have been added later by someone else, perhaps one of the Augustinian canons, to help readers find their way around the text. For the reader's convenience, I have repeated the headings at the beginning of each chapter and have placed them within angle brackets to indicate that they are not actually repeated in the manuscript itself.

⁷ The world-soul is meant here (see *Timaeus* 35a–36b); I have capitalized the word to distinguish it from the human soul, which is mentioned in the headings for Chapters 1 and 3.

⁸ See *Contra Wolfelmum*, ed. Hartmann, p. 20; idem, "Manegold von Lautenbach und die Anfänge der Frühscholastik," pp. 65–66. See also Tullio Gregory, *Platonismo medievale: Studi e ricerche*, Studi storici 26–27 (Rome: Istituto storico italiano per il Medio Evo, 1958), pp. 17–21.

⁹ Consider Augustine's praise of the Platonists in *De vera religione* 4.23 (CCSL 32: 192).

¹⁰ Cf. Psalm 115.11; Romans 3.4.

¹¹ Cf. Ephesians 4.14. See also Boethius, *De consolatione philosophiae* 1 pr. 6.21 (CCSL 94: 16).

¹² On Pythagoras as the most innovative and influential of the early philosophers, see Augustine, *De civitate dei* 8.2 (CCSL 47: 217). See also Ovid, *Metamorphoses* 15.72–74; Calcidius, *Commentarius* 45, in *Timaeus a Calcidio translatus commentarioque instructus*, ed. J. H. Waszink, Plato Latinus 4, 2nd ed. (London: Warburg Institute, 1975), p. 93; Macrobius, *Commentarii in Somnium Scipionis* 2.1.8, ed. James Willis (Leipzig: G.B. Teubner, 1970), p. 96; Lactantius, *Divinae institutiones* 3.2 (CSEL 19: 180); Boethius, *De institutione arithmetica* 1.1 (CCSL 94A: 9); idem, *De musica* 2.2 (PL 63: 1195D); Isidore of Seville, *Etymologiae* 8.6.2 (PL 82: 305B).

¹³ That is, the human being. See Chapter 22: "Therefore, the philosopher is in error when he announces that 'man is a rational, mortal animal'…."

¹⁴ The phrase *perpetua ratione* recalls Boethius, *De consolatione philosophiae* 3 metrum 9.1 (CC 94: 51), where it is applied to the creator of the universe. Here it is applied to the human being, who is made in the image and likeness of the creator, as Manegold notes at the end of the paragraph.

¹⁵ Macrobius, *Commentarii* 1.11.11, p. 47.

¹⁶ See Macrobius, *Commentarii* 2.17.13, p. 153. See also Augustine, *De civitate dei* 12.12, 12.14 (CCSL 48: 366, 368–69). Neither source, however, associates this doctrine specifically with Pythagoras; see note 18.

¹⁷ Cf. Macrobius, *Commentarii* 1.10.9, 1.11.3, pp. 43, 45. See H. Silvestre, "La prison de l'âme (Phédon, 62b): Nouveaux témoignages du moyen âge latin," *Latomus* 38 (1979), pp. 982–86. See also Chapter 22 (at note 272).

¹⁸ It is curious that Manegold should have condemned Pythagoras alone for the doctrine of the transmigration of souls, and not also Plato, since the latter clearly taught the same doctrine at *Timaeus* 41d–42d; indeed, Manegold seems to have read this passage in Calcidius's translation (see note 270). In Chapter 2 Manegold dissociates Plato from the doctrine of metempsychosis by counting him among the philosophers who rejected "that crude belief." Patristic sources, on the other hand, generally associate the doctrine with both Pythagoras and Plato. Augustine attributes it to Plato, without referring to Pythagoras, in *De civitate dei* 13.19 (CCSL 48: 401–02). Jerome links the two in *Epistula* 120.10 (CSEL 55: 500) and *Epistula* 126.1 (CSEL 56: 143). Lactantius attributes the doctrine to Pythagoras in *Divinae institutiones* 3.18, 7.12, and 7.23, but he also notes at 3.19 that Plato followed Pythagoras in this teaching (see CSEL 19: 236–45, 624, 655–56). Among the ancient poets, however, Ovid attributes it specifically to Pythagoras in *Metamorphoses* 15.153–75 and 15.453–62. Thus, Manegold had some authoritative foundations for identifying Pythagoras as the originator of the doctrine of metempsychosis, but his motive in singling Pythagoras out for exclusive denunciation seems to have been rhetorical in nature. Since Pythagoras was reputed to be the most innovative and influential of the early philosophers, he was guilty of misleading others with his delusions; he therefore stood in relation to Plato as heresiarch to heretic, and thus deserved the harsher condemnation. Manegold's dissociation of Plato from the doctrine of metempsychosis, then, seems tendentious rather than due to ignorance and was probably motivated by the desire to maximize contrast for the sake of rhetorical effect; compare Manegold's unusual depiction of Satan in Chapter 11 as a solitary figure rather than the commander of demonic legions — a characterization that contradicts a basic feature of the Christian world-view in order to serve the rhetorical purposes of its immediate context (see note 125). For additional patristic sources on metempsychosis, see Hartmann, "Manegold von Lautenbach und die Anfänge der Frühscholastik," pp. 65–66. For a general introduction

to the medieval reception of the doctrine, see Lodi Nauta, "The Preexistence of the Soul in Medieval Thought," *Recherches de théologie ancienne et médiévale* 63 (1996), pp. 93–135.

[19] Cf. Ambrose, *De excessu fratris* 2.130 (CSEL 73: 323): "those who have been made in the image and likeness of God cannot pass into the forms of beasts."

[20] The two parts of this robe are the body and the soul, respectively. Consider Apocalypse 6.11 ("And to each of them was given a single white robe") in light of Gregory the Great's comment (*Dialogues* 4.25; PL 77: 357B–C): "Those who have presently received a single robe will have two robes at the Last Judgment, for now they enjoy only the glory of souls, but then they will enjoy the glory both of souls and of bodies." See also note 232.

[21] The address from this point to the end of the paragraph is plural rather than singular.

[22] Despite Manegold's vehement insistence that there is no point of contact between Christian soteriology and Pythagorean metempsychosis, there is a certain harmony between the Christian doctrine of damnation for sin and the pagan doctrine of reincarnation as punishment for moral failings, and Manegold exploits this consonance effectively here in his ironic hyperbole. Certain twelfth-century thinkers would use such resonances between Christianity and Platonism to elaborate an argument that Plato and his followers used mythological metaphors to hint at doctrines that were clearly and openly expressed among Christian thinkers. The hermeneutic device that the Platonists of the twelfth century employed to describe this perceived agreement between Platonism and Christianity was the *involucrum* or *integumentum*; see notes 26 and 109.

[23] See *Contra Wolfelmum*, ed. Hartmann, p. 19; idem, "Manegold von Lautenbach und die Anfänge der Frühscholastik," pp. 66–67. On the medieval reception of the world-soul, see Tullio Gregory, *Anima mundi: La filosofia di Guglielmo di Conches e la scuola di Chartres*, Pubblicazioni dell'Istituto di Filosofia dell'Università di Roma (Florence: G.C. Sansoni, 1955), pp. 123–74. See also the recent studies by Irene Caiazzo, "La discussione sull'*Anima mundi* nel secolo XII," *Studi filosofici* 16 (1993), pp. 27–62, and "L'âme du monde: un thème privilégié des auteurs chartrains au XIIe siècle," *Le temps de Fulbert: Actes de l'Université d'été* (Chartres: Société archéologique d'Eure-et-Loir, 1996), pp. 79–89.

[24] See Augustine, *De civitate dei* 8.4 (CCSL 47: 219).

[25] Manegold employs the word *anima* alone, but the context makes it clear that he is speaking of the Platonic world-soul specifically. I have indicated this distinction by capitalizing the word. Macrobius likewise speaks simply of *anima* at times when the context makes it clear that he is referring to the world-soul, as at *Commentarii* 2.3.15, p. 107.

[26] The word I have translated "mythological metaphors" is *involucra* (nominative plural). The Latin word is significant, for the *involucrum*, or *integumentum*, was used as a hermeneutic device by scholars in the twelfth century to minimize doctrinal differences between Christianity and the philosophy of the ancients, yet the word bore the stigma of heterodoxy in the opinion of conservative thinkers. Thus, when one writer criticized Peter Abelard's theologies, he noted Abelard's use of the word *involucrum*, which he associated with the heterodox thinking of John Scot Eriugena; see *Disputatio catholicorum patrum* (PL 180: 322A). Curiously, the word *involucrum* does not occur in any of Eriugena's own texts, but it does occur in a manuscript of Honorius Augustodunensis's *Clavis physicae*, which is an adaptation of Eriugena's *Periphyseon*. See Marie-Thérèse d'Alverny, "Le cosmos symbolique du XIIe siècle," *Archives d'histoire doctrinale et littéraire du moyen âge* 20 (1953), pp. 31–81, at 35 n. 1.

For the medieval use of the terms *integumentum* and *involucrum*, see M.-D. Chenu, "*Involucrum*: Le mythe selon les théologiens médiévaux," *Archives d'histoire doctrinale et littéraire du moyen âge* 22 (1955), pp. 75–79; Edouard Jeauneau, "L'Usage de la notion d'*integumentum* à travers les gloses de Guillaume de Conches," *Archives d'histoire doctrinale et littéraire du moyen âge* 24 (1957), pp. 35–100, reprinted in his '*Lectio philosophorum*': *Recherches sur l'Ecole de Chartres* (Amsterdam: Adolf M. Hakkert, 1973), pp. 127–92; Henri de Lubac, *Exégèse médiévale: Les quatre sens de l'Écriture* 2.2 (Paris: Aubier, 1964), pp. 182–262; Brian

Stock, *Myth and Science in the Twelfth Century: A Study of Bernard Silvester* (Princeton, N.J.: Princeton University Press, 1972), pp. 31–62; Winthrop Wetherbee, *Platonism and Poetry in the Twelfth Century: The Literary Influence of the School of Chartres* (Princeton, N.J.: Princeton University Press, 1972), pp. 36–48; Peter Dronke, *Fabula: Explorations into the Uses of Myth in Medieval Platonism*, Mittellateinische Studien und Texte 9 (Leiden and Cologne: E.J. Brill, 1974), pp. 1–78; Haijo Jan Westra, *The Commentary on Martianus Capella's De nuptiis Philologiae et Mercurii Attributed to Bernardus Silvestris*, Studies and Texts 80 (Toronto: Pontifical Institute of Mediaeval Studies, 1986), pp. 23–33; Frank Bezner, *"Latet Omne Verum?* Mittelalterliche 'Literatur'-Theorie interpretieren," *Text und Kultur: Mittelalterliche Literatur, 1150–1450,* ed. Ursula Peters, Germanistische Symposien Berichtsbände 23 (Stuttgart and Weimar: J.B. Metzler, 2001), pp. 575–611. See also the forthcoming monograph by Frank Bezner, *"Vela veritatis": Hermeneutik, Wissen und Sprache in der Ideengeschichte des 12. Jahrhunderts* (Leiden, New York, and Cologne: Brill Academic Publishers).

[27] Plato, *Timaeus* 35a, trans. Calcidius, p. 27. See Macrobius, *Commentarii* 1.12.6, pp. 48–49; Calcidius, *Commentarius* 27–28, 53, 102, pp. 78, 101, 152.

[28] In other words, the world-soul gives life to material bodies and inhibits their natural tendency to degenerate. This active power within the world-soul was associated with fire. Cf. Virgil, *Aeneid* 6.730–32; Macrobius, *Commentarii* 1.21.35, p. 91; Calcidius, *Commentarius* 54, p. 102.

[29] On the doctrine of the life-giving power of the world-soul, see especially *Commentarii* 1.14.7–9, pp. 56–57. On Cicero, see *Commentarii* 1.14.1–3, p. 55, which precedes the discussion of the Neoplatonic trinity that Manegold cites verbatim in Chapter 6. On Virgil, see *Commentarii* 1.14.14, pp. 57–58.

[30] See Macrobius, *Commentarii* 2.2.14, p. 101. Cf. Calcidius, *Commentarius* 227, p. 242, lines 19–20: "it penetrates and vivifies every body."

[31] Macrobius, *Commentarii* 1.12.6, p. 49, lines 1–2: "which he describes in the *Timaeus* when he speaks about the fashioning of the world-soul."

[32] It is only in Macrobius that the substance of the world-soul is called "yeast"; see *Commentarii* 2.2.15, p. 101. The Latin word is *fermentum.* I have translated it more literally than William Harris Stahl, who renders the word "mixture"; see Stahl, *Commentary on the Dream of Scipio by Macrobius,* p. 191.

[33] The passage is lifted verbatim from Macrobius, *Commentarii* 2.2.15, p. 101, lines 27–29, where Macrobius provides his own Latin translation of Plato's text. Cf. Calcidius's translation at *Timaeus* 35b, p. 27, lines 18–20; and at *Commentarius* 32, p. 81, lines 20–22.

[34] Cf. Macrobius, *Commentarii* 2.3.15, p. 107, lines 1–2: "Porphyry includes this conviction of the Platonists in his books which pour light upon the obscurities in the *Timaeus.*" Translation by Stahl, *Commentary on the Dream of Scipio by Macrobius,* pp. 196–97.

[35] Macrobius, *Commentarii* 1.14.19–20, pp. 58–59. See *Contra Wolfelmum,* ed. Hartmann, p. 15. The list of philosophers here given by Manegold roughly follows the sequence in Macrobius, but some names have been omitted or corrupted; the corruptions are presumably due to scribal errors in the manuscript of the *Commentarii* that Manegold consulted, or were introduced afterwards by copyists of the *Contra Wolfelmum.* The philosophers presented by Macrobius are as follows (brackets indicate names omitted by Manegold): Plato, Xenocrates, Aristotle, Pythagoras [and Philolaus], Posidonius, [Asclepiades], Hippocrates, Heraclides, Heraclitus, Zeno, Democritus, Critolaus, Hipparchus, Anaximenes, Empedocles [and Critias], Parmenides, Xenophanes, Boethos, Epicurus. Macrobius provides the definition of the soul maintained by each philosopher immediately after that philosopher's name in the enumeration, whereas Manegold first lists the philosophers, then separately lists the definitions of the soul without linking them to their authors. Since Manegold omits three of the names and one of the definitions, and follows a slightly different sequence in each list, the two lists do not correspond precisely. It was not Manegold's concern to identify the authors of the definitions, but to demonstrate the uselessness of philosophical speculation by attesting that there are as many definitions of the soul as there are

philosophers (he provides eighteen names and eighteen definitions). This chapter is discussed by Heinrich Fichtenau, *Heretics and Scholars in the High Middle Ages, 1000–1200*, trans. Denise A. Kaiser (University Park, Penn.: Pennsylvania State University Press, 1998), pp. 47–48, 174. Unfortunately, his discussion is flawed. On pp. 47–48 Fichtenau observes that Manegold's source was Macrobius, who provided "the opinions of eighteen ancient philosophers on the soul." Yet on p. 174 he contradicts himself and erroneously asserts that Manegold presents twenty-three definitions of the soul, and that all twenty-three were drawn from Plato.

[36] This name should actually be "Heraclides," but I have preserved Manegold's error because the third philosopher after this one is identified as "another Heraclitus." Macrobius reports only one Heraclitus.

[37] The manuscript has "Crisolaum."

[38] The manuscript has "Hypantum."

[39] The manuscript has "Zenophontem." Hence, Xenophon rather than Xenophanes.

[40] The lack of agreement among the ancient philosophers was a common theme in patristic literature. See Lactantius, *Divinae institutiones* 5.3, 7.2 (CSEL 19: 407, 586); Hilary, *De Trinitate* 1.4 (CCSL 62: 3–4); Augustine, *De civitate dei* 11.25, 18.41 (CCSL 48: 344–45, 635–38). For additional examples, see *Contra Wolfelmum*, ed. Hartmann, p. 49 n. 2.

[41] Cf. Lactantius, *Epitome divinarum institutionum* 38.1 (CSEL 19: 708; PL 6: 1045B–C): "Plato, …alone of them all, philosophized in such a way that he came fairly close to the truth."

[42] This definition, as the others that follow, are drawn from Macrobius, *Commentarii* 1.14.19–20, pp. 58–59. On Plato's definition of the soul, compare Calcidius, *Commentarius* 226, p. 241, lines 8–9: "Therefore, according to Plato the soul is a rational substance that moves itself without a body." For Manegold's probable understanding of this definition, see the Introduction, p. 14, above.

[43] Xenocrates.

[44] Aristotle. In addition to Macrobius, see Calcidius, *Commentarius* 222 (pp. 235, 237), 225 (p. 240).

[45] Compare the definition by the eleventh-century grammarian Papias: "Entelechy — the absolute perfection or form of the body." See *Papias vocabulista* (Venice: Philippus de Pincis Mantuanus, 1496; facsimile reproduction, Torino: Bottega d'Erasmo, 1966), p. 106. See also Dronke, *Fabula*, pp. 109–10.

[46] Pythagoras and Philolaus.

[47] Posidonius.

[48] Asclepiades. Note that Manegold does not list Asclepiades in his catalogue of philosophers. Although Manegold lists Boethos, he does not provide his definition: "a mixture of air and fire."

[49] Hippocrates.

[50] Heraclides.

[51] Heraclitus.

[52] Zeno.

[53] Democritus.

[54] Critolaus.

[55] Hipparchus.

[56] Anaximenes.

[57] Empedocles and Critias.

[58] Parmenides.

[59] Xenophanes.

[60] Epicurus.

[61] Although Manegold drew his lists from Macrobius, the use to which he put them resembles Augustine's discussion of the soul in *De Trinitate* 10.7.9 (CCSL 50: 322–23). See also Lactantius, *Divinae institutiones* 3.4, 3.7 (CSEL 19: 184, 190–92).

⁶² As noted, Macrobius attributes this position to Empedocles and Critias. See also Calcidius, who asserts that the Jews, in addition to Empedocles, identified the soul with the blood; he cites as proof texts Genesis 4.10 and 9.4, as well as Leviticus 17.11 and 17.14 (*Commentarius* 218–19, pp. 231–32). For additional sources, see *Contra Wolfelmum*, ed. Hartmann, p. 50 n. 8. As Hartmann supposes, Manegold may have singled out this definition of the soul for emphatic denunciation in response to an opinion that was being taught in the schools during his lifetime. Among the theological opinions taught at the early twelfth-century school of Laon on the sacrament of the Eucharist (which may reflect earlier discussions), one finds the following assertions: blood is the "seat of the soul"; blood represents the soul; and blood is said to be the soul and life of the flesh "according to the philosophers." See Odon Lottin, *Psychologie et morale aux XIIe et XIIIe siècles* 5: *Problèmes d'histoire littéraire: L'école d'Anselm de Laon et de Guillaume de Champeaux* (Gembloux: J. Duculot, 1959), pp. 27 (no. 27, lines 6–7), 108 (no. 139, lines 26–27), 277–78 (no. 375, lines 22–23), respectively. See also Honorius Augustodunensis, *Elucidarium* 1.180 ("our soul…is in the blood"), in *L'Elucidarium et les lucidaires*, ed. Yves Lefèvre (Paris: E. de Boccard, 1954), p. 395.

There is a fragment of a commentary on the Pauline epistles attributed to one "Manig." — presumably "Manegold" — in Oxford, Bodleian Library, MS. Laud Misc. 216, fols. 153ra–53vb, which asserts, "nothing is found…that could represent <the soul> more closely than blood, which is said to be the seat of the soul itself." See Lottin, *Psychologie et morale* 5, p. 148 (no. 229, lines 18–20). Lottin identifies "Manig." with Manegold of Lautenbach; see his article, "Manegold de Lautenbach, source d'Anselme de Laon," *Recherches de théologie ancienne et médiévale* 14 (1947), pp. 218–23. This identification, however, is doubted by François Châtillon, particularly since "Manig." maintains a position that Manegold so vehemently opposes here in the *Contra Wolfelmum*; see Châtillon, "Recherches critiques sur les différents personnages nommés Manegold," *Revue du moyen âge latin* 9 (1953), pp. 153–70, at 163. Hartmann suggests that Lottin's attribution is correct and that the commentary represents Manegold's opinion before he became a canon regular and wrote the *Contra Wolfelmum*, that is, when he was still a teacher of philosophy in the schools. If so, Manegold self-consciously singled out this definition in the *Contra Wolfelmum* in order to repudiate an error that he had taught earlier in his career. See Hartmann, "Manegold von Lautenbach und die Anfänge der Frühscholastik," p. 94, and the extended discussion on pp. 90–99, 147–48.

⁶³ See *Contra Wolfelmum*, ed. Hartmann, pp. 18–19; idem, "Manegold von Lautenbach und die Anfänge der Frühscholastik," pp. 67–69. See also Gregory, *Platonismo medievale*, pp. 25–26; John Kirkland Wright, *The Geographical Lore of the Time of the Crusades: A Study in the History of Medieval Science and Tradition in Western Europe* (1925; repr. New York: Dover Publications, 1965), pp. 47, 161, 429–30 n. 148; Duhem, *Le système du monde*, vol. 2, pp. 408–17; ibid., vol. 3, pp. 64–67.

⁶⁴ Macrobius, *Commentarii* 1.14.22–25, pp. 59–60. Manegold's objection to the study of "the sphere and the orbs" (*de spera et de orbibus*) seems to be an objection to the study of astronomy in general, not to the shape of the earth in particular, for the universe was regarded by ancient cosmologists as an immense sphere filled with the orbs of the planets. Manegold did not reject the presumed shape of the universe, but contended only that there is little value in studying the physical world; see Chapter 20. On Manegold's probable views about the shape of the earth, see note 66.

⁶⁵ Macrobius, *Commentarii* 1.19.20–22, 2.1–4, pp. 77, 95–109.

⁶⁶ Macrobius, *Commentarii* 1.16.8–13, 1.20.8–32, pp. 65–66, 79–84. When Manegold mentions the *orbis terrę*, he was probably thinking of the earth as a sphere rather than disk-shaped; there is no reason to suppose that Manegold thought the earth was flat. Nowhere does Manegold object to a spherical earth (which was clearly taught by Macrobius; see *Commentarii* 2.5, pp. 110–16), nor even to the idea that there might be a continent on the opposite side of the globe, but strictly speaking he objected only to the idea that such a continent might be inhabited if it were true that the equator was impassable because of intolerable heat. In the third century Lactantius had ridiculed the idea that the earth was round, and in the

fourth century Augustine expressed some reservations about the earth's sphericity without rejecting it out-right. As late as the eighth century a debate on the subject arose between Boniface and Virgil of Salzburg which had to be settled by the pope. Nevertheless, in the same century Bede had accepted the cosmological doctrine that the earth was spherical, and in the eleventh century belief in a spherical earth was apparently the norm among educated men. The monk Hermannus Contractus, or Hermann of Reichenau (1013–1054), had in fact corrected Macrobius's calculation of the earth's circumference; see Loris Sturlese, *Die deutsche Philosophie im Mittelalter: Von Bonifatius bis zu Albert dem Großen (748–1280)*, trans. Johanna Baumann (Munich: C.H. Beck, 1993), pp. 54–65. The texts of Macrobius, Calcidius, and Martianus Capella were largely responsible for medieval belief in the sphericity of the earth. For references to the patristic texts, see Gregory, *Platonismo medievale*, p. 26 n. 1. For studies on medieval notions of the earth's shape, see Francis S. Betten, "St. Boniface and the Doctrine of the Antipodes," *American Catholic Quarterly Review* 43 (1918), pp. 654–63; idem, "The Knowledge of the Sphericity of the Earth during the Earlier Middle Ages," *The Catholic Historical Review*, new series 3 (1924), pp. 74–90; Arthur Percival Newton, "Introduction: The Conception of the World in the Middle Ages," *Travel and Travellers of the Middle Ages* (London: Routledge & Kegan Paul, 1926), pp. 1–18; George Sarton, *Introduction to the History of Science* 2: *From Rabbi ben Ezra to Roger Bacon* (Baltimore: The William & Williams Company, 1931), pp. 44–46; Charles W. Jones, "The Flat Earth," *Thought* 9 (1934), pp. 296–307; George H.T. Kimble, *Geography in the Middle Ages* (New York: Russel & Russell, 1938), pp. 1–43; Wesley M. Stevens, "The Figure of the Earth in Isidore's 'De Natura Rerum,'" *Isis* 71 (1980), pp. 268–77. See also Wright, *The Geographical Lore of the Time of the Crusades* (cited in note 63); Rudolf Simek, *Heaven and Earth in the Middle Ages: The Physical World before Columbus*, trans. Angela Hall (Woodbridge: Boydell Press, 1996); Patrick Gautier Dalché, *Géographie et culture: La representation de l'espace du VIe au XIIe siècle*, Variorum Collected Studies Series (Aldershot: Ashgate, 1997); J.R.S. Phillips, *The Medieval Expansion of Europe*, 2nd ed. (Oxford: Clarendon Press, 1998).

67 On the habitable "spots" (*maculae*), see Macrobius, *Commentarii* 2.5.28–30, 2.5.34, pp. 114–15. On the earth as a mere "point" (*punctum*) in relation to the rest of the universe, see ibid., 1.16.10, 2.5.10, pp. 66, 111. Cicero calls the habitable regions "spots" at *Somnium Scipionis* 6.1 (ibid., p. 160); he likens the Roman Empire to a mere point on the earth's surface at 3.7 (ibid., p. 158).

68 Macrobius, *Commentarii* 1.22.13, 2.5.22, 2.5.31–36, pp. 93, 113, 115–16. On the Antipodes, see the literature cited in note 66, as well as Gabriella Moretti, *Gli antipodi: Avventure letterarie di un mito scientifico* (Parma: Pratiche Editrice, 1994), pp. 84–85; Alison Peden, "The Medieval Antipodes," *History Today* 45.12 (1995), pp. 27–33.

69 See Macrobius, *Commentarii* 2.5.1–18, pp. 110–13, on the climatic zones. Hartmann is under the impression that Manegold's argument has no precedent in patristic literature (see "Manegold von Lautenbach und die Anfänge der Frühscholastik," p. 69), but H. Silvestre sees a fundamental affinity between Manegold's critique of the Antipodes and that of Augustine; see Silvestre's review of Hartmann's edition and study, in *Revue d'histoire ecclésiastique* 68 (1973), pp. 933–35, at 935.

70 That is, the Psalmist, David.

71 Cf. Isaiah 52.10. Note that Psalm 97.3 actually employs the past tense, whereas the future tense appears in Isaiah 52.10.

72 On Manegold's use of the phrase *quadratura christianę doctrinę*, which I have translated "the perfect measure of Christian doctrine," see *Contra Wolfelmum*, ed. Hartmann, p. 53 n. 6. In addition to the literature he cites, one might also consult the study on the perfection of the number four in medieval esthetics by Edgar de Bruyne, *Études d'esthétique médiévale* 2: *L'époque romane*, Rijksuniversiteit te Gent: Werken Uitgegeven door de Faculteit van de Wijsbegeerte en Letteren 98 (Bruges: "De Tempel," 1946), pp. 343–70.

73 The paragraph that begins Chapter 6 is drawn from Macrobius, *Commentarii* 1.14.6–7, p. 56. Manegold counters it in Chapter 11 with the orthodox Trinitarian confession of faith. Enzo Maccagnolo cites

this passage in his article, "Il secondo assioma del *De hebdomadibus* di Boezio e la *rerum universitas*," *Sandalion* 4 (1981), pp. 191–99, at 196–97, but he does not seem to be aware that it is drawn from Macrobius and that Manegold is citing it in disapproval.

[74] See Hartmann, "Manegold von Lautenbach und die Anfänge der Frühscholastik," pp. 82–83.

[75] As Macrobius explains in an earlier passage (*Commentarii* 1.6.19, pp. 21–22), the distinction between things that "are" and things that "seem to be" concerns intelligible and material beings, respectively: "We speak of things intelligible as 'being' and of things material as 'seeming to be,' whether they have a divine or mortal body" (Stahl, *Commentary on the Dream of Scipio by Macrobius*, p. 104). The passage reflects Plato's distinction between 'being' and 'becoming,' expressed at *Timaeus* 27d–29a.

[76] Macrobius's passage contains only "the Father," whereas Manegold's contains "Nous" and "the Father," but without a copulative (*Contra Wolfelmum*, ed. Hartmann, p. 55, lines 1–2): "Rursus anima noym patrem qua intuetur, induitur…."

[77] Cf. Stahl, *Commentary on the Dream of Scipio by Macrobius*, p. 143. In this passage Macrobius preserved and passed on to medieval readers of Latin the teaching of Plotinus (*Enneads* 5.2.1; see also *Enneads* 5.1.7–8). See Pierre Courcelle, *Late Latin Writers and their Greek Sources*, trans. Harry E. Wedeck (Cambridge, Mass.: Harvard University Press, 1969), pp. 32–33; Stephen Gersh, *Middle Platonism and Neoplatonism: The Latin Tradition* 2, pp. 518–19.

[78] Arius of Alexandria (ca. 250–ca. 336). On the Arian heresy, see Augustine, *De haeresibus* 49, ed. and trans. Liguori G. Müller, Patristic Studies 90 (Washington, D.C.: Catholic University of America Press, 1956), pp. 96–99, 174–78; Jaroslav Pelikan, *The Christian Tradition: A History in the Development of Christian Doctrine* 1: *The Emergence of the Catholic Tradition (100–600)* (Chicago and London: The University of Chicago Press, 1971), pp. 191–200.

[79] Mani (216–277). On Manichaeism, see Augustine, *De haeresibus* 46, pp. 84–97, 158–72. Augustine notes that the Greek followers of the Persian religious leader named "Manes" rendered his name "Manichaeus" because *manes* in Greek would suggest insanity (*De haeresibus* 46, pp. 84–85).

[80] Origen of Alexandria (ca. 185–254). See Augustine, *De haeresibus* 43, pp. 82–85, 156; Pelikan, *The Christian Tradition* 1, pp. 48–49. On Origen's place in the ecclesiastical imagination, see Henri de Lubac, *Exégèse médiévale* 1.1, pp. 221–304, especially Chapter 4.3, pp. 257–74. This part of de Lubac's study is available in English translation; see Henri de Lubac, *Medieval Exegesis: The Four Senses of Scripture*, vol. 1, trans. Mark Sebanc (Grand Rapids, Mich. and Edinburgh: William B. Eerdmans, T&T Clark, 1998), pp. 161–224, especially pp. 184–98.

[81] De Lubac quotes this passage in Latin in *Exégèse médiévale* 1.1, p. 265, but introduces an error, presenting the word *metuit* instead of *meruit*; the edition used by de Lubac actually has *meruit* (PL 155: 156A). The English translation by Mark Sebanc preserves this error (*Medieval Exegesis*, pp. 191–92). Sebanc's translation of Manegold's text continues on p. 403 n. 45, then resumes on p. 192, with a digression to p. 403 n. 46, following de Lubac's presentation of the passages.

[82] This remark does not appear in Origen's commentary on the Song of Songs. To the contrary, in that text he asserts, "not only does Christ Himself see the Father, but He makes Him seen by others"; see Origen, *In Canticum Canticorum* 3, PG 13: 178A. Moreover, Jerome reports that the error is found in Origen's *Peri Archon*, not in the commentary on the Song of Songs; see Jerome, *Contra Ioannem Hierosolymitanum* 7 (PL 23: 360B; later edition, 376B). The passage that Manegold cites in the following sentence, however, is found in Jerome's prologue to a translation of Origen's homilies on the Song of Songs (as well as in one of Jerome's letters); hence, Manegold's error may derive from a conflation of sources. See the following note.

[83] Jerome, *Epistula* 84.7 (CSEL 55: 129); idem, *Interpretatio homiliarum duarum Origenis in Canticum Canticorum*, Prologus (PL 23: 1173/1174).

[84] Cf. Jerome, *Contra Ioannem Hierosolymitanum* 7 (PL 23: 360C, later edition 376B). See the Latin translation of Origen, *De principiis* 2.10.1–3, by Rufinus of Aquileia (PG 11: 233B–36C); see also Origen, *On First Principles*, trans. G.W. Butterworth (Gloucester, Mass.: Peter Smith, 1973), pp. 138–41.

⁸⁵ Cf. Psalm 8.3: "Out of the mouth of infants and of sucklings thou hast perfected praise." Note, however, that the word *infantium*, which Manegold uses here, may refer to any person lacking the power of speech.

⁸⁶ See 1 Corinthians 12; Ephesians 4. In Manegold's text, this sentence (*Contra Wolfelmum*, ed. Hartmann, p. 58, lines 10–14: *et…detestatur*) actually follows the one I have placed after it (ibid., p. 58, lines 8–10: *Hic…contempnit*). I have reversed the sequence for the sake of clarifying the idea that Manegold apparently intended to convey. The original order of the clauses implies that the chapter's logical progression was interrupted by an afterthought. As with the incongruities found in Chapter 3 regarding the lists of the philosophers and their definitions of the soul, the staggered order of Manegold's thoughts here may imply the haste with which the *Contra Wolfelmum* was written.

⁸⁷ See *Contra Wolfelmum*, ed. Hartmann, pp. 20–21; idem, "Manegold von Lautenbach und die Anfänge der Frühscholastik," pp. 69–77; Gregory, *Platonismo medievale*, pp. 23–24.

⁸⁸ That is, Jesus Christ.

⁸⁹ Calcidius spends the concluding quarter of his massive commentary on Plato's *Timaeus* (Chapters 268–354, pp. 273–346) in a detailed discussion of prime matter. See J. Reginald O'Donnell, "The Meaning of 'Silva' in the Commentary on the *Timaeus* of Plato by Chalcidius," *Mediaeval Studies* 7 (1945), pp. 1–20; J.C.M. Van Winden, *Calcidius on Matter: His Doctrine and Sources — A Chapter in the History of Platonism*, Philosophia Antiqua 9 (Leiden: E.J. Brill, 1959). Medieval audiences, however, seem to have regarded Calcidius as a Christian. For general studies, see B.W. Switalski, *Des Chalcidius Kommentar zu Plato's Timaeus: Eine historisch-kritische Untersuchung*, Beiträge zur Geschichte der Philosophie des Mittelalters 3.6 (Münster: Aschendorff, 1902); Stephen Gersh, *Middle Platonism and Neoplatonism: The Latin Tradition* 2, pp. 421–92; John Dillon, *The Middle Platonists: 80 B.C. to A.D. 220*, rev. ed. (Ithaca, N.Y.: Cornell University Press, 1996), pp. 401–08. See also the forthcoming article by Paul Edward Dutton, "Medieval Approaches to Calcidius," in *Plato's 'Timaeus' as Cultural Icon*, ed. Gretchen Reydams-Schills (Notre Dame, Ind.: University of Notre Dame Press).

⁹⁰ Macrobius, *Commentarii* 1.6.24, p. 22.

⁹¹ Cf. Calcidius, *Commentarius* 125, p. 168: "the stars do not cause future events, but foretell them." Astrology, however, receives little attention in the works of Macrobius and Calcidius; see S.J. Tester, *A History of Western Astrology* (Woodbridge: Boydell Press, 1987), pp. 114–15, 117–20. A critique of ancient astrology is found in Augustine's *De civitate dei* 5.1–6 (CCSL 47: 128–34).

⁹² Cf. Calcidius, *Commentarius* 153, 180, 185, pp. 188, 208, 211. See J. den Boeft, *Calcidius on Fate: His Doctrine and Sources*, Philosophia Antiqua 18 (Leiden: E.J. Brill, 1970).

⁹³ On the errors of the philosophers in their opinions about what constitutes the highest good, see Lactantius, *Divinae institutiones* 3.7 (CSEL 19: 190–92) and Augustine, *De civitate dei* 8.8 (CCSL 47: 224–25).

⁹⁴ That is, God. Manegold is critical of the philosophers because they studied the creature but did not recognize the creator. Cf. Romans 1.18–22.

⁹⁵ The "threefold mystery" refers to Father, Son, and Holy Spirit — the three persons who are the "single majesty," that is, the one God.

⁹⁶ See Apuleius, *De Platone et eius dogmate* 1.5.190, in *Apulei Platonici Madaurensis opera quae supersunt* 3: *De philosophia libri*, ed. Paul Thomas (1908; repr. Stuttgart: B.G. Teubner, 1970), p. 86; Calcidius, *Commentarius* 307, pp. 308–09. Perhaps the most influential source for the medieval tradition was Ambrose, *Hexameron* 1.1.1 (CSEL 32: 3). Additional references by patristic and medieval authors can be found in *Contra Wolfelmum*, ed. Hartmann, p. 60 n. 13. While medieval writers were keen on repeating the formula popularized by Ambrose, the twelfth-century theologian Robert of Melun criticized this schematization of Plato's cosmogonic doctrine, claiming that it does not correspond to what one reads in the *Timaeus*, and he castigated all those who thoughtlessly repeated the formula without bothering to check its accuracy. See Robert of Melun, *Sententie* 1.1.19, in *Oeuvres de Robert de Melun* 3: *Sententie* 1, ed.

Raymond P. Martin, Spicilegium sacrum Lovaniense: Études et documents 21 (Louvain: "Spicilegium sacrum Lovaniense" Administration, 1947), pp. 210–23.

Note that the excerpt from a commentary on Plato's *Timaeus* to which Hartmann draws attention is not a unique text, as his note seems to imply (*Contra Wolfelmum*, ed. Hartmann, p. 60 n. 14; see also "Manegold von Lautenbach und die Anfänge der Frühscholastik," p. 73 n. 131). The text cited by Hartmann is drawn from Paris, Bibliothèque Nationale, MS. lat. 14065, fol. 59r, in the edition by Victor Cousin, *Ouvrages inédits d'Abélard* (Paris: Imprimerie royale, 1836), p. 656. As Hartmann notes, Cousin suspected the text to be a work of Honorius Augustodunensis. However, it was actually written by William of Conches, as Charles Jourdain demonstrated in 1838; see Guillaume de Conches, *Glosae super Platonem*, ed. Édouard Jeauneau, Textes philosophiques du Moyen Age 13 (Paris: Librairie philosophique J. Vrin, 1965), p. 39 n. 1. For the passage cited by Hartmann, see Jeauneau, ibid., p. 126; on the manuscript itself, see ibid., pp. 37–40.

[97] According to Tullio Gregory, Manegold intended the reading "intelligible matter" in the preceding clause, rather than "intelligible world" in the present clause; see *Platonismo medievale*, p. 24. Wilfried Hartmann adopted Gregory's interpretation and consequently spent several pages in his article on Manegold attempting to contextualize this strange, indeed unprecedented, concept; see "Manegold von Lautenbach und die Anfänge der Frühscholastik," pp. 69–77, as well as *Contra Wolfelmum*, ed. Hartmann, pp. 20–21. However, I am convinced that Gregory and Hartmann's reading of the passage is incorrect. The question turns on how to divide the clauses in this sentence: "Unde factum est, ut tria sibi principia ponerent, artificem, formas et materiam intelligibilem etiam, mundum in mente divina collocantes, qui exemplum huius sensilis secundum numerorum rationem cuncta, que sub sensibus casura erant, in se intelligibiliter contineret" (*Contra Wolfelmum*, ed. Hartmann, p. 60, line 7, to p. 61, line 3); the punctuation is supplied by Hartmann rather than the manuscript. Challenging Hartmann's editorial intervention, I believe the comma placed between *etiam* and *mundum* should instead be placed between *materiam* and *intelligibilem*, for the following reasons. First of all, the formula "God, forms, matter" is extremely common in medieval discussions of Platonic cosmology, whereas the formula "God, forms, intelligible matter" would be unique; and since Manegold's intention was to attack the commonplaces within the philosophical tradition that he was denouncing, it is unlikely that he would have intended the unprecedented concept of "intelligible matter." Furthermore, since the curious formula suggested by Gregory and Hartmann occurs within a context that would allow one to adopt the traditional formula simply by shifting the adjective to the following clause, it is untenable to insist on the unusual reading. Finally, in medieval Platonism, "intelligible world" is a standard expression used to describe its counterpart, the "sensory world." See Calcidius, *Commentarius* 105, p. 154, lines 10–11: "mundus intelligibilis exemplum est mundi sensilis"; see also *Commentarius* 268, p. 273, lines 10–14. Manegold is clearly thinking along these lines, for he identifies the world in the mind of God as the exemplar of this sensory world, and he does so in words that echo Calcidius; since it is clear that Manegold was thinking that the world in the mind of God is intelligible (as indicated by the presence of the adverb *intelligibiliter*), it is more reasonable to conclude that the adjective "intelligible" here is being applied to "world" (according to the standard formula) than to suppose that it is being used in the novel combination, "intelligible matter." For an independent critique of Gregory and Hartmann's reading, see the recent article by Frank Bezner (whom I thank for notifying me of its imminent publication), "'Simmistes Veri': Das Bild Platons in der Theologie des 12. Jahrhunderts," *The Platonic Tradition in the Middle Ages: A Doxographic Approach*, ed. S. Gersh and J.F.M. Hoenen (Berlin: De Gruyter, 2002), pp. 93–137, at 102 n. 39.

[98] Calcidius, *Commentarius* 105, 268, pp. 154, 273. See also Priscian, *Institutiones grammaticae* 17.44, in *Grammatici Latini* 3, ed. Martin Hertz (Leipzig: B.G. Teubner, 1859), p. 135.

99 Cf. Peter Damian, *De divina omnipotentia* 11 (PL 145: 612B–C). The principle "nothing comes from nothing" can also be found in Boethius, *De consolatione philosophiae* 5 pr. 1.9 (CCSL 94: 89).

100 The language is vaguely reminiscent of Ovid, *Metamorphoses* 2.232, and Ausonius, *Gratiarum actio* 16.74. Manegold seems to be hearkening back to the planetary orbs of classical cosmology, which in his estimation were as insubstantial and obstructive to vision as smoke; see the opening sentences of Chapters 4 and 5.

101 That is, Satan, who fell through pride. See Augustine, *De Genesi ad litteram* 11.23–26 (CSEL 28/1: 355–59).

102 Cf. Job 1.6–12, 2.1–7.

103 Virgil, *Aeneid* 7.338.

104 Cf. Augustine, *De civitate dei* 2.26 (CCSL 47: 61–62).

105 Here Manegold is particularly obscure (*Contra Wolfelmum*, ed. Hartmann, p. 62, lines 7–9): "… et per turpe suum inficit eorum bonum miserandoque nimis commercio de precioso alieno, vilitatem suę confusionis circumtegit." Apparently "another" (*alieno*) refers to God, and "treasure" (*precioso*, taken substantively) refers to the human race, which God made as the consummation of the creative act (Genesis 1.26–31). Manegold is employing the idea of Satan's ability to disguise himself as an angel of light; see 2 Corinthians 11.14, and the text by Augustine cited in the preceding note.

106 Cf. Peter Damian, *De divina omnipotentia* 6 (PL 145: 604C).

107 See R.R. Bolgar, *The Classical Heritage and its Beneficiaries: From the Carolingian Age to the End of the Renaissance* (1954; repr. New York, Evanston, and London: Harper & Row, 1964), pp. 192, 415.

108 Cf. Philippians 3.19. See also Calcidius, *Commentarius* 128, p. 171; for a translation, see J. den Boeft, *Calcidius on Demons (Commentarius Ch. 127–136)*, Philosophia Antiqua 33 (Leiden: E.J. Brill, 1977), pp. 14–15.

109 On "mythological metaphors" (*involucra*), see note 26. The myths that were studied and interpreted by the twelfth-century Platonists (and presumably by eleventh-century masters as well) often depicted the gods behaving immorally, yet the immorality was given a noble gloss when the tales were read as *involucra*. For example, Vulcan's attempted rape of Minerva in the founding myth of Athens at *Timaeus* 23d–e (trans. Calcidius, p. 15) was interpreted as a representation of the mind that desires wisdom but finds itself frustrated in the attempt to possess knowledge completely (see Guillaume de Conches, *Glosae super Platonem* 28, ed. Édouard Jeauneau, p. 93). Manegold is objecting to the idea that tales describing the immoral behavior of the gods can conceal any worthwhile lessons — perhaps in response to an attempt by Wolfhelm to defend classical literature by invoking the concept of the *involucrum*. In Manegold's view, the *involucrum* customarily took as its subject an immoral deed (for example, an attempted rape) and glorified it by presenting the perpetrators as divine beings involved in some noble undertaking (such as founding a city). Thus, for Manegold, the *involucrum* itself was immoral inasmuch as it glorified vice. It may be noted, however, that Macrobius condemns the poets who depict the gods in scurrilous fables; see *Commentarii* 1.2, pp. 3–8.

110 Manegold may be referring to the worship of idols in the form of reproductive organs. See Richard Payne Knight, *A Discourse on the Worship of Priapus and its Connection with the Mystic Theology of the Ancients,* A new edition to which is added an *Essay on the Worship of the Generative Powers during the Middle Ages of Western Europe*, Foreword by O.V. Garrison (Secaucus, N.J.: University Books, 1974).

111 The patristic literature on this theme is extensive. For a classic statement, see Augustine, *De doctrina christiana* 2.40.60–2.42.63 (CCSL 32: 73–77), or 2.144–2.152 according to the numbering in CSEL 80: 75–78. Hartmann enumerates many other sources; see *Contra Wolfelmum*, ed. Hartmann, p. 63 n. 1.

112 That is, the human being's innate capacity for reason.

113 Psalm 38.12 (Vulgate/Douay). The Latin word *aranea* can be taken to mean "spider" or "cobweb." Augustine specified the animal in *Enarrationes in Psalmos: Enarratio in Psalmum* 38, §18 (CCSL 38: 418), as did a medieval commentary on the Psalms which Manegold's text echoes; see the following note.

[114] Cf. Pseudo-Haimo, *Explanatio in Psalmos: In Psalmum* 38 (PL 116: 331B): "Just as the spider draws out its innards as it toils in useless work, so does the sinner exhaust his own soul as he strives after worldly things."

[115] Cf. Psalm 140.9–10.

[116] "Vessels for common use" presumably refers to the writings of the pagans, and "carrion" refers to the glorified vice that classical texts contain.

[117] See Hartmann, "Manegold von Lautenbach und die Anfänge der Frühscholastik," pp. 105–06. With this chapter, Manegold launches into an extended digression on salvation history, for the sake of correcting Wolfhelm's supposed ignorance of the basic tenets of Christianity. Manegold explains the purpose of the digression at the beginning of Chapter 22, where he returns to his attack on the philosophers.

[118] That is, Jesus Christ, the second person of the Trinity, who in Christian interpretation was thought to be prefigured in the Old Testament as the wisdom of God. See Pelikan, *The Christian Tradition* 1, pp. 191–92.

[119] This passage is Manegold's answer to the "confession" of the philosophers quoted in Chapter 6 (from Macrobius, *Commentarii* 1.14.6–7, p. 56).

[120] Cf. Deuteronomy 32.39, 33.26.

[121] Cf. Hebrews 12.22–23. See also Odon Lottin, *Psychologie et morale* 5, pp. 50–52 (no. 54: Anselm of Laon), 343–44 (no. 523: School of Laon); Franz Bliemetzrieder, *Anselms von Laon systematische Sentenzen*, Beiträge zur Geschichte der Philosophie des Mittelalters 18.2–3 (Münster: Aschendorff, 1919), pp. 11 (*Sententiae divinae paginae*) and 48 (*Sententiae Anselmi*).

[122] See Lottin, *Psychologie et morale* 5, pp. 126 (no. 176: Anselm of Laon), 244 (no. 307: School of Laon); *Dialogus inter Christianum et Iudaeum de fide catholica* (PL 163: 1060D).

[123] Cf. Augustine, *De Genesi ad litteram* 11.15 (CSEL 28/1: 347); see St. Augustine, *The Literal Meaning of Genesis*, vol. 2, trans. John Hammond Taylor, Ancient Christian Writers 42 (New York and Mahwah, N.J.: Newman Press, 1982), p. 147: "…*Avarice is the root of all evils.* For it was by this vice that the Devil fell, and yet he certainly did not love money but rather his own power."

[124] Cf. Job 1.6–12, 2.1–7; 1 Peter 5.8.

[125] The Satan depicted by Manegold is a curiously solitary figure. This characterization of the devil seems to have been inspired by a strict adherence to the Book of Job, without heed to the Gospel accounts (see especially Mark 5.9 and Luke 8.30). Christian demonology generally regarded Satan as having seduced numerous angels when he fell, although the angels that remained faithful were thought to be free of temptation thereafter. Gregory the Great had asserted that there was once a tenth rank of angels in addition to the nine ranks described by Pseudo-Dionysius, and that the entire rank fell *en masse* along with Satan; human beings were created to replace the fallen angels. This theory, however, was rejected at the school of Laon and by Honorius Augustodunensis early in the twelfth century. Manegold seems to have taken no interest in such questions. His motivation for depicting a solitary Satan may have been guided by rhetorical considerations rather than doctrinal ones. By assuming that the other angels were beyond Satan's reach, the human race, which was the only other rational form of life, was an obvious target for his designs. For the demonology of the school of Laon, see Bliemetzrieder, *Anselms von Laon systematische Sentenzen*, pp. 15, 18–19, 55; for Honorius, see *Libellus octo quaestionum* 2 (PL 172: 1187–88) and *Liber duodecim quaestionum* 3, 5 (PL 172: 1180A, 1180D). For a general introduction to medieval demonology, see Jeffrey Burton Russell, *Lucifer: The Devil in the Middle Ages* (Ithaca and London: Cornell University Press, 1984).

[126] Genesis 2.16–17.

[127] That is, man, who was created from "the mud of the earth," according to Genesis 2.7.

[128] Cf. the opinions on this question by Anselm and Ralph of Laon; Lottin, *Psychologie et morale* 5, pp. 44–46, 50–52 (nos. 47, 54: Anselm), 184–86 (nos. 231, 232: Ralph). For an extended discussion, see Hartmann, "Manegold von Lautenbach und die Anfänge der Frühscholastik," pp. 100–05.

129 See Genesis 14.18–20, Psalm 109.4, Hebrews 5.6, 7.1–28.

130 See Genesis 17.1–14, 22.1–18. See also Augustine, *De civitate dei* 16.32 (CCSL 48: 536–38). "Immolation" (*immolationem*) apparently refers to the institution of offering holocausts, that is, sacrificial animals (see Genesis 22.10–13), whereas "sacrifice" (*sacrificium*), which appears in the preceding and following clauses, seems to emphasize the offering of bread and wine; see Genesis 14.18: "Melchizedek, the king of Salem, brought forth bread and wine, for he was a priest of God the Most High."

131 Cf. Genesis 28.18–22, which describes how Jacob erected a memorial stone at the place where he dreamed about the ladder between heaven and earth. According to Augustine, the crucial act was not so much the erection of the stone as its anointing with oil, since the anointing suggests the mystery of Christ, "the anointed one"; see Augustine, *De civitate dei* 16.38 (CCSL 48: 543–44). Manegold differs from the tradition by emphasizing the person of Jacob rather than Melchizedek as the prefiguration of the high priest and of the true sacrifice. In this connection, see *Contra Wolfelmum*, ed. Hartmann, pp. 68–69 n. 3.

132 See Exodus 35–40, and Leviticus as a whole.

133 Cf. Genesis 15.6, Romans 4.3, Galatians 3.6, James 2.23.

134 See 2 Kings (2 Samuel) 11.

135 That is, David. See 1 Kings (1 Samuel) 16.1–13.

136 2 Kings (2 Samuel) 15–18. Note that Absalom was David's son by his legitimate wife, Maacah (2 Samuel 3.3), not by the wife of Uriah the Hittite, Bathsheba, who gave birth to Solomon (2 Samuel 12.24).

137 That is, David.

138 2 Kings (2 Samuel) 16.5–13.

139 That is, David.

140 Here I disagree with the punctuation in Hartmann's edition (*Contra Wolfelmum*, ed. Hartmann, p. 70, lines 22–23). Hartman has "…poposcerat, emundatum; aptum fieret…"; I have shifted the semi-colon to precede *emundatum*, thus: "…poposcerat; emundatum, aptum fieret…."

141 That is, the Blessed Virgin Mary.

142 That is, Elizabeth (the mother of John the Baptist), whose greeting served as the inspiration for the prayer, the Hail Mary. See Luke 1.5, 1.39–45. For "the rod of Aaron," which is here given a typological reading, see Numbers 17.8.

143 That is, Jesus Christ. See Isaiah 7.14.

144 That is, David.

145 That is, Jesus Christ.

146 That is, David.

147 See also Psalm 143.9, 149.1.

148 2 Kings (2 Samuel) 6.14.

149 See Tertullian, *Apologeticum* 21.15 (CSEL 69: 56) and *Adversus Marcionem* 3.7 (CSEL 47: 386). Manegold cites Tertullian in the *Liber ad Gebehardum* 43 (MGH Ldl 1: 385).

150 That is, the Incarnation.

151 That is, the Day of Judgment.

152 The "time of indulgence" refers to the First Coming, that is, the Incarnation when God was born in a manger, lived as a carpenter, and died on a cross.

153 See Isaiah 13.13. According to Wolfger of Prüfening, Manegold glossed the Book of Isaiah; see Appendix, Text 23.

154 See Lamentations 1.12.

155 Cf. Malachi 3.1 and 1 Paralipomenon (1 Chronicles) 29.11–12.

156 On this theme, see de Lubac, *Exégèse médiévale* 2.1, pp. 153–81.

157 Manegold is addressing Wolfhelm (the verbs in this paragraph are singular). He hearkens back to the theme of the prologue.

[158] See Hartmann, "Manegold von Lautenbach und die Anfänge der Frühscholastik," pp. 100–01; Gregory, *Platonismo medievale*, p. 26.

[159] Cf. 1 Timothy 2.4.

[160] See Chapter 11.

[161] Luke 1.34–35.

[162] See *Decrees of the Ecumenical Councils* 1: *Nicaea I to Lateran V*, ed. and trans. Norman P. Tanner (London and Washington, D.C.: Sheed & Ward, Georgetown University Press, 1990), p. 5.

[163] For several patristic and medieval references on this theme, see *Contra Wolfelmum*, ed. Hartmann, pp. 74–75 n. 8.

[164] That is, St. Paul. The metaphor may be drawn from 2 Timothy 2.20–21.

[165] Manegold seems to be referring to hylomorphism, according to which a given natural object is considered to be made up of two parts: form and matter. Neither of these two parts by itself is identical with the object; the two must be combined so that the object can exist, as a *tertium quid*. This metaphysical framework does not apply to God, for although the Father and the Son are distinct persons, they nevertheless share the same substance; by contrast, there can be no natural object that is made up of two distinct and equal forms which share the same matter. Hence, the nature of the distinction between the persons of the Godhead is unlike that between the objects which human beings experience in the natural world. Nevertheless, St. Paul uses the word "form" to give an inkling of the very close union between the Father and the Son — as Manegold suggests in the sentences that follow.

[166] That is, St. Paul. See 1 Timothy 2.7.

[167] In other words, "emptying" does not mean that the second person of the Trinity lost His divine status when He became human; it indicates, rather, that He added the lowly status of humanity to His divine nature. Thus, by deigning to assume the form of a creature that is a slave to sin, He displayed the greatness of His honor.

[168] Cf. Fulgentius Ruspensis, *De fide* 10–11 (CCSL 91A: 718): "The only-begotten God was born twice: once from the Father, once from the mother. For He was born from the Father as the Word; He was born from the mother when the Word became flesh. Therefore God, the Son of God, one and the same, was born before all time and in time; and each of the two nativities pertains to the one Son of God." Cf. Peter Abelard, *Sermo* 2 (PL 178: 388C): "Therefore each of His two nativities is wondrous; each of His two acts of generation is ineffable."

[169] Cf. Cicero, *De inventione* 1.29.44; Boethius, *De topicis differentiis* 3 (PL 64: 1198D). For additional references, see *Contra Wolfelmum*, ed. Hartmann, p. 76 n. 22, as well as "Manegold von Lautenbach und die Anfänge der Frühscholastik," pp. 115–16.

[170] See Wilfried Hartmann, "Rhetorik und Dialektik in der Streitschriftenliteratur des 11./12. Jahrhunderts," *Dialektik und Rhetorik im früheren und hohen Mittelalter: Rezeption, Überlieferung und gesellschaftliche Wirkung antiker Gelehrsamkeit vornehmlich im 9. und 12. Jahrhundert*, ed. Johannes Fried (Munich: R. Oldenbourg, 1997), pp. 73–95, at 85.

[171] See Hartmann, "Manegold von Lautenbach und die Anfänge der Frühscholastik," pp. 103–04.

[172] That is, St. Paul. See Romans 15.15–16; Galatians 2.7–8; 1 Timothy 2.7; 2 Timothy 1.11.

[173] On the salvation of those who lived before the First Coming, see the opinions of Anselm of Laon and William of Champeaux in Lottin, *Psychologie et morale* 5, pp. 96, 211–13 (nos. 118, 261).

[174] That is, the cross.

[175] See 1 Corinthians 1.23.

[176] That is, the cross. Cf. Genesis 2.9, 3.22, 3.24, and Apocalypse 22.2, 22.14.

[177] The grammatical constructions in Chapter 16 are exceptionally convoluted; the chapter may have been written in haste and never revised.

[178] Luke 2.21.

[179] See Matthew 5.17–18; Luke 16.16–17.

[180] Since Christ was both God and Man, He was able to perform the function of a Mediator. Only the God-man could make reparation for sin.

[181] Matthew 9.18–26; Mark 5.21–43; Luke 8.41–56.

[182] Luke 7.11–16.

[183] John 11.17–44.

[184] Manegold recapitulates his three examples in sequence.

[185] That is, if the Lord can raise the dead, he can also forgive the sins of those who have not yet died. The "part" to which Manegold here refers is presumably the soul.

[186] In this momentary address to Wolfhelm, Manegold hearkens back to the prologue, where he warns that minor sins often lead to major ones.

[187] Luke 1.26–2.20.

[188] Luke 2.21–24.

[189] That is, St. John the Baptist. Matthew 3.1–17; Mark 1.1–11; Luke 3.1–22; John 1.6–9, 1.15, 1.19–36.

[190] Matthew 4.1–11; Mark 1.12–13; Luke 4.1–13.

[191] Matthew 4.18–22, 9.9–13, 10.2–4; Mark 1.16–20, 2.13–17, 3.13–19; Luke 5.1–11, 5.27–32, 6.13–16; John 1.35–51.

[192] See Augustine, *Sermo* 87.10 (PL 38: 537).

[193] That is, "*Who do you say that I am?*" (Matthew 16.15).

[194] Matthew 16.19.

[195] That is, excommunication.

[196] Acts 5.1–11.

[197] Psalm 23.4, 50.12; Matthew 5.8.

[198] See Romans 1.17, "The just man shall live by faith" (repeating Habakkuk 2.4); likewise Galatians 3.11 and Hebrews 10.38.

[199] Cf. Matthew 5.20, 18.3, 19.23–24.

[200] This is a paraphrase of John 20.23, where, however, the power of forgiving and not forgiving is given to the disciples in general, not to Peter specifically, as Manegold observes in the following sentence. Cf. Matthew 18.18.

[201] John 20.23; cf. Matthew 16.19, 18.18.

[202] John 21.15–17.

[203] That is, baptism and the Eucharist, respectively.

[204] See Hartmann, "Manegold von Lautenbach und die Anfänge der Frühscholastik," pp. 94–99. Manegold seems to have regarded the washing of the feet at the Last Supper (John 13.1–20) as a sign of the spiritual cleansing offered by the sacrament of baptism. For the institution of the Eucharist at the Last Supper, see Matthew 26.26–29, Mark 14.22–25, and Luke 22.15–20.

[205] The "plan of humility and love" refers to Christ's death on the cross, by which He would redeem the human race from sin and grant His followers the inheritance of eternal life.

[206] At the Last Supper and in the Mass.

[207] Mark 16.19; Luke 24.51; Acts 1.9–11.

[208] See Matthew 26.64; Mark 16.19; Colossians 3.1; Hebrews 1.3.

[209] Cf. Luke 24.36; John 20.19, 20.26. The phrase describes Christ's sudden appearance after the Crucifixion in the midst of His disciples, when they were hiding behind locked doors. Manegold uses the phrase here to explain that the priest, as a conduit of grace, makes the actual presence of God tangible through the ministry of the sacraments. On the role of the priest in the sacrament, see Paschasius Radbertus, *De corpore et sanguine Domini* 12 (CCCM 16: 76–77; PL 120: 1310C). As Hartmann observes

(*Contra Wolfelmum*, pp. 83–84 n. 11), this passage from Paschasius Radbertus is cited by the author of a commentary on the Pauline epistles who is identified in an Oxford manuscript as "Manig.," and who may be Manegold of Lautenbach. Compare the edition of the text by "Manig." in Lottin, *Morale et psychologie* 5, p. 149, lines 83–88, with the passage from Paschasius.

210   This chapter seems to have been included as a denunciation of the eucharistic theology of Berengar of Tours (d. 1088), who doubted that the bread and wine consecrated during the Mass truly become the body and blood of Christ. His statements were condemned at the Roman synod of 1079, where he recanted in the presence of Gregory VII. Manegold seems to imply that Wolfhelm and his fellows were in danger of adopting heretical beliefs concerning the sacraments, although the indirectness of the discussion here suggests that Wolfhelm did not actually maintain any such beliefs. To the contrary, Wolfhelm wrote a condemnation of Berengar's doctrine; see *Vita Wolfhelmi*, in *Acta Sanctorum: Aprilis*, ed. Godefridus Henschenius and Daniel van Papenbroeck, vol. 3 (Paris and Rome: Victor Palmé, 1866), pp. 80–81; MGH SS 12: 185–86. Manegold seems to have thought that an uncritical acceptance of philosophical doctrines and a rejection of the papal privilege of determining orthodoxy could easily lead to unorthodox experimentation with sacramental theology that would deny the efficacy of the sacraments. Yet the fact that Wolfhelm maintained an orthodox stance on the Berengarian controversy, even though he was an avid reader of the philosophers and a supporter of the emperor, contradicts Manegold's radical thesis of the inseparability of political, philosophical, and theological attitudes.

On the Berengarian controversy, see Charles E. Sheedy, *The Eucharistic Controversy of the Eleventh Century against the Background of Pre-scholastic Theology* (Washington, D.C.: Catholic University of America Press, 1947); Gary Macy, *The Theologies of the Eucharist in the Early Scholastic Period: A Study of the Salvific Function of the Sacrament according to the Theologians c. 1080–c.1220* (Oxford: Clarendon Press, 1984); idem, *Treasures from the Storeroom: Medieval Religion and the Eucharist* (Collegeville, Minn.: Liturgical Press, 1999).

211   See Matthew 26.26–28; 1 Corinthians 11.23–25.

212   Ambrose, *De mysteriis* 9.50 (CSEL 73: 110).

213   See Hartmann, "Manegold von Lautenbach und die Anfänge der Frühscholastik," pp. 104–05.

214   See John 15.1–8 for the metaphor of the vine and the branches, and John 15.9–17 for the discourse on love. The Passover sermon comprises John 13–17.

215   See John 10.17–18.

216   Cf. Hebrews 9.15–18.

217   See Matthew 26.64; Mark 16.19; Colossians 3.1; Hebrews 1.3.

218   See Luke 23.34.

219   See Romans 10.9–10.

220   Matthew 16.24; Mark 8.34; Luke 9.23.

221   Cf. 2 Timothy 2.20–21.

222   Cf. Ephesians 4.8–10.

223   Cf. Job 38.17; Psalm, 106.18; Wisdom 16.13.

224   Cf. Luke 1.79; Matthew 4.16, citing Isaiah 9.2.

225   Cf. 1 Corinthians 15.22, 15.45.

226   Cf. Galatians 4.31 (5.1): "the freedom for which Christ freed us."

227   That is, the Jews of the old covenant and the Gentiles who accepted the new covenant.

228   That is, rising from the dead. See 3 Kings (1 Kings) 17.17–24, 4 Kings (2 Kings) 4.32–37.

229   Cf. 1 John 1.2: "we announce to you eternal life."

230   See Chapter 13.

231   Genesis 3.17–19.

232   Cf. Augustine, *De civitate dei* 20.6 (CCSL 48: 706–08).

233   See John 1.4, 11.25, 14.6.

[234] The phrase "contrary to the nature of things that are incorruptible" (*contra naturam incorruptibilium*) is an allusion to souls, since Manegold has just discussed their superior dignity in the preceding paragraph. Thus, whereas souls are incorruptible but not palpable, Christ's immortalized body was both.

[235] John 20.19–29. Cf. Luke 24.36–43, Matthew 28.16–17, Mark 16.14.

[236] The phrase "that which was blessed with immortality" (*inmortalitate beatificatum*) refers to Christ's resurrected body. On the forty days before the Ascension, see Acts 1.1–11.

[237] Matthew 28.9. See also John 20.17, Mark 16.9, Luke 24.10–11.

[238] See Acts 1.3.

[239] That is, the disciples.

[240] See Macrobius, *Commentarii* 1.20.20–24, pp. 82–83.

[241] Cf. Lactantius, *Divinae institutiones* 3.5.2 (CSEL 19: 186); Peter Damian, *De divina omnipotentia* 12 (PL 145: 615B) and *Epistola* 5.1 (PL 144: 337A). As Hartmann suspects (*Contra Wolfelmum*, p. 89 n. 15), Manegold may have had the work of eleventh-century astronomers in mind, such as Hermannus Contractus (1013–1054); see Mary Catherine Welborn, "Lotharingia as a Center of Arabic and Scientific Influence in the Eleventh Century," *Isis* 16 (1931), pp. 188–99.

[242] See 1 John 2.15; James 4.4; 2 Peter 1.4.

[243] Cf. Macrobius, *Commentarii* 1.5.2, 1.6.83, pp. 14, 34; Calcidius, *Commentarius* 123, p. 166; Augustine, *De civitate dei* 12.14, CCSL 48: 368–69.

[244] Cf. Calcidius, *Commentarius* 70, p. 117.

[245] Acts 2.1–3.

[246] Acts 4.5–22, 5.17–42.

[247] The word "heavens" in Psalm 18.2 was commonly interpreted as a reference to the apostles; see Augustine, *Enarrationes in Psalmos: In Psalmum* 18, *Enarratio* 2 (CCSL 38: 106, lines 19–20). Hartmann provides additional sources; see *Contra Wolfelmum*, p. 90 n. 10.

[248] Psalm 28.3, 8, 4 (Manegold has altered the sequence of the verses).

[249] Acts 2.3–12.

[250] See 1 Corinthians 13.13; Luke 10.27.

[251] See John 15.26.

[252] Matthew 27.51; Mark 15.38; Luke 23.45.

[253] Cf. Ephesians 2.19–22.

[254] Manegold's text seems to be unrefined from the beginning of the paragraph to the end of the chapter; it is beset with problems that render its meaning unusually obscure.

[255] Acts 8.18.

[256] The Council of Jerusalem, ca. 50 A.D. See Acts 15.1–29; Galatians 2.1–10.

[257] That is, the popes, who stand in the line of apostolic succession.

[258] See, for example, Acts 12.

[259] Cf. 1 Corinthians 13.3.

[260] Manegold supplements *quid desit michi* ("what I lack") with *debitum* (literally, "something owed"), which I have translated "promise" in the sense of something owed by God to man, through the grace of divine generosity. For the completion of the meaning, see the following note.

[261] That is, the Holy Spirit makes us jump the chasm of death in order to enjoy the infinite number of days that remain in heaven. This sentence provides the answers to the questions posed by the Psalmist in the preceding sentence: thus, through the Holy Spirit the Lord makes known that the "end" is eternal life with Jesus Christ, "the number of days" is infinite, and "what I lack" presently (before death) is the fulfillment of God's generous promise of eternal life. Compare this interpretation with the glosses on Psalm 38.5 in the commentary attributed to Manegold (PL 93: 688A–D).

²⁶² The passage is used here to supplement the citation from Psalm 38.5; thus, it is the Holy Spirit who "teaches all things" and thereby "makes known" one's end, the number of one's days, and what one lacks. Manegold seems to consider the anointing mentioned in 1 John 2.27 as a reference to the sacrament of extreme unction.

²⁶³ Philippians 3.13: "Brothers, I do not consider myself to have attained it" — referring to the resurrection of the dead (see Philippians 3.11–12). Manegold does not express himself clearly in this passage, but the substantive adjective *totum* ("everything") is apparently a reference to the fullness of eternal life, which includes the restoration of one's physical body and the enjoyment of the direct presence of Christ. Manegold's point is that the sacraments enable salvation, but do not guarantee it.

²⁶⁴ The commentary on the Psalms attributed to Manegold draws upon Philippians 3.12–14 when glossing Psalm 38.5; see PL 93: 688A–B. This commentary also introduces the word *transilire* ("leap across"), as Manegold does here; see PL 93: 686C–91D. The reference to 1 John 2.27, however, is absent from the commentary on the Psalms.

²⁶⁵ Manegold is referring to the direct, physical presence of Christ that the faithful will enjoy after the resurrection of the dead.

²⁶⁶ That is, the sacraments, which were foretold typologically in the Old Testament.

²⁶⁷ At last Manegold concludes his lengthy digression on salvation history (Chapters 11–21), an ironic exercise affecting to offer Wolfhelm basic instruction in the Christian faith for the sake of correcting his abysmal ignorance. The present chapter serves as a reprise and conclusion of Manegold's attack on the philosophers.

²⁶⁸ Macrobius, *Commentarii* 1.8.5, p. 37 (cf. Plotinus, *Enneads* 1.2; Porphyry, *Sententiae* 32). Abelard refers to the same passage in his *Theologia Christiana* 2.64 (CCCM 12: 157; PL 178: 1115C), but he cites all four categories provided by Macrobius, whereas Manegold omits the fourth category, that is, the "exemplary" virtues. For literature on the medieval reception of Plotinus, see Hartmann, "Manegold von Lautenbach und die Anfänge der Frühscholastik," p. 81 n. 164; also *Contra Wolfelmum*, ed. Hartmann, pp. 23–24 n. 64.

²⁶⁹ Cf. Macrobius, *Commentarii* 1.6.36, 1.22.9, pp. 25, 93. The idea that the human body is composed of the four elements was a cosmological commonplace. Augustine had accepted the doctrine; see *De Genesi ad litteram* 7.13–7.15 (CSEL 28/1: 212–13). Hence, Manegold's criticisms are directed not against the doctrine itself but against the conclusion that the body cannot be restored after death because the weight of the elements would prevent it from leaving the earth into which it had decomposed. See Augustine, *De civitate dei* 22.11, CCSL 48: 829–31.

²⁷⁰ Plato wrote in the *Timaeus* (41d–42d) that every human soul has its individual star, in which the creator placed it before its incarnation on earth. After death, souls that have lived immoral lives will be reincarnated as lower life-forms as punishment for their misdeeds, whereas souls that have lived moral lives will return to the bliss of their native star, or "companion star." Manegold seems in fact to have drawn this reference from Calcidius's translation, for there is a verbal echo between Manegold's text (*comparem stellam*) and Calcidius's rendition (*comparis stellae*; ed. Waszink, p. 37, line 10). The doctrine is outlined by Augustine in *De civitate dei* 13.19, but his expression for "native star" is *astrum congruum* (occurring in the phrase *in astro sibi congruo*; CCSL 48: 402, lines 29–30). Macrobius does not specify native stars when describing the place where souls dwell before their incarnation; cf. *Commentarii* 1.11.11, 1.12.2, 1.12.17, pp. 47, 48, 51.

²⁷¹ By "essences" Manegold means the four elements (fire, air, water, earth). His language resembles that of Jerome, *Contra Johannem Hierosolymitanum* 25 (PL 23: 376B, first edition): "When, therefore, at God's command the soul will have forsaken its cold and lifeless remnant of a body, all the components will eventually return to the substances from which they were born: the flesh will go back to the earth, breath will mingle

with the air, fluid will return to the deeps, heat will rise up to the ether." Manegold uses "essences" (*essencias*) in place of "substances" (*substantias*), but the words were interchangeable according to Calcidius (*Commentarius* 27, p. 78). Most notably, Manegold and Jerome make unusual use of the word *matrices* ("wombs"), which is set in apposition to *essencias* and *substantias* respectively, and which I have translated "from which they were born" in order to approximate the required sense of emerging from the "womb" of generation.

[272] See Macrobius, *Commentarii* 1.10.9–10, 1.11.3, pp. 43, 45. See also Manegold's earlier statement in Chapter 1 (at note 17).

[273] Cf. Augustine, *De civitate dei* 22.11, CCSL 48: 829–31.

[274] Macrobius, *Commentarii* 1.22.13, p. 93. Manegold may be playing on the double meaning of *nutus* as physical "inclination" (that is, gravity) and "nod, assent" (that is, acceptance of the truth of this doctrine). Thus, the implied meaning may also be, "by your assent, your heavy bodies will be dragged into the earth." Compare the concluding sentence of Chapter 1.

[275] The early twelfth-century Platonist, William of Conches, criticized the anti-intellectual practice of appealing to miraculous intervention in order to circumvent the need to think through scientific problems. However, his criticism focused on the creation of the firmament described in Genesis 1.6–8, rather than the resurrection of bodies. See his *Philosophia mundi* 2.2–3 in PL 172: 57D–58D, or *Philosophia mundi* 2.2.4–6, ed. Gregor Maurach (Pretoria: University of South Africa, 1980), p. 43; a new critical edition is being prepared by Paul Dutton for Corpus Christianorum Continuatio Mediaevalis (Brepols: Turnhout). See also William's *Dragmaticon* 3.2.3–9 (CCCM 152: 58–60), which has been translated into English by Italo Ronca and Matthew Curr, under the title *A Dialogue on Natural Philosophy*, Notre Dame Texts in Medieval Culture 2 (Notre Dame, Ind.: University of Notre Dame Press, 1997), pp. 38–40. Although William suffered for his freethinking, his career is evidence that the naturalistic attitude which Manegold opposed made considerable progress in the following generation.

[276] The phrase *prima creatio*, which I have translated "the first moment of creation," was used with some frequency in the cosmogonic discussions of the twelfth century and acquired a technical sense in the thought of Peter Abelard, who distinguished between *prima creatio* (the creation of formless matter *ex nihilo*) and *secunda creatio* (the application of specific forms to formless matter, which is the creation of individual entities); see Petrus Abaelardus, *Dialectica*, ed. L.M. De Rijk, 2nd ed. (Assen: Van Gorcum & Co., 1970), p. 419.

[277] William of Conches (see note 275), rejected the doctrine that the universe had been created in a state of chaos. See his *Philosophia mundi* 1.21 (PL 172: 53A–54B; or *Philosophia mundi* 1.11.35–39, ed. Maurach, pp. 33–36). In his denunciation of the doctrine of chaos, William was opposing the idea that the elements had ever behaved in a manner implying the absence of natural laws, so that divine intervention was necessary to prevent the universe from tearing itself apart. The independence of mind and the confidence in the powers of an autonomous nature that William of Conches displayed early in the twelfth century reflect an ethos that seems to have been pioneered by men like Wolfhelm of Cologne.

[278] Compare the discussion concerning God's freedom of will and action by Peter Damian, in *De divina omnipotentia* 1, PL 145: 596B–97A.

[279] Cf. Isaiah 22.22; Matthew 16.19.

[280] See Luke 1.55; Acts 3.25; Galatians 3.8.

[281] Exodus 13.21–22, 14.19–20, 14.24; Numbers 9.15–22; 1 Corinthians 10.1–2.

[282] Exodus 14.21; 1 Corinthians 10.1–2.

[283] Cf. Peter Damian, *De divina omnipotentia* 11, PL 145: 612B.

[284] John 11.1–44.

[285] For this common definition, see Augustine, *De civitate dei* 9.13, 16.8 (CCSL 47: 260–61, 48: 508–10); idem, *De Trinitate* 7.4.7 (CCSL 50: 255); Boethius, *In Isagogen Porphirii commenta* 1.25 (CSEL 48: 76); idem, *De consolatione philosophiae* 1 pr. 6.15 (CCSL 94: 15); Priscian, *Institutiones grammaticae* 17.44, p. 135.

286 That is, in devising an accurate definition of "man."

287 Manegold's language reflects Boethius, *In Isagogen* 2.7 (CSEL 48: 97, lines 8–9): "Likewise, although gods and men are both rational, nevertheless they differ and are divided from one another by the addition of the word 'mortal.'" Manegold concludes the paragraph by noting that man, who is mortal, and God, who is immortal, "come together in a single definition" — that is, God's immortality, conferred upon Christ and through Him extended to the entire human race, does away with the mortality in the philosopher's definition of man. Consequently, because God became man, the definition must be revised: man should now be considered "a rational, immortal animal."

288 That is, God and man; the Latin *quos* (*Contra Wolfelmum*, ed. Hartmann, p. 97, line 7) implies *homo* and *deus*.

289 That is, mortality, according to the hypothetical philosopher's definition of man as "a rational, mortal animal." Recall the discussion in Boethius, *In Isagogen* 2.7 (see note 287), wherein divinity and humanity are separated by the addition of the word "mortal" — hence, mortality is the "transitory quality" to which Manegold is referring.

290 See also Romans 8.1–13.

291 Manegold's list is a combination of the vices enumerated in Galatians 5.19–21 and Colossians 3.5.

292 For the first time in the text since Chapter 1, the address is plural rather than singular (*vos…studuistis*; ed. Hartmann, p. 97, lines 21–22). Thus, in the long digression on salvation history, Manegold directs his words to Wolfhelm alone; from this point on, however, he once again includes Wolfhelm's compatriots in his obloquy, as he did in Chapter 1. See also note 296.

293 Romans 6.23: "The wages of sin is death, but the grace of God is life eternal in Christ Jesus our Lord."

294 Manegold's prologue concludes with a variation of this phrase, which reflects the language of Gregory the Great; see note 5.

295 See 1 Kings (1 Samuel) 15.22.

296 The address is plural. Hartmann notes that from this point to the end of the text Manegold broadens the scope of his attack (*Contra Wolfelmum*, pp. 98–99 n. 2), but this shift in address actually begins in the preceding chapter (ibid., p. 97, lines 21–22); see note 292.

297 Manegold is referring to the councils in which many of the German bishops rejected the authority of Pope Gregory VII in response to his excommunication of Emperor Henry IV, especially the council of Worms in 1076 and the council of Brixen in 1080.

298 Manegold is referring to the pronouncements of the councils held by Gregory VII and the canon law collections that he promoted. See I.S. Robinson, *Authority and Resistance in the Investiture Contest: The Polemical Literature of the Late Eleventh Century* (Manchester and New York: Manchester University Press, Holmes & Meier Publishers, 1978), pp. 39–44. Gregory's canonical principles are outlined in the *Dictatus papae*, the twenty-seven theses edited in Gregory's *Register* as Letter 2.55a; see *Das Register Gregors VII.*, ed. Erich Caspar, MGH Epistolae selectae 2, rev. ed. (Berlin: Weidmannsche Verlagsbuchhandlung, 1955), pp. 201–08. However, H.E.J. Cowdrey observes that the theses of the *Dictatus papae* "were in no sense published," and "it is puzzling that they should have remained largely unused and unnoticed in subsequent years both by Gregory and by his friends and foes." See H.E.J. Cowdrey, *Pope Gregory VII, 1073–1085* (Oxford: Clarendon Press, 1998), p. 502. Cf. Robinson, *Authority and Resistance in the Investiture Contest*, pp. 41–42.

299 Manegold repeats the personification of mother Church later in the chapter. Cf. Appendix, Text 9 — a poem which employs the same personification in its mockery of Manegold. The poem was apparently written in response to Chapters 23–24 of the *Contra Wolfelmum*, by someone styling himself "Hugh the Orthodox."

300 Manegold is apparently referring to five of Henry IV's most trusted advisors, among whom were Count Eberhard "the Bearded," Udalric of Godesheim, and a certain Hartmann. The five imperial advisors were excommunicated by Pope Alexander II in 1073. Gregory VII repeated the measure, and in 1076

he excommunicated Henry IV himself, in part for continued association with the advisors. It was on the advice of his excommunicated counselors that Henry IV summoned the council of Worms to depose Gregory VII. Manegold may also have had in mind Cardinal Hugh Candidus and Wibert (or Guibert), the archbishop of Ravenna. The former was excommunicated by 1075 and took refuge at the imperial court; the latter was excommunicated in 1078 and became antipope in 1080. See Cowdrey, *Pope Gregory VII*, pp. 130–31; I.S. Robinson, *Henry IV of Germany, 1056–1106* (Cambridge: Cambridge University Press, 1999), pp. 125, 139, 143, 360–61. For more on Wibert of Ravenna, see notes 305 and 319.

301 In this passage, "Judaic perfidy" seems simply to herald the next sentence, in which Manegold quotes the cry of the Jewish priests and people who rejected the authority of Christ by clamoring for his crucifixion. Yet see also *Liber ad Gebehardum* 42 and 76 (MGH Ldl 1: 384, 429), where Manegold rather fancifully accuses his enemies of Ebionitism, which was an ancient heresy that attempted to combine Christianity and Judaism by continuing to observe Mosaic law; see Augustine, *De haeresibus* 10, ed. Müller, pp. 68–69, 140–41.

302 Cf. John 19.15: "Pilate said to them, 'Shall I crucify your king?' The chief priests answered, 'We have no king but Caesar.'"

303 See Augustine, *De Genesi ad litteram* 11.22, 24–25 (CSEL 28 /1: 354–58); Alcuin, *Commentarii in Apocalypsin* 6.7, 8.7 (PL 100: 1125D, 1136D). This image is a negative reflection of the Pauline theme of the Church as the mystical body of Christ; see 1 Corinthians 12.

304 See also Matthew 27.20; Mark 15.11; Luke 23.18–19; John 18.40.

305 The antipope, Clement III (1080–1100), who was chosen at the council of Brixen. See Cowdrey, *Pope Gregory VII*, pp. 201–03; Robinson, *Henry IV of Germany*, pp. 198–202.

306 The Roman synod of 1078. See Cowdrey, *Pope Gregory VII*, pp. 309–10; Robinson, *Henry IV of Germany*, p. 200.

307 Cf. John 19.15.

308 See also 3 Kings (1 Kings) 19.18.

309 A similar compliment is paid to Manegold by Wolfger of Prüfening in his catalogue of ecclesiastical writers; see Appendix, Text 23.

310 Gregory VII was elected pope on 22 April 1073 and died on 25 May 1085. The sentence implies that he is no longer alive; see also notes 318 and 344.

311 This account by Gebhard, archbishop of Salzburg (1060–1088), is either lost or is identical with his *Epistola ad Herimannum Mettensem episcopum*, MGH Ldl 1: 261–79. See Max Manitius, *Geschichte der lateinischen Literatur des Mittelalters* 3, Handbuch der Altertumswissenschaft 9/2 (Munich: C.H. Beck'sche Verlagsbuchhandlung, 1931), pp. 25–26. This is the Gebhard to whom Manegold addressed his *Liber ad Gebehardum*.

312 Matthew 10.24; Luke 6.40.

313 Cf. Manegold, *Liber ad Gebehardum* 25 (MGH Ldl 1: 357, line 31); Gregory VII, *Dictatus pape* 19 (*Epistola* 2.55a), MGH Epistolae selectae 2: 206. See Robinson, *Henry IV of Germany*, p. 144.

314 On the collections of canonical decrees promoted by Gregory VII, see Robinson, *Authority and Resistance in the Investiture Contest*, pp. 39–44.

315 Manegold's *Liber ad Gebehardum* is itself largely a collection of canonical sources intended to oppose the arguments of the anti-Gregorians; see, for example, John Gilchrist, *The Collection in Seventy-Four Titles: A Canon Law Manual of the Gregorian Reform*, Mediaeval Sources in Translation 22 (Toronto: Pontifical Institute of Mediaeval Studies, 1980), p. 43. The supporters of the emperor regarded the use of the new collections made by members of the Gregorian party to be "tendentious and deceptive." They were able, however, to turn the new collections against the Gregorians themselves. See Robinson, *Authority and Resistance in the Investiture Contest*, pp. 40 (n. 162), 41, 44–48; quotation from p. 41.

316 See Augustine, *De civitate dei* 21.1 (CCSL 48: 758); idem, *Enchiridion* 111 (CCSL 46: 109).

317 Genesis 4.2–4. Manegold implies that Cain incurred God's displeasure by offering Him unwinnowed grain; similarly, the anti-Gregorians neglected to remove the chaff of secular entanglement from the offering of their religious observance. For the division of the two cities beginning with Cain and Abel, see Augustine, *De civitate dei* 15.1 (CCSL 48: 453–54).

318 This phrase is presented in the ablative absolute (*vivente patre et domino nostro*); in the context of verbal past tense (*usurpare et polluere conatus sit*) it implies that Gregory is no longer alive. Since Gregory died 25 May 1085, the *Contra Wolfelmum* must have been written after this date. See *Contra Wolfelmum*, ed. Hartmann, p. 102, lines 14–19. See also notes 310 and 344.

319 Wibert was elected antipope at the council of Brixen in 1080 and was enthroned in Rome on 24 March 1084, after Henry IV's army had seized the city. The imperial forces abandoned Rome, however, on 21 May at the approach of Robert Guiscard, the Norman duke of Apulia and Calabria, vassal of Gregory VII. See Robinson, *Henry IV of Germany*, pp. 227–33.

320 On 31 March 1084, Wibert crowned Henry IV emperor in Rome — in return, as it were, for his enthronement there as pope, an event made possible only when Henry's armies captured the city. Hence Manegold considers one to have obliged the other in sin. See Robinson, *Henry IV of Germany*, pp. 229–30.

321 See Robinson, *Henry IV of Germany*, pp. 211–35, on the invasion of Italy during the years 1081–1084, which culminated in the capture of Rome. Henry IV decided to invade Italy after Gregory VII excommunicated him a second time, in March 1080. He intended to replace an unworthy pope with an obedient one, as his father, Henry III, had done in 1046. At the council of Brixen in June 1080, Henry IV had announced his intention of presiding at the papal enthronement of Wibert of Ravenna in Rome the following year. As it turned out, however, the event did not take place until 1084. On the events leading up to the invasion, see Robinson, ibid., pp. 194–202.

322 The council of Worms that met on 24 January 1076 at Henry IV's instigation urged Gregory VII to abdicate the see of Rome which, they claimed, "he had usurped contrary to the laws of the Church"; see Robinson, *Henry IV of Germany*, pp. 143–46; quotation from p. 144. For the letter by the German bishops, see *Die Briefe Heinrichs IV.*, ed. Carl Erdmann, MGH Deutsches Mittelalter 1 (1937; Stuttgart: Anton Hiersemann, 1978), pp. 65–68.

323 See Gregory VII, *Registrum* 1.1, MGH Epistolae selectae 2: 2.

324 Gregory VII was elected on 22 April 1073. This passage echoes the phrases of the official election protocol found in Gregory VII's *Registrum* 1.1 and answers the letter of the German bishops of 24 January 1076, which questioned the legality of Gregory's election. On the canonical validity of Gregory's election, particularly in light of the Papal Election Decree of 1059 (which stipulated that a pope must be elected by the cardinals, approved by the people, and confirmed by the authoritative consent of the king), see Robinson, *Henry IV of Germany*, pp. 128–29; Cowdrey, *Pope Gregory VII*, pp. 44–45, 71–74. On Manegold's portrayal of Gregory VII's election in the *Liber ad Gebehardum* 14 (MGH Ldl 1: 336–37), see Robinson, *Authority and Resistance in the Investiture Contest*, pp. 35–36.

325 *Contra Wolfelmum*, ed. Hartmann, p. 104, line 10: "Talia eos canones docuerunt." Manegold seems to mean that Gregory's reform of ecclesiastical discipline through his "revival of the canons" has made faithful Christians appreciate the excellence of his pontificate.

326 That is, the Church.

327 That is, St. Peter. See Matthew 16.17.

328 See "Bariona" in *Papias Vocabulista*, p. 39. See also Jerome, *Commentarii in Mattheum* 3.16, CCSL 77: 141.

329 See Horst Fuhrmann, "'Volkssouveränität' und 'Herrschaftsvertrag' bei Manegold von Lautenbach," *Festschrift für Hermann Krause*, ed. Sten Gagnér, Hans Schlosser, and Wolfgang Wiegand (Cologne and Vienna: Böhlau, 1975), pp. 21–42, at 34–35 n. 29.

330 Henry IV was excommunicated in February 1076 and repented at Canossa in January 1077 in a desperate attempt to stay in power after military reversals in Germany; he was excommunicated a second time
by Gregory VII in March 1080. On Henry's dramatic repentance at Canossa and the events leading up to
it, see Robinson, *Henry IV of Germany*, pp. 147–64.

331 That is, Gebhard, the archbishop of Salzburg. See note 311.

332 The letter, which was written by Wenrich of Trier, is printed in MGH Ldl 1: 280–99. On Wenrich,
see note 335.

333 1 Kings (1 Samuel) 24.7, here applied to Gregory VII, as the vicar of Christ. For additional references,
see *Contra Wolfelmum*, ed. Hartmann, p. 106 n. 4. The Latin is *christo domini* (ibid., p. 106, line 1). The
epithet was associated with kingship in the Old Testament, and although it continued to have such con-
notations during the Middle Ages, its application to Jesus, who was both king and priest, tended to associate it with the priesthood, and hence with the supreme pontiff.

334 Manegold seems to have been misinformed; he must have been thinking of the council held at Mainz
on 31 May 1080, where nineteen bishops summoned by Henry IV repudiated Gregory VII's authority in
response to the second excommunication of the emperor. Manegold may have made the association with
Trier because the letter that was supposedly conceived at the council was written by a master at the cathedral school of Trier, as Manegold notes later in the paragraph. It is believed that the pamphlet was written
between the middle of 1080 and the end of 1081. See Robinson, *Authority and Resistance*, p. 154; *Die
deutsche Literatur des Mittelalters: Verfasserlexikon*, 2nd ed., vol. 10, cols. 1221–22.

335 Wenrich was later appointed imperial bishop of Piacenza (ca. 1090/1091). He died after 1095. See *Die
deutsche Literatur des Mittelalters: Verfasserlexikon*, 2nd ed., vol. 10, cols. 1219–24.

336 That is, Theodoric (alternatively, Dietrich or Thierry) of Verdun (1046–1089). See Robinson, *Authority and Resistance*, pp. 152–56.

337 One of the three figures whose speech tormented Job in his misfortune; see Job 2.11, 4.1, and passim.
Isidore of Seville, in *Allegoriae* 55 (PL 83: 108B), writes: "The three friends of Job represent a type of
heretic — those who try to seduce another under the pretense of offering consolation." Cf. Gregory the
Great, *Moralia* 3.21.44 (PL 75: 621D): "'Eliphaz' is said to mean 'One who has contempt for God.'"

338 This sentence draws phrases from Job 2.8 and 2 Maccabees 9.9.

339 Cf. 1 Kings (1 Samuel) 17.26. Manegold is identifying Wenrich with Goliath. The poem by "Hugh
the Orthodox," in turn, identifies Manegold with Goliath; see Appendix, Text 9.

340 Manegold's phrase, *more scolarium*, also appears in the opening sentence of the *Contra Wolfelmum*. In
both instances "the manner of the schoolmen" implies a method of education that involves intellectual
opposition in a charged emotional environment, but here it also implies an objectionable emphasis on
technical skill without regard for truth.

341 See Wilfried Hartmann, "Rhetorik und Dialektik in der Streitschriftenliteratur des 11./12. Jahrhun-
derts," p. 91; Robinson, "The Bible in the Investiture Contest: The South German Gregorian Circle," *The
Bible in the Medieval World: Essays in Memory of Beryl Smalley*, ed. Katherine Walsh and Diana Wood,
Studies in Church History, Subsidia 4 (Oxford: Basil Blackwell, 1985), pp. 61–84, at 77; Peter Godman,
The Silent Masters: Latin Literature and Its Censors in the High Middle Ages (Princeton, N.J.: Princeton
University Press, 2000), p. 58.

342 Manegold's very substantial response to Wenrich's brief letter is the *Liber ad Gebehardum* (MGH Ldl 1:
308–430). It seems Manegold had already been at work on the *Ad Gebehardum* when he was interrupted
by the argument with Wolfhelm. See the Introduction, pp. 17–18 above, where my discussion is indebted
to the article by Paul Ewald, "Chronologie der Schriften Manegolds von Lautenbach," *Forschungen zur
deutschen Geschichte* 16 (1876), pp. 383–85. Ewald rightly rejected the emendation of this passage suggested
by Wilhelm von Giesebrecht, "Ueber Magister Manegold von Lautenbach und seine Schrift gegen den

Scholasticus Wenrich," *Sitzungsberichte der königlich-bayerischen Akademie der Wissenschaften zu München*, Jahrgang 1868, Band 2 (Munich: Akademische Buchdruckerei von F. Straub), pp. 297–330, at 304.

[343] Manegold's evaluation of the pamphlet's motives has been adopted as the standard view among modern scholars. However, I.S. Robinson thinks that Manegold's interpretation has been accepted too readily. He observes that Theodoric of Verdun was concerned to defend his own actions following the council of Mainz; for when Theodoric returned to Verdun, he found the city held against him, and he was able to regain entry only by submitting to the pope — a submission he repudiated at the end of 1081. Since the pamphlet is thought to have been written during the interim, it may have been designed more as a piece of self-justification than as a subtle attack against Gregory VII. Thus, Theodoric may have been more concerned with local politics than with the larger drama. See Robinson, *Authority and Resistance in the Investiture Contest*, pp. 154–56. There is, in any event, a measure of restraint in the pamphlet composed by Wenrich that makes it a more magnanimous statement than Manegold's *Contra Wolfelmum* and his even more vehement *Ad Gebehardum*. Of course, to Manegold's way of thinking, Wenrich's pamphlet was all the more insidious for its restraint. On the pamphlet, see also Cowdrey, *Pope Gregory VII*, pp. 216–17.

[344] As Hartmann notes (*Contra Wolfelmum*, pp. 12 n. 24, 107 n. 18), this verse was used in reference to the dead. Even apart from this evidence, however, the remainder of the text clearly indicates that Gregory VII has died. See also Manegold's briefer indications in Chapter 23 (at notes 310 and 318).

Bibliographical Essay

LIBER CONTRA WOLFELMUM: MANUSCRIPT AND EDITIONS

The *Liber contra Wolfelmum* is preserved in a single twelfth-century manuscript: Milan, Biblioteca Ambrosiana, MS. N 118 sup., fols. 117r–134r. For a description of this manuscript and information on provenance, see Manegold von Lautenbach, *Liber contra Wolfelmum*, ed. Wilfried Hartmann, MGH Quellen zur Geistesgeschichte des Mittelalters 8 (Weimar: Hermann Böhlaus Nachfolger, 1972), pp. 32, 34–36.

The *Contra Wolfelmum* was first edited in the eighteenth century by Lodovico Antonio Muratori, "Magistri Manegaldi contra Wolfelmum Coloniensem opusculum," *Anecdota quae ex Ambrosianae Bibliothecae codicibus…* 4 (Padua: Giovanni Manfrè, 1713), pp. 167–208. This edition was reprinted in *Opere del proposto Lodovico Antonio Muratori* 11/2 (Arezzo: M. Bellotti, 1770), pp. 102–36, and again in J.-P. Migne's *Patrologia Latina*, vol. 155, cols. 149–76. In 1891 Kuno Francke published a partial edition, including prologue, table of contents, and Chapters 22–24, in MGH Ldl 1: 303–08, as an accompaniment to his edition of the *Liber ad Gebehardum*. The text was re-edited and supplied with critical notes and an abundant source apparatus in 1972 by Wilfried Hartmann (cited in the preceding paragraph).

LIBER AD GEBEHARDUM: MANUSCRIPT AND EDITION

Manegold's far lengthier polemical treatise, the *Liber ad Gebehardum*, presents his political ideas and engages the issues of the Investiture Controversy more directly than the *Contra Wolfelmum* does. Like the *Contra Wolfelmum*, the *Ad Gebehardum* is also preserved in a single twelfth-century manuscript: Karlsruhe, Badische Landesbibliothek, MS. Rastatt 27 (formerly Codex 93), fols. 1r–102v. For a description of this manuscript, see Alfred Holder, *Die Durlacher und Rastatter Handschriften*, Die Handschriften der Badischen Landesbibliothek in Karlsruhe 3 (1895; repr. Wiesbaden: Otto Harrassowitz, 1970), pp. 117–19; see also Horst Fuhrmann, "'Volkssouveranität' und 'Herrschaftsvertrag' bei Manegold von Lautenbach," *Festschrift für Hermann Krause*, ed. Sten Gagnér, Hans Schlosser, and Wolfgang Wiegand (Cologne and Vienna: Böhlau, 1975), p. 31 n. 22.

The text was edited in 1891 by Kuno Francke, "Manegoldi ad Gebehardum Liber," MGH Ldl 1: 308–430. As with the *Contra Wolfelmum*, only brief portions have been translated into modern languages. In English, one may consult Ewart Lewis, *Medieval Political Ideas* 1 (London: Routledge & Kegan Paul, 1954), pp. 164–65, which presents the oft-cited analogy of kingship and swineherding (*Liber ad Gebehardum* 30); see also Reginald Lane Poole, *Illustrations of the History of Medieval Thought and Learning*, 2nd ed. (1920; repr. New York: Dover Publications, 1960), p. 203.

Consuetudines Marbacenses

As the first prior of the new house of Augustinian canons at Marbach in Alsace, Manegold undoubtedly had great influence on the life of his community and probably on the movement of canons regular more generally. The priory of Marbach, in fact, produced a supplement to the rule of St. Augustine that was highly influential in southern Germany. The recent editor of this Marbach customal, or *Consuetudines Marbacenses*, believes that Manegold was largely responsible for its contents. See Joseph Siegwart, *Die Consuetudines des Augustiner-Chorherrenstiftes Marbach im Elsass (12. Jahrhundert)*, Spicilegium Friburgense 10 (Freiburg: Universitätsverlag Freiburg, 1965), pp. 18–31. Siegwart provides a detailed philological comparison of the *Consuetudines Marbacenses* and the *Liber contra Wolfelmum*, in "Die Consuetudines von Marbach und Schwarzenthann," *Le Codex Guta-Sintram: Manuscrit 37 de la bibliothèque du Grand Séminaire de Strasbourg*, 2 vols.: facsimile and commentary (Lucerne and Strasbourg: Éditions Fac-similés, en co-édition avec les Éditions Coprur, 1982, 1983), commentary volume, pp. 192–233, at 197–201. Unfortunately, the availability of this publication is extremely limited.

Biblical Commentaries

Several commentaries, on both biblical and classical texts, have been attributed to Manegold of Lautenbach. See Max Manitius, *Geschichte der lateinischen Literatur des Mittelalters* 3, Handbuch der Altertumswissenschaft 9/2 (Munich: C.H. Beck'sche Verlagsbuchhandlung, 1931), pp. 175–80; Wilfried Hartmann, "Manegold von Lautenbach und die Anfänge der Frühscholastik," *Deutsches Archiv für Erforschung des Mittelalters* 26 (1970), pp. 47–149, at 52–53; see also Hartmann's article in *Die deutsche Literatur des Mittelalters: Verfasserlexikon*, ed. Wolfgang Stammler et al., 2nd ed., vol. 5 (Berlin and New York: Walter de Gruyter, 1985), cols. 1214–18, at 1215–16.

A twelfth-century catalogue of ecclesiastical authors, which is thought to have been compiled by Wolfger of Prüfening, asserts that Manegold the polemicist annotated the

Book of Isaiah and wrote full-length commentaries on the Gospel of Matthew and on the Psalms.[1] No trace remains of the first two works, but the last may still be extant as the text of Pseudo-Bede printed in Migne's *Patrologia Latina*, vol. 93, cols. 477–1098. There is some concern, however, that Wolfger may have conflated two different Manegolds in his catalogue-entry.[2] The matter is debated in the following articles (arranged in chronological order):

> Germain Morin, "Le Pseudo-Bède sur les Psaumes et l'*Opus super Psalterium* de Maître Manegold de Lautenbach," *Revue Bénédictine* 28 (1911), pp. 331–40.
>
> Bernhard Bischoff, "Zur Kritik der Heerwagenschen Ausgabe von Bedas Werken, Basel 1563," *Studien und Mitteilungen zur Geschichte des Benediktiner-Ordens* 51 (1933), pp. 171–76.
>
> Heinrich Weisweiler, "Die handschriftlichen Vorlagen zum Erstdruck von Pseudo-Beda, *In Psalmorum Librum Exegesis*," *Biblica* 18 (1937), pp. 197–204.
>
> François Châtillon, "Recherches critiques sur les différents personnages nommés Manegold," *Revue du moyen âge latin* 9 (1953), pp. 153–70.
>
> Damian van den Eynde, "Literary Note on the Earliest Scholastic *Commentarii in Psalmos*," *Franciscan Studies* 14 (1954), pp. 121–54, at 139–47.
>
> Julia Gross, "Die Erbsündenlehre Manegolds von Lautenbach nach seinem Psalmenkommentar," *Zeitschrift für Kirchengeschichte* 71 (1960), pp. 253–61.
>
> Valerie I.J. Flint, "Some Notes on the Early Twelfth-Century Commentaries on the Psalms," *Recherches de théologie ancienne et médiévale* 38 (1971), pp. 80–88.
>
> Wilfried Hartmann, "Psalmenkommentare aus der Zeit der Reform und der Früh-scholastik," *Studi Gregoriani* 9 (1972), pp. 313–66, at 319–27.
>
> Joseph Siegwart, "Erziehung, Gerechtigkeit Gottes und Strafe im Psalmenkommentar Manegolds von Lautenbach," *Ordo sapientiae et amoris…Hommage au Professeur Jean-Pierre Torell, O.P. à l'occasion de son 65e anniversaire*, ed. Carlos-Josaphat Pinto de Oliveira, Studia Friburgensia, new series 78 (Fribourg: Éditions Universitaires, 1993), pp. 595–616.

---

[1] See Appendix, Text 23. Consider also the entry in a catalogue attributed to Henry of Ghent (d. 1293): "Manegold (*Manegundus*) left to posterity the monuments of his genius in commentaries on the Psalms and on Paul's Letters." See Henricus Gandavensis, *De scriptoribus ecclesiasticis*, ed. Aubert Le Mire (Miraeus), in *Bibliotheca ecclesiastica*, 2 vols. in 1 (Antwerp: J. Mesium, 1639–1649), p. 167 of vol. 1. A later edition of this text was published by Johann Albert Fabricius, *Bibliotheca ecclesiastica*, 4 vols. in 1 (Hamburg: Christian. Liebezeit & Theodor. Christoph. Felginer, 1718), p. 122 of vol. 2; repr. Farnborough, U.K.: Gregg Press, 1967. For additional stray references in catalogues and manuscripts, see Manitius, *Geschichte der lateinischen Literatur des Mittelalters* 3, p. 177.

[2] See the Introduction, p. 24.

The exposition of Psalm 2 (PL 93: 489C–94B) has been translated into French by Baptista Landry, in *Les psaumes commentés par les Pères*, preface by A.-G. Hamman, Collection "les Pères dans la foi" (Paris: Desclée de Brouwer, 1983), pp. 53–66.

Manegold is also thought to have written a commentary on the Pauline epistles.[3] A fragment of this text may be preserved in the florilegium of theological opinions collected in Oxford, Bodleian Library, MS. Laud Misc. 216, under the heading "Manig. in glosis super Apostolum."[4] This portion of the Oxford florilegium (fols. 153ra–vb) has been edited; see Odon Lottin, *Psychologie et morale aux XIIe et XIIIe siècles* 5: *Problèmes d'histoire littéraire: L'école d'Anselm de Laon et de Guillaume de Champeaux* (Gembloux: J. Duculot, 1959), pp. 146–53; and Lottin's earlier discussion, in "Manegold de Lautenbach, source d'Anselme de Laon," *Recherches de théologie ancienne et médiévale* 14 (1947), pp. 218–23.

The last of the biblical commentaries attributed to Manegold of Lautenbach is an exposition of the Apocalypse; the text is preserved in Verdun, Bibliothèque municipale, MS. 63. This twelfth-century manuscript identifies its author as "Master Manegold."[5] François Châtillon once planned to edit the text, and in the article cited above he offered some observations by way of preparation (see pp. 165–70), but nothing else has come of the project. Châtillon was firmly of the opinion that Manegold of Lautenbach did not write the commentary, yet he did not advance proofs to support his conviction. For a discussion of this commentary, see Wilhelm Kamlah, *Apokalypse und Geschichtstheologie: Die mittelalterliche Auslegung der Apokalypse vor Joachim von Fiore*, Historische Studien 285 (Berlin: Fr. Emil Ebering, 1935; repr., Vaduz: Kraus Reprint, 1965), pp. 25–38. The commentary receives brief mention in an article by Yves Christie, "Le *visiones* dell'Apocalisse dall'undicesimo al trecesimo secolo: immagini, testi e contesti," trans. Marina Massaglia, *Schede medievali: Rassegna dell'officina di studi medievali* 19 (1990), pp. 278–96, at 282.

COMMENTARIES ON CLASSICAL TEXTS

Of the commentaries on classical texts attributed to Manegold of Lautenbach, one that has long been recognized in modern scholarship is a commentary on Ovid's *Metamorphoses*. The complete text is not known, but the opinions of a certain Manegold

---

[3] See note 1, above.

[4] See Hartmann, "Manegold von Lautenbach und die Anfänge der Frühscholastik," pp. 93–94; see also his article in *Die deutsche Literatur des Mittelalters: Verfasserlexikon*, 2nd ed., vol. 5, col. 1217.

[5] The title is *Stille verborum magistri Menegaudi in Apocalipsim*.

(*Manogaldus*) can be gleaned from references found in an early twelfth-century manuscript: Munich, Bayerische Staatsbibliothek, MS. Clm 4610. One may consult the following studies: Moritz Haupt, "Coniectanea," *Hermes: Zeitschrift für classische Philologie* 7 (1873), pp. 190–92; Carl Meiser, "Über einen Commentar zu den Metamorphosen des Ovid," *Sitzungsberichte der königlich-bayerische Akademie der Wissenschaften zu München, philosophisch-philologischen und historischen Classe*, Jahrgang 1885 (Munich: Akademische Buchdruckerei von F. Staub, 1886), pp. 47–89, especially pp. 71–72. Most recently, see Claudia Villa, "Tra *fabula* e *historia*: Manegoldo di Lautenbach e il 'Maestro di Orazio,'" *Aevum* 70 (1996), pp. 245–56.

Villa's article also reviews the evidence that Manegold wrote commentaries on two other classical texts: Horace's *Ars Poetica* (according to the twelfth/thirteenth-century manuscript at Bern, Burgerbibliothek, MS. 327) and Priscian's *Institutiones grammaticae* (according to the twelfth-century manuscript at Durham, Cathedral Library, MS. C.IV.29, as well as the grammatical summa of the twelfth-century scholar Peter Helias; see Manitius, *Geschichte der lateinischen Literatur des Mittelalters* 3, pp. 177–78).

The evidence that Manegold wrote commentaries on Plato's *Timaeus* and Boethius's *De consolatione philosophiae* is meager. The attribution of the Platonic commentary is based on an entry in a fourteenth-century catalogue from Peterborough; see Margaret T. Gibson, "The Study of the *Timaeus* in the Eleventh and Twelfth Centuries," *Pensamiento* 25 (1969), pp. 183–94, at 185, available in her volume, *"Artes" and Bible in the Medieval West*, Variorum Collected Studies Series (Aldershot: Ashgate, 1993), no. IX; see also Charles Burnett, "Adelard, Music and the Quadrivium," *Adelard of Bath: An English Scientist and Arabist of the Early Twelfth Century*, ed. Charles Burnett, Warburg Institute Surveys and Texts 14 (London: Warburg Institute, 1987), p. 81 n. 37. Such a commentary would be of great interest, considering Manegold's critique of Plato's cosmological doctrines, but if Manegold ever wrote a set of glosses on the *Timaeus*, it has not survived. The commentary listed in the Peterborough catalogue, whether by the author of the *Contra Wolfelmum* or by another Manegold, has no likely candidate among the manuscripts surveyed by Paul Edward Dutton, "Material Remains of the Study of the *Timaeus* in the Later Middle Ages," *L'enseignement de la philosophie au XIIIe siècle: Autour du "Guide de l'étudiant" du ms. Ripoll 109*, ed. Claude Lafleur and Joanne Carrier, Studia artistarum 5 (Brepols: Turnhout, 1997), pp. 203–30.

There is a reference to a certain "Master Manegold" in a commentary on Boethius's *De consolatione philosophiae*, preserved in the twelfth-century manuscript at Kues, Hospitalbibliothek, MS. 191, but it does not necessarily imply that Manegold wrote a commentary on the famous Boethian prosimetrum; see *Die deutsche Literatur des Mittelalters: Verfasserlexikon*, 2nd ed., vol. 5, cols. 1217–18. Likewise, the marginal reference to a Manegold in a twelfth-century manuscript of Boethius's *De musica* (Oxford, Trinity

College, MS. D.47) need not imply that Manegold wrote a commentary on that text; see Alison White, "Boethius in the Medieval Quadrivium," *Boethius: His Life, Thought and Influence*, ed. Margaret T. Gibson (Oxford: B. Blackwell, 1981), pp. 182–84.

Finally, an anonymous commentary on Cicero's *De inventione* preserved in the eleventh/twelfth-century manuscript at Cologne, Dombibliothek MS. 197 has been ascribed to Manegold of Lautenbach by Mary Dickey, "Some Commentaries on the *De inventione* and *Ad Herennium* of the Eleventh and Early Twelfth Centuries," *Mediaeval and Renaissance Studies* 6 (1968), pp. 1–41. Dickey made this connection on the basis of a reference to a Master Manegold in the twelfth-century manuscript of York, Minster Library, MS. XVI.M.7. See also Karin Margareta Fredborg, "The Commentaries on Cicero's *De inventione* and *Rhetorica ad Herennium* by William of Champeaux," *Cahiers de l'Institut du moyen âge grec et latin* 17 (1976), pp. 1–39.

STUDIES OF MANEGOLD'S THOUGHT

Scholarly analysis of Manegold's thought tends to be divided between his views on philosophy, enunciated in the *Liber contra Wolfelmum*, and his political and ecclesiological conceptions, which are elaborated in the *Liber ad Gebehardum*. The major exception to this tendency is the essential article by Wilfried Hartmann, "Manegold von Lautenbach und die Anfänge der Frühscholastik," *Deutsches Archiv für Erforschung des Mittelalters* 26 (1970), pp. 47–149. In tying together the different strands within the scholarly tradition, Hartmann offers a thorough attempt to locate Manegold within the intellectual culture of the late eleventh and early twelfth centuries, with commendable sensitivity to the considerable problems surrounding Manegold's biography. Despite a few questionable passages,[6] Hartmann admirably answers Peter Classen's appeal: "eine neue Untersuchung Manegolds als Scholastiker wäre wünschenswert." See Peter Classen, "Zur Geschichte der Frühscholastik in Österreich und Bayern," *Mitteilungen des Instituts für Österreichische Geschichtsforschung* 67 (1959), pp. 249–77, at 250 n. 3. See also Hartmann's more general study, "Rhetorik und Dialektik in der Streitschriftlichenliteratur des 11./12. Jahrhunderts," *Dialektik und Rhetorik im früheren und hohen Mittelalter: Rezeption, Überlieferung und gesellschaftliche Wirkung antiker Gelehrsamkeit vornehmlich im 9. und 12. Jahrhundert*, ed. Johannes Fried, Schriften des Historischen Kollegs, Kolloquien 27 (Munich: R. Oldenbourg, 1997), pp. 73–95.

---

[6] See H. Silvestre's comments in *Revue d'histoire ecclésiastique* 68 (1973), pp. 933–35, as well as my criticism of Hartmann's discussion of "intelligible matter" (p. 78 n. 97 above).

PHILOSOPHICAL STUDIES (*LIBER CONTRA WOLFELMUM*)

Studies devoted to Manegold's anti-philosophical polemic include the following:

Joseph Anton Endres, *Forschungen zur Geschichte der frühmittelalterlichen Philosophie*, Beiträge zur Geschichte der Philosophie des Mittelalters 17.2–3 (Münster: Aschendorff, 1915), pp. 98–109.

Eugenio Garin, *Studi sul platonismo medievale* (Florence: Felice le monnier, 1958), pp. 23–33.

Tullio Gregory, *Platonismo medievale: Studi e ricerche*, Studi storici 26–27 (Rome: Istituto storico italiano per il Medio Evo, 1958), pp. 17–30.

Tullio Gregory, "*Das Opusculum contra Wolfelmum* und die antiplatonische Polemik des Manegold von Lautenbach," trans. Markus Lakebrink, *Platonismus in der Philosophie des Mittelalters*, ed. Werner Beierwaltes, Wege der Forschung 197 (Darmstadt: Wissenschaftliche Buchgesellschaft, 1969), pp. 366–80. This is a translation of the Italian text of 1958.

Loris Sturlese, *Storia della filosofia tedesca nel medioevo: Dagli inizi alla fine del XII secolo*, Accademia toscana di scienze e lettere "La Colombaria," Studi 105 (Florence: Leo S. Olschki, 1990), pp. 62–69.

Loris Sturlese, *Die deutsche Philosophie im Mittelalter: Von Bonifatius bis zu Albert dem Großen (748–1280)*, trans. Johanna Baumann (Munich: C.H. Beck, 1993), pp. 77–86. This is a translation of the Italian text of 1990.

POLITICAL AND ECCLESIOLOGICAL STUDIES (*LIBER AD GEBEHARDUM*)

Most studies of Manegold's thought are devoted to his political ideas, which he developed in the course of the Investiture Controversy and elaborated in his massive and more trenchant polemic, the *Liber ad Gebehardum*. Opinions have been divided on the value of this text. Some scholars have esteemed Manegold for developing a theory of the "social contract." Consider Reginald Lane Poole, *Illustrations of the History of Medieval Thought and Learning*, 2nd ed. (1920; repr. New York: Dover Publications, 1960), pp. 203–04, where he cites *Liber ad Gebehardum* 47 (MGH Ldl 1: 391–92):

It is impossible to express the theory of "social contract" more clearly than Manegold does: *since*, he says, *no one can create himself emperor or king, the people elevates a certain one person over itself to this end that he govern and rule it according to the principle of righteous government; but if in any wise he transgresses the contract by virtue of which he is chosen, he absolves the people from the obligation of submission, because he has first broken faith with it.*

It should be remembered, however, that "the people" for Manegold referred primarily to the German landed nobility, who enjoyed the privilege of electing their king, even though this right was regularly exercised in affirming a hereditary ruler. In the opinion of Alois Fauser (see below), Manegold was fundamentally a monarchist, but his monarch was the pope. Thus, far from proclaiming a nascent democratic theory, Manegold was defending theocracy, particularly the right of popes to depose emperors. For a recent statement on Manegold's political theory and its reception, including abundant references to scholarship not listed here, see p. 27 n. 13 of the article by Horst Fuhrmann cited below. The following list also contains ecclesiological studies that consider Manegold's place in the Investiture Controversy.

Georg Koch, *Manegold von Lautenbach und die Lehre von der Volkssouveränität unter Heinrich IV*, Historische Studien 34 (Berlin: E. Ebering, 1902; repr. Vaduz: Kraus Reprint, 1965).

M.T. Stead, "Manegold of Lautenbach," *English Historical Review* 29 (1914), pp. 1–15.

Alois Fauser, *Die Publizisten des Investiturstreites: Persönlichkeiten und Ideen*, Inaugural-Dissertation (Würzburg: Dissertationsdruckerei und Verlag Konrad Triltsch, 1935), pp. 45–50.

Reinhold Laakmann, *Die Königsgewalt bei Manegold von Lautenbach*, Dissertation (Hamburg: Dissertations-Druck, 1969).

Pietro De Leo, "Ricerche sul *Liber ad Gebehardum* di Manegoldo di Lautenbach," *Rivista di storia e letteratura religiosa* 10 (1974), pp. 112–53.

Horst Fuhrmann, "'Volkssouveränität' und 'Herrschaftsvertrag' bei Manegold von Lautenbach," *Festschrift für Hermann Krause*, ed. Sten Gagnér, Hans Schlosser, and Wolfgang Wiegand (Cologne and Vienna: Böhlau, 1975), pp. 21–42.

I.S. Robinson, *Authority and Resistance in the Investiture Contest: The Polemical Literature of the Late Eleventh Century* (Manchester and New York: Manchester University Press, Holmes & Meier Publishers, 1978), especially pp. 124–31.

I.S. Robinson, "Pope Gregory VII, the Princes and the *Pactum* 1077–1080," *English Historical Review* 94 (1979), pp. 721–56, at 738 and 746–47.

I.S. Robinson, "The Bible in the Investiture Contest: The South German Gregorian Circle," *The Bible in the Medieval World: Essays in Memory of Beryl Smalley*, ed. Katherine Walsh and Diana Wood (Oxford: Basil Blackwell, 1985), pp. 61–84. See also the article in the same volume by Jean Dunbabin, "The Maccabees as Exemplars in the Tenth and Eleventh Centuries," pp. 31–41, at 39–40.

Allen Brent, "The Investiture Controversy: An Issue in Sacramental Theology?" *Ephemerides theologicae Lovanienses* 63 (1987), pp. 59–89, at 69–72.

Tilman Struve, "Das Problem der Eideslösung in der Streitschriften des Investiturstreites," *Zeitschrift der Savigny-Stiftung für Rechtsgeschichte: Kanonistische Abteilung* 75 (1989), pp. 107–32, at 122–26.

Ovidio Capitani, "Il papato di Gregorio VII nella pubblicistica del suo tempo: notazioni sul *Liber ad Gebehardum*," *Tradizione ed interpretazione: dialettiche ecclesiologiche del secolo XI* (Rome: Jouvence, 1990), pp. 233–60.

Irene Scaravelli, "'Utilitas' nella libellistica dell'XI secolo: un primo sondaggio," *Studi medievali*, Spoleto 32 (1991), pp. 191–229, at 200–08.

John Gilchrist, "The Reception of Pope Gregory VII into the Canon Law (1073–1141)," *Canon Law in the Age of Reform, 11th–12th Centuries*, Variorum Collected Studies Series (Aldershot: Ashgate, 1993), no. IX, pp. 192–229, at 214–16, 225.

Wilhelm Kölmel, "*Juditio rationis*: Manegolds Theorie der Königsmacht," *Festschrift für Eduard Hlawitschka zum 65. Geburtstag*, ed. Karl Rudolf Schnith and Roland Pauler, Münchener historische Studien, Abteilung Mittelalterliche Geschichte 5 (Kallmünz Opf.: Michael Lassleben, 1993), pp. 267–82.

BIOGRAPHICAL STUDIES AND GENERAL TREATMENTS

The problems with the evidence for Manegold's biography — particularly the question of whether it applies to one Manegold or to more than one — has generated a substantial body of scholarship. Here I offer a representative sampling that includes the more noteworthy publications, which in turn will lead the reader to additional sources. In the nineteenth century, some scholars reacted against the general tendency to accept the evidence uncritically. They concluded that there were at least two Manegolds: a famous teacher born ca. 1030 or 1040, and the polemicist from Lautenbach, born ca. 1060; see the articles by Wilhelm von Giesebrecht and N. Paulus in the following list. Joseph A. Endres initially accepted Giesebrecht's argument (see his publication of 1901, in the list below), but soon thereafter rejected it upon a reconsideration of the evidence. He presented critical arguments to defend the thesis that the famous teacher and the polemicist were one and the same. François Châtillon vehemently rejected the position defended by Endres but failed to advance arguments that would disprove it. Wilfried Hartmann's study, noted above, tends toward Endres's view, although with due caution; he suggests that the disparity between the famous teacher of philosophy and the outspoken critic of the philosophers probably reflects two phases of Manegold's career. The question is by no means settled. For example, in response to Charles Haaby's deplorably uncritical discussion, Yves Ritter has reasserted the position of Giesebrecht with all the vehemence of Châtillon. Peter Godman, on the other hand, accepts with conviction what Hartmann suggested with a measure of caution; Godman observes that repentant philosophers were not all that uncommon in the eleventh and twelfth centuries. John Marenbon suggests a third possibility between the two extremes, which respects the ambiguity of the evidence: "…Manegold may have taught about pagan philosophy before he became a monk; but he is probably not to be identified with the Manegold who taught William of Champeaux and is treated by twelfth-century chroniclers as one of the forerunners of the intellectual life of their time." In the final analysis, every reader must decide what seems likeliest. It is for this purpose that I have appended the biographical dossier.

The following selective list of studies is arranged chronologically. It should be noted that the texts preceding Giesebrecht's article, with the exception of Fabricius, are marked by a lack of critical rigor; they have been included as a sampling of earlier scholarship.

César Égasse Du Boulay (Caesar Egassius Bulaeus), *Historia Universitatis Parisiensis* 1 (1665; repr. Franfurt am Main: Minerva, 1966), pp. 587–88, 621.

Johann Albert Fabricius, *Bibliotheca latina mediae et infimae aetatis* 5 (Hamburg: Sumtu Viduae Felgineriae ex officina piscatoria, 1736), pp. 33–36.

Histoire littéraire de la France 9 (1750; repr. Paris: Victor Palmé, 1868), pp. 280–90.

Philippe André Grandidier, *Œuvres historiques inédits*, ed. J. Liblin, vol. 2 (Colmar: Revue d'Alsace, 1865), pp. 257–86. Published posthumously; Grandidier died in 1787.

Wilhelm von Giesebrecht, "Ueber Magister Manegold von Lautenbach und seine Schrift gegen den Scholasticus Wenrich," *Sitzungsberichte der königlich- bayerischen Akademie der Wissenschaften zu München*, Jahrgang 1868, Band 2 (Munich: Akademische Buchdruckerei von F. Straub), pp. 297–330.

N. Paulus, "Études nouvelles sur Manegold de Lautenbach," *Revue catholique d'Alsace* (1886), pp. 209–20, 279–89, 337–45.

Joseph Anton Endres, "Manegold von Lautenbach: Ein Beitrag zur Philosophiegeschichte des 11. Jahrhunderts," *Historisch-politische Blätter für das katholische Deutschland* 127 (1901), pp. 389–401, 486–95.

Joseph Anton Endres, "Manegold von Lautenbach, 'modernorum magister magistrorum,'" *Historisches Jahrbuch* 25 (1904), pp. 168–76.

Édouard Sitzmann, *Dictionnaire de biographie des hommes célèbres de l'Alsace* 2 (1910; repr. Paris: Éditions du Palais Royal, 1973), pp. 232–34 ("Manegold de Lautenbach"), 234–35 ("Manegold le Philosophe").

Joseph Anton Endres, *Forschungen zur Geschichte der frühmittelalterlichen Philosophie*, Beiträge zur Geschichte der Philosophie des Mittelalters 17.2–3 (Münster: Aschendorff, 1915), pp. 87–113.

É. Amann, "Manegold de Lautenbach," *Dictionnaire de théologie catholique* 9 (Paris: Letouzey et Ané, 1927), cols. 1825–30.

Max Manitius, *Geschichte der lateinischen Literatur des Mittelalters* 3, Handbuch der Altertumswissenschaft 9/2 (Munich: C.H. Beck'sche Verlagsbuchhandlung, 1931), pp. 25–28, 175–80.

François Châtillon, "Recherches critiques sur les différents personnages nommés Manegold," *Revue du moyen âge latin* 9 (1953), pp. 153–70.

Jakob Mois, *Das Stift Rottenbuch in der Kirchenreformation des XI.–XII. Jahrhunderts: Ein Beitrag zur Ordens-Geschichte der Augustiner-Chorherren*, Beiträge zur altbayerischen Kirchengeschichte 19 (Munich: Verlag des Erzbischöflichen Ordinariats München und Freising, 1953), pp. 99–107.

Charles Haaby, *Stift Lautenbach*, Alsatia Monastica: Forschungen herausgegeben von der Gesellschaft für Elsässische Kirchengeschichte zu Strassburg 2 (Kevelaer: Butzon & Bercker, 1958), pp. 22–39.

Yves Ritter, "Manégold de Lautenbach, sa parole valait une épée," *Recherches médiévales* 6–7 (1984), pp. 63–66.

John Marenbon, *Early Medieval Philosophy (480–1150)*, rev. ed. (London and New York: Routledge, 1988), p. 87.

Peter Godman, *The Silent Masters: Latin Literature and Its Censors in the High Middle Ages* (Princeton, N.J.: Princeton University Press, 2000), pp. 57–60, 348.

Appendix: Biographical Dossier

Table of Contents

Text 1: *Untitled Poem in the Margin of a Manuscript.*[1]
Date: Late eleventh century.[2]

Pythagoras is weeping, and you, good Cicero, are weeping too.
   Aristotle the soldier of logic is weeping.

   The greatest of all men, both Plato and Socrates, are weeping.
Here is the reason why: they are weeping for philosophy,
   Which once did prosper, flourish, gleam —
But now has become tawdry, now has been reduced to such baseness
   That female hearts even study it.

Text 2: **Bernold of Constance,**[3] *Pamphlet 16: On Sending a Book.*[4]
Date: Before 21 December 1084?[5]

   To the venerable dom A.,[6] who like Martha is concerned about many things when only one thing is necessary, B.,[7] who is not so intent on many things but only on one.[8]

---

[1] Gabriel Silagi, "Marginalien zur Bildungsgeschichte," *Lateinische Dichtungen des X. und XI. Jahrhunderts: Festgabe für Walter Bulst zum 80. Geburtstag,* ed. Walter Berschin and Reinhard Düchting (Heidelberg: Lambert Schneider, 1981), pp. 221–26, at 223–24. Silagi suggests that the text may apply to Manegold, according to the report by Richard of Poitiers that "Master Manegold" had a wife and that his daughters were so well educated that they taught their own students (see Text 21). The manuscript is Munich, Bayerische Staatsbibliothek, MS. Clm 9545, fol. 38r.

[2] The editor offers this date on the basis of paleographical evidence.

[3] Also known as Bernold of St. Blaise (Sankt Blasien).

[4] *Libellus XVI: De libro mittendo,* ed. F. Thaner, MGH Ldl 2: 160.

[5] Since Bernold does not identify himself as a priest, as he does in other letters, it is likely that he wrote this letter before 21 December 1084, the date of his ordination; see Bernold's chronicle, MGH SS 5: 441; see also *Die deutsche Literatur des Mittelalters: Verfasserlexikon,* 2nd ed., vol. 1, col. 795. However, the editor notes that this letter poses special problems with regard to its placement among the others (see MGH Ldl 2: 1–2).

[6] Possibly Alboin, to whom Bernold addressed other polemical letters. See *Libellus 1: De incontinentia sacerdotum* (MGH Ldl 2: 4–26). If the present pamphlet was written during the exchange of letters that were collected to form *Libellus* 1, it should be dated ca. 1074 (ibid., p. 6). However, the question in *Libellus* 16 is not about priestly marriage but about contact with excommunicates. It may be that the opening remark, which hearkens to Luke 10.41–42, represents a sigh of impatience for Alboin's straying from the principal question of priestly marriage; hence, Bernold asserts that only one thing is necessary—presumably, obedience to the pope. However, it is not certain that "A." refers to Alboin.

[7] Bernold. Since the present letter appears among the works of Bernold and repeats passages from other *libelli* that he wrote, there is little trouble in identifying him as the author.

[8] See Luke 10.41–42.

Our brother Manegold[9] passed on the news you gave him that you were not able to keep the book which you might have sent to us presently, in which some passages were found that seem to support your position, and which we would be most eager to peruse, especially since it is said to be a work of Blessed Augustine.[10] But we cannot stop wondering why you did not want to tell us the name [of the author] and the title of this book.[11] For we could acquire it most easily in our parts. By all means you should have given us the title of the book and briefly noted the reasons why the book seems to support your position. We would certainly have submitted mostly willingly to arguments based on authority. Wherefore again and again we steadfastly urge you and hope either that you may be willing now to send us that book, which is your defender, or, if this seems impossible, at least that you may not consider it irksome to send us the name [of the author] and the title of the book in which he seems to assent to your position.

In any event, we wish you to know that we have not yet found, nor do we expect eventually to find, anything authoritative which promises eternal salvation to anyone who, against the statutes of the holy fathers and of the apostles themselves, does not cease to communicate with those who have been excommunicated, whether in salutation, in the kiss of greeting, in speech, or in sharing a meal.[12] How, indeed, can eternal salvation be promised to one whom the apostles themselves have condemned under the sentence of excommunication, as the saintly Pope Calixtus attests?[13] Their judgment on one who communicates with the excommunicated has been confirmed time and again by later saintly fathers, both in the decrees of apostolic men[14] and in the councils of Catholic bishops. In the council of 217 bishops,[15] Blessed Augustine

---

[9] "Frater noster Manegoldus…." The reference to Manegold as "brother" does not necessarily imply that Bernold and Manegold belonged to the same order. Bernold, who was a Benedictine, addresses the canons regular of Rottenbuch as "brothers"; see *Libellus* 11, MGH Ldl 2: 142.

[10] The manuscript in question probably contained Augustine's *Sermon* 88 (PL 38: 539–53), which discusses the question of contact with schismatics. See *The Works of Saint Augustine (A Translation for the 21st Century): Sermons III/3*, trans. Edmund Hill (Brooklyn and New York: New City Press, 1991), pp. 419–38 (especially pp. 435–36).

[11] "Us" refers to Bernold, not to both Bernold and Manegold; the preceding remark suggests that Manegold was the source for Bernold's knowledge that the book in question was a work of St. Augustine, and it implies that they were living in different cloisters. Bernold similarly addresses A. in the plural, but this stylistic point is lost in translation.

[12] This list also appears in Bernold's *Libelli* 5, 7, and 10 (MGH Ldl 2: 95, 104, 113).

[13] Calixtus I (217–222). Bernold mentions Calixtus I in the same context in *Libelli* 5, 7, and 10, cited in the preceding note.

[14] That is, popes.

[15] Bernold identifies this as "the Fourth Council of Carthage attended by 217 bishops" (A.D. 419) in *Libellus* 10, and as "the council of 217 bishops" in *Libellus* 5 (MGH Ldl 2: 95, 114). The text of *Libellus* 16 actually reads "CCXIIII," but this error is presumably a scribal corruption of "CCXVII."

himself condemned under the sentence of excommunication those who communicated with excommunicates even just in speech. Therefore it seems incredible that the same man should in any of his writings have expressed anything contradicting this judgment, to the effect of asserting that communion with excommunicates is not unlawful.

By no means do we say this because we have already come to a verdict, as it were, on what you have discovered. Rather, we ask that you may include us as sharers of your discovery, so that when our positions have been considered in light of it, all of us may share what is seen to be the better part. So then, please grant our petition, and kindly send back to us your opinion on this matter in detail.

Text 3: Manegold of Lautenbach, *The Book against Wolfhelm*, Chapters 23–24.[16]
Date: ca. 25 May 1085–ca. 24 May 1086.[17]

[*See pp. 64–68 above.*]

Text 4: Manegold of Lautenbach, *The Book for Gebhard*, Prologue.[18]
Date: ca. 1085–ca. 1086.[19]

To Gebhard, most vigilant watchman of the citadel of Zion, indeed like a creature with eyes in front and back,[20] Manegold, one who is *a worm, not a man* [Ps. 21.7], offers the fervent devotion of a sinner and that which befits a suppliant.

Although being unknown, I dare to trouble with my letter one who is not unknown,[21] and being so inconsequential, one who is of great consequence, and being rustic, one who is urbane — yet it is not the presumption of temerity that impels me; rather, the gentleness of your clemency, which is known far and wide, commands me, even though you are not present. For it is, indeed, as Father Augustine says: "Familiarity with a person is not acquired by seeing his face; rather, we recognize someone

---

[16] *Contra Wolfelmum*, ed. Hartmann, pp. 98–108.
[17] See Introduction, pp. 15, 20–21 above.
[18] *Manegoldi ad Gebehardum liber*, ed. Kuno Francke, MGH Ldl 1: 310–12, 313.
[19] See Introduction, pp. 18, 20 above.
[20] Cf. Apocalypse 4.8.
[21] The text has left out the negation, but the context requires it. The emended text should read (MGH Ldl 1: 310): "Quod ignotus <non> ignotum, tantillus tantum, rusticus urbanum literis inquietare audeo...."

clearly when his life and morals reveal him; otherwise one cannot even know oneself, since one can never see one's own face."[22] To us, moreover, the copious indications and examples of your constancy, discretion, and wisdom — by virtue of which the Church blooms so richly indeed on every side — make your presence known even though you are not seen directly. Indeed, I do not speak out of ignorance, for I have enjoyed unnumbered blessings from your friendship and favor.

O reverend father, when day after day we heave with frequent sighs as we desire that the rage and madness of our adversaries be weakened and the unity of Catholic peace be restored, alas! not only do we not yet enjoy the outcome for which we long with yearning, but daily we groan with a most truculent impatience for the same unity to extend itself further, and we shudder with all sorrow and bitterness of heart. For that which until now they presumed to whisper in the privacy of the places where they met with their women, and preached only with great restraint by way of furtive assertions (since they were muted and astounded at the enormity of their own crime), now they do not blush to defend nor fear to promulgate in writing. For the bishop of Verdun, or rather Wenrich, master at the school of Trier who used his name and speech, recently composed a pamphlet against the Apostolic See, against ecclesiastical discipline, and against the Catholic religion. In it he even supplied several proof-texts drawn from Scripture, distorting some passages which he found therein, according to the manner in which he misunderstood them, while other passages which he did not find therein he presented as scriptural with a false attribution, since he lacks all shame and is more depraved than any prostitute. He slandered even the apostolic bishop with filthy abuse, and with the bitterest reproaches he derided the rest of the leaders and teachers of the Catholic religion, hinting at some of them obliquely and reviling others openly — a testimony to his capriciousness! In short, this pamphlet has been published for the mockery of the Church, since it is circulated by them on all sides as authoritative and even canonical; indeed, it has found its way into nearly every street and inglenook.

When it had found its way even into our hands, then Harmann — formerly the prior of our little monastery, which has now been destroyed by the same culprits — enjoined upon my foolishness the command that I undertake the task of opposing this pamphlet and strive to deprive it of its force by means of canonical demonstration. I believe he thought it would have been too mean to burden anyone with such easy exercises, if that person were engaged in a weightier project, or if he possessed more

---

[22] *Tractatus in Iohannis Evangelium* 90 (not 100, as printed in MGH Ldl 1: 310 n. 1); PL 35: 1858–1860. See St. Augustine, *Tractates on the Gospel of John 55–111*, trans. John W. Rettig, The Fathers of the Church: A New Translation 90 (Washington, D.C.: The Catholic University of America Press, 1994), p. 160.

natural talent; but it would also be more glorious for the Church and more humbling for her adversaries if a youth, and one who is almost entirely ignorant, should put their vain assertions to rout. It seemed to him that if only I applied myself diligently to the matter as it really is, then these paltry abilities of mine would suffice to discredit the many prominent and illustrious men who are greater in wisdom and importance — or actually, greater only in the influence of their status and title — and to discredit their innumerable opinions and treatises on this matter, which have been published in a form that is perhaps more elegant or attractive than my own. He[23] would first look over their pamphlets, he would then read my words and line up my arguments against theirs, he would at times turn me aside from what I had intended in order to make sure he had not compelled me to undertake something that would expose me to spitting from every side, something that would have deserved the mockery of all, especially since I have not yet matured in age, since I am undisciplined in manners, uncultivated in talent, impeded in speech, lowly in birth, rustic in my manner of address — and if I am scarcely capable of stammering out something in ordinary conversation, much less can I contrive anything in writing.

Some of the brothers, siding with him, very tenaciously began to insist that I should be compelled with pressure to complete that which I wanted to abandon. The sentiment of one of the poets occurred to me, which although pagan in origin, is nevertheless not entirely contemptible: "You who write, choose a subject equal to your powers, and consider carefully what will make your shoulders buckle and what they have the strength to bear."[24] In my objections I also used the words of Solomon: *A fool, if he keeps silent, is considered wise; and if he keeps his lips tightly closed,* he is deemed *intelligent* [Prov. 17.28]. And this too: *The mouth of a fool is near to his own undoing* [Prov. 10.14]. And: *He who is foolish discloses his own stupidity* [Prov. 13.16]. I also recalled that *in many words you will not avoid sin* [Prov. 10.19]. And finally in order to confess to your paternity the full character of my own cowardice, I turned pale at the thought of stirring up the hatred of antagonists against me. I was indeed afraid: if it became known that this text had been written by me, whom they had driven out from the places that are fit for human habitation, they might search even in the woods, and I might find no safety in the lairs of wild animals and in caves hidden by ravines. It was only by using these hiding places that I saved my life before.

For these reasons I felt compelled to forsake the service I owed to my brothers, even though I have always been eager to apply myself on their behalf, in any capacity whatsoever. I resisted even when some of them finally found the prolixity of my impudent protests so odious that they could bear it no longer; induced by the boisterousness of

---

[23] That is, Harmann the prior.
[24] Horace, *Ars poetica* 38–40.

my intemperate objections, they even drove our brothers out from their spare guest-rooms.[25] But to be brief about the whole sorry affair, I decided it would be better to put an end to their fury through my acquiescence, by writing what they wanted, than to worry about provoking the rage of antagonists. Of course, a certain historian stated the matter elegantly enough when he admonished, "It is foolish, and the height of madness, to exert onself and earn nothing for one's efforts except contempt."[26] Accordingly, I might make a pretext of this line, and many others of its kind, as an excuse — but the Apostle would respond with this objection: *Each must seek the interests of others, not his own* [Phil. 2.4]. And: *Love is not self-seeking* [1 Cor. 13.5]. And also: *He that shall be ashamed of me and of my words*, and so forth.[27] This, too, should be adduced: if I concur with the wishes of my brothers, I shall not incur the offense of temerity nor the stigma of obstinacy, which I fear more than anything else, since they have been unanimous in what they have commanded.

Finally then, overcome with these objections, I submitted to their will, since I was unable to escape the necessity of obedience; and although I am a fool, I have not been foolish to obey them. I have done what I could. I have said what I thought.

[*There follows a synopsis of the book. The prologue concludes*:]

Yet I wish your well-instructed paternity to know that the scarcity of books has considerably reduced the abundance of passages that I have drawn from authoritative texts. It was not for lack of resolve that I have omitted them, for I would of course have heaped them up more copiously, if only the libraries of the churches were as open to me as are the caves and lairs of the forests! Since enemies surround these[28] on every side, who neither draw fruit from them by reading the books, nor allow us to draw from them either — as the common proverb has it: "The ox cannot reach his trough, the dog that does not eat from it prevents him"[29] — therefore you alone, reverend one, by your paternal grace do advance the duty of our labor. Thus you will consecrate the work of our insignificance with your most learned judgment, and the author will not be considered greater in merit than the one who approves his work.[30]

---

[25] Manegold's text is obscure at this point (MGH Ldl 1: 312): "...ut meae levitatis inquietudine incitati fratres nostros de sibi etiam superfluis eiecerint hospiciis."

[26] Sallust, *Bellum Iugurthinum* 3. See *Sallust*, ed. and trans. J.C. Rolfe, Loeb Classical Library (London and New York: William Heinemann and G. P. Putnam's Sons, 1931), pp. 136–39.

[27] Luke 9.26: "For he that shall be ashamed of me and of my words, of him the Son of Man shall be ashamed, when He shall come in His majesty and that of His Father and of the holy angels."

[28] That is, the libraries.

[29] See *Denkmäler deutscher Poesie und Prosa aus dem VIII–XII Jahrhundert*, ed. K. Müllenhoff and W. Scherer, 2nd ed. (Berlin: Weidmannsche Buchhandlung, 1873), p. 45, verse 19.

[30] The concluding clauses, beginning with "therefore," are borrowed (and slightly adapted) from the prologue to Boethius's *De institutione arithmetica* (CCSL 94A: 6).

Text 5: Ivo of Chartres, *Letter* 38 (40).[31]
Date: 1090–1115 (1094–1095?)[32]

Ivo, unworthy minister of the church of Chartres, to brother Manegold[33] — may he sedulously bear the cross of Christ and, using it like an oar, traverse the sea of this world.

Since, after many winding paths, *you have elected to live in obscurity in the house of God* [Ps. 83.11], bearing the light burden of Christ and despising the flowers of this world, knowing that *the poverty of the just is better than the abounding riches of sinners* [Ps. 36.16], we offer thanks to the divine goodness, *which gives grace to the humble* [1 Pet. 5.5]; and we insistently beseech you, that from the sum committed to you by your creditor, you may as a faithful banker return the same divine goodness with accumulated interest.[34] For thus the command of reason demanded that you, who have guided many with your words to *the path that leads to life* [Matt. 7.14], should one day inform and affirm others by your example. Like the long-time servant Zilpah who gave birth to sons from the seed of Father Jacob, so you have given birth to sons beneath the slavish yoke of philosophy;[35] but now you should not hesitate to establish a spiritual lineage in the liberty of interior vision, just as the beautiful Rachel gave birth from the seed of the same father.[36] In speaking thus, I do indeed instruct Minerva,[37] from whom I have greater need to be instructed. However, rejoicing in the progress of my brothers, I yearn that good beginnings may be granted even better outcomes.

At the same time I implore you to aid me with your prayers, so that the dread which besets me as I navigate the high seas, risking the peril of shipwreck, may be assuaged by the wholesome advice you can give, firm as you are in a port of tranquillity. For I believe

---

[31] The letter is identified as no. 38 in Yves de Chartres, *Correspondance*, ed. and trans. Jean Leclercq (Paris: Société d'Édition "Les Belles Lettres," 1949), pp. 156–61. It is identified as no. 40 in PL 162: 51B–52B.

[32] The range of dates corresponds to the episcopate of Ivo at Chartres; the date in parentheses is the one assigned by the editor, Jean Leclercq, on the assumption that the Manegold mentioned here was in fact Manegold of Lautenbach (ibid., p. 156 n. 3), and that he joined the canons regular at Marbach in 1094, as Bernold of Constance reports (see Text 11). See, however, the Introduction, p. 25 above.

[33] Ibid., p. 156: "Ivo, Carnotensis ecclesiae non satis aptus minister, fratri Manegaldo...."

[34] Cf. Matthew 25.13–30.

[35] Cf. Texts 21 and 28; see also the Introduction, pp. 27–31 above. Although Ivo is presumably using "sons" here in a figurative sense as a reference to Manegold's students in the schools, it is possible that he meant it literally.

[36] Genesis 30.9–24.

[37] This phrase was used by another figure who had a connection to Chartres, namely, Bernardus Silvestris; see *The Cosmographia of Bernardus Silvestris*, trans. Winthrop Wetherbee, Records of Western Civilization Series (New York: Columbia University Press, 1973), p. 69. However, as Leclercq indicates (*Correspondance*, p. 158 n. 2), the phrase is of Ciceronian inspiration and was used widely.

you are well aware that although I strove for the hand of Rachel, Leah was substituted in the night. Against my will I received her, against my will I tolerate her; for her vision is poor, she bears few children, and she provokes me much.[38] I am often dispirited with the tedium of these annoyances and, looking back at the beauty of the peace I have lost, I sigh with heavy heart. I wish I could *fly away on the wings of a dove* [Ps. 54.7] and be free once again. In my agitation, my sole refuge is to pray and to await the one who *will save me from the cowering of my spirit and from the tempest* [Ps. 54.9]. If only I did not fear to disobey His will, I would gladly shake off this burden which is too much for me to bear.

When, therefore, you find someone who is journeying in our direction or who is returning hereto, send a letter that I may know your *inner self*,[39] just as you know mine through my letter. For the rest, I commend to your fraternal hospitality the brother who is bearing the present letter, that you may treat him as a member of your household and answer his questions kindly during your lectures. Inasmuch as we can judge the man, *he seeks to be edified, not puffed up* [1 Cor. 8.1].

Text 6: Pope Urban II, *Letters and Privileges* 182.[40]
Date: 24 March 1096.

Urban, bishop, servant of the servants of God, to his beloved sons in the church of Marbach professing the canonical life, and to their successors persisting in the same religious life, in perpetuity.

It is right and agreeable to grant consent to those who desire to lead a religious life, since faithful devotion leads to a praiseworthy conclusion. Wherefore we, assenting to the prayers of our dear servant Manegold,[41] who is your prior, place you and all that is yours under the protection of the Apostolic See, and we furnish you with the authority of the present privilege. [...]

Issued at Tours by the hand of John, cardinal deacon of the holy Roman Church, on the 24th of March, in the 4th indiction, in the year of the Lord's Incarnation 1096, and in the 9th [year] of the pontificate of Pope Urban II.

---

[38] Genesis 29.14–30. In this passage Ivo may be referring to his frustration at the unsuccessful attempt to establish the canons regular at Chartres. See Grover A. Zinn, "The Regular Canons," *Christian Spirituality I: Origins to the Twelfth Century*, ed. Bernard McGinn and John Meyendorff with Jean Leclercq, World Spirituality 16 (New York: Crossroad, 1985), pp. 218–28, at 220.

[39] Romans 7.22; Ephesians 3.16; et al.

[40] PL 151: 455A–56A. See *Regesta Pontificum Romanorum*, ed. Philipp Jaffé et al., 2nd rev. ed., vol. 1 (Leipzig: Veit & Co., 1885), p. 686, no. 5629 (4212).

[41] PL 151: 455A: "Proinde nos vestris per familiarem nostrum, vestrum autem praepositum Manegaldum precibus annuentes…."

Text 7: Pope Urban II, *Letters and Privileges* 208.[42]
Date: 7 August 1096.

Urban, bishop, servant of the servants of God, to the venerable brother Gebhard, bishop of Constance, greeting and apostolic blessing.

It is perfectly clear to your fraternal lordship why there has been for a very long time discord between the congregations of Schaffhausen and Rottenbuch.[43] Recently when we were at Tours, we heard from our son Manegold, master of the schools, that they had settled the matter.[44] However, one of the community's brothers, Gerhard, a monk from Schaffhausen, came to us and repeated the same complaint as before, to wit, that those brothers[45] did not want to return the monk. Therefore we entrust to your loving concern that you continue to watch over these religious men in order to restore concord between them. But if they are unwilling to obey now, and have not, within 30 days of receiving our letter, returned to the abbot of Schaffhausen that monk on whose account discord between them has arisen, then you will be aware of our sentence of interdiction against them.

Issued on the 7th of August at Forcalquier.

Text 8: Pope Urban II, *Letters and Privileges* 209.[46]
Date: 7 August 1096 (issued together with Text 7).

Urban, bishop, servant of the servants of God, to his beloved sons O. the prior and M. the dean of Rottenbuch,[47] greeting and apostolic blessing.

---

[42] Horst Fuhrmann, "Papst Urban II. und der Stand der Regularkanoniker," *Sitzungsberichte der Bayerische Akademie der Wissenschaften, philosophisch-historische Klasse*, Jahrgang 1984, Heft 2, pp. 39–40. The text is also printed in PL 151: 482B.–D. See *Regesta Pontificum Romanorum*, ed. Philipp Jaffé et al., 2nd rev. ed., vol. 1, p. 690, no. 5665 (4242).

[43] Schaffhausen was a Benedictine monastery, and Rottenbuch was a house of canons regular.

[44] Fuhrmann, ibid., pp. 39–40: "Nuper enim cum Turonis essemus, per filium nostrum Manegoldum magistrum scolarum eos pacificos audieramus."

[45] That is, of Rottenbuch.

[46] Fuhrmann, "Papst Urban II. und der Stand der Regularkanoniker," pp. 40–41. The text is also printed in PL 151: 482D–83B. See *Regesta Pontificum Romanorum*, ed. Philipp Jaffé et al., 2nd rev. ed., vol. 1, p. 690, no. 5666 (4243).

[47] "O." refers to Oudalricus, that is, Ulrich (d. 1126); it is not clear, however, that "M." refers to Manegold, as some scholars have supposed; see Fuhrmann, ibid., pp. 35–36 n. 82 (and p. 41 n. 101).

For a long time now we have urged your love with letters of exhortation sent again and again,[48] and to our exhortations we have added prayerful entreaties, that you resume peaceful relations with the venerable abbot and the congregation of Schaffhausen by restoring to them the brother whom you smuggled out of their cloister by deceitful schemes.[49] You, however, in a way that is least befitting your religious vocation, have spurned our prayers and have shown little respect for the authority of the Apostolic See, which we possess. Surely you have offended even *God*, who *is love*,[50] since you presumed to ridicule the religious men who gathered in order to be reconciled with you, including the venerable abbot of Schaffhausen. You insulted all of them when they came into your presence seeking only the interests of love, by deceiving them with a promise which you did not fulfill. We must punish such guilt of disobedience and deception with severity, for we despair that we are not able to read *in the tablet of your heart*[51] the prudence that you should observe. After the reception of this letter, therefore, if you have not within 30 days made satisfaction to the aforesaid abbot, as a consequence [you must desist from the exercise of your] religious functions.[52]

---

[48] See the letter edited by Fuhrmann, ibid., pp. 35–38. This text, issued by Urban II on 8 October 1095 at Lyons, is addressed to the prior Ulrich (whose name is spelled out fully), and the dean "M." (only the initial is provided): "Urbanus episcopus servus servorum dei in Christo dilectis filiis Oudalrico praeposito, M. decano et ceteris Reitenbuochensibus salutem et apostolicam benedictionem."

[49] Urban's letter of 8 October 1095 (Fuhrmann, ibid., p. 37) summarizes the crime thus: "…dearest sons, you exceeded your bounds not a little and incurred great peril to yourselves and to the monk, Eppo, when you deceitfully led him out of the monastery of Schaffhausen and impetuously (*violenter*) stripped him of his monastic garments." Urban's adverb, *violenter*, does not imply that Eppo was abducted against his will; the violence consisted in helping Eppo break the vow of stability that he had made at Schaffhausen.

[50] 1 John 4.8, 4.16.

[51] Proverbs 3.3, 7.3; 2 Corinthians 3.3.

[52] The letter ends imperfectly; it survives in only one manscript (Munich, Bayerische Staatsbibliothek, MS. Clm 4631, fol. 114v): "Post harum igitur litterarum acceptionem, nisi infra dies XXX eidem abbati satisfeceritis, divinorum deinceps officiorum […]." The following summary (in translation) is provided by the *Regesta Pontificum Romanorum*, ed. Philipp Jaffé et al., 2nd rev. ed., vol. 1, p. 690, no. 5666 (4243): "He warns O(udalric) the provost and M(anegold) the dean of Rottenbuch that unless they have made satisfaction to (Siegfried) the abbot of Schaffhausen within 30 days, they must abstain from the exercise of their sacred offices."

Text 9: Hugh the Orthodox, *To Manegold the Hildebrandine*.[53]
Date: 1098?[54]

Every honest man declines unfair advantages.
O Manegold, if you would be wise, you would shun every untrue word!
While Goliath struts about brandishing his arms,
His own sword slashes his throat and kills him.
You too have slit your throat, though with your words instead of a sword:
With a word you used to terrorize the peoples, but you were easily conquered.
The light of the mind is what you lack; since you lack the light of the mind,
Cruel delusion drives you; indeed you are driven whither delusion leads.
Your mother is here, calling you back: listen to the calls of your mother![55]
She has prepared a potent spice, she has prepared lotion to heal your eyes,
Which if you would apply, you could then acquire sight.
You are falling down a steep slope; she stretches out her arms
To catch you as you fall: do not despise the arms of your mother!
Maternal power holds you: since it is by the power of your mother that you are held,
You are untrue in your bitter complaints; do not complain against such a good mother!
It is often a failing of the deluded mind, beset with the phantasms of night,
To regard shadows as though they were real.
O Hildebrand, as you pass along a cup that makes the mind forgetful,
You make the mind of the one who drinks go mad!
There is a potent medicine that counteracts your poisons,
And this is given by the hand of the mother, not of another.
This cleanses the brain, cleanses the heart of the mind.

---

[53] *Versus Hugonis contra Manegoldum*, ed. Ernst Dümmler, MGH Ldl 1: 430–31. The text was first edited by Wilhelm Wattenbach, "Mittheilungen aus zwei Handschriften der k. Hof- und Staatsbibliothek," *Sitzungsberichte der königlich-bayerischen Akademie der Wissenschaften zu München, philosophisch-philologischen und historischen Classe* 3 (1873), pp. 685–747, at 732–33. "Hildebrand" was Gregory VII's name before his elevation to the papal see; the form "Hildebrandine," following Hugh's assertion of his own status as a defender of orthodoxy, implies that Manegold is a heretic who follows the heresiarch Hildebrand. The identity of Hugh is not known. His poem echoes passages in Chapters 23–24 of the *Contra Wolfelmum*.
[54] The ambiguity of the poem makes it difficult to date. The dire situation in which Manegold is found corresponds with the report that he was imprisoned in 1098, during the pontificate of Urban II, as a consequence of his preaching on behalf of the papal party; see Text 11. The poem survives in only one manuscript: Munich, Bayerische Staatsbibliothek, MS. Clm 17142; see Wattenbach, ibid., p. 710.
[55] Manegold's "mother" is apparently the German church, as seen from the perspective of the imperial party, who of course regarded themselves as the upholders of orthodoxy.

Whoever you are who reject this medicine, by pushing it away, you die.

O Manegold, your motherly healer holds it out to you,

She is the pity of your father, the voice that calls back those despairing of hope.[56]

The office of Peter remains; may the pious office of Peter indeed remain!

He reigns with hope, with tears; with this office you, too, may reign.

Paul persecutes, and sets out to spill sacred blood.

For this reason he is prostrated, and piously learns to love the persecuted.[57]

"I do not believe that 'Turban' disturbed the faith," you will say in denial.[58]

What you assert is not a confession of faith, yet you insist it is the truth.

How new the law! How new the dogma, newly contrived!

He[59] has strayed from the faith in the midst of synods, and thus has escaped reproof.

One who did not strike down Saul, claimed to have dispatched him;

But because of his report, he was killed at David's command.[60]

Often in such a way confession punishes those swollen with pride,

Often in many ways it unites the humble with the heavens.

If you look upon the human race since the beginning of the world:

Adam's defense of his sin casts him down to the depths;

David's confession absolves his more grievous sin;

The less serious transgression of Saul, when pleaded as an excuse, condemns him;

The confession of guilt frees Vigilius[61] from wrath;

---

[56] "Father" probably refers to the antipope, Clement III (Wibert of Ravenna, d. 1100), whom Hugh would have regarded as the rightful pope.

[57] Acts 8.1–4, 9.1–22.

[58] This passage is exceedingly obscure. The text, as printed, runs thus: "Turbantum turbasse fidem, non credo negabis." Wattenbach suggests that "Turbantum" should be read "Turbanum" (from the verb *turbare*, "to disturb, throw into confusion"), a derisive name applied to Urban II by his enemies. It implied that Urban, as the perpetuator of the Hildebrandine heresy, was the cause of the ongoing schism. Wattenbach's emendation is reasonable, given the fact that the scribe has clearly made an error of a proper name elsewhere, in misspelling "Anastasius" in line 53 ("Anathasius"); I have followed Wattenbach's suggestion in my translation. See MGH Ldl 1: 431 n. *d*; Wattenbach, "Mittheilungen aus zwei Handschriften der k. Hof- und Staatsbibliothek," p. 734.

[59] Presumably Urban II, if we are to accept Wattenbach's suggested emendation; otherwise, Hildebrand. No subject is specified: "In sinodis errasse fide, nec sic reprobatum."

[60] 2 Kings (2 Samuel) 1.1–16.

[61] Pope Vigilius (537–555). Caught between Justinian and Theodora on the question of the Monophysite heresy, Vigilius temporized; the "confession of guilt" probably refers to his eventual condemnation of the "Three Chapters," as Justinian required. However, Vigilius actually died in disgrace. See P.G. Maxwell-Stuart, *Chronicle of the Popes* (London: Thames and Hudson, 1997), pp. 43–44.

The dire defense of crime condemns Liberius.[62]
No one will assert that a bishop is the equal of the supreme pontiff,
Only that the see of Peter is sometimes held by one who is equal or one who is greater.
One who follows the precepts of the laws is equal to the pontifical office;
And a greater [holder of the office] will judge one who errs with a voice of power.[63]
With these holy flowers, discretion prepares its spice:
Carefully collect the fruits from the old law and the new.
The confession of guilt, when it comes forth sincerely, brings healing;
He who defends his guilt, ties for himself a noose that brings death.
One Roman priest condemns Liberius;[64]
Anastasius errs,[65] and he too is removed from his see.[66]
O Hildebrand, you deserved to be removed by a like fate!
The fathers forsook their faults because they feared to be condemned.

---

[62] Pope Liberius (352–366) was the first Roman pontiff not to be canonized. He was forced by Emperor Constantius II into communion with the Arian heretics, and despite his later return to an orthodox stance, his reputation was ruined: he had already been deposed by the Roman Church and replaced with the antipope Felix II. See Maxwell-Stuart, *Chronicle of the Popes*, pp. 26, 28.

[63] This line seems to be a defense of the practice of electing an antipope in order to depose a pontiff who is deemed unworthy of his office. As noted above, this measure had been taken against Pope Liberius.

[64] The "Roman priest" was apparently the antipope Felix II, who as noted had been elected in Liberius's place when Liberius had discredited himself through communion with the Arians.

[65] Anastasius II (496–498). He, like Vigilius, was caught in the web of imperial politics that attended the Monophysite controversy; his attempts to re-establish unity with the Eastern Church caused a schism within the Western Church. See Maxwell-Stuart, *Chronicle of the Popes*, pp. 39–40.

[66] On Liberius and Anastasius, see I.S. Robinson, *Authority and Resistance in the Investiture Contest* (Manchester and New York: Manchester University Press, Holmes & Meier Publishers, 1978), p. 47. Robinson cites the pamphlet entitled *Contra decreta Turbani* ("Against the decrees of Turban," that is, Urban II): "Hildebrand perversely turned the sword of excommunication upon himself, while he excommunicated the emperor and, by exempting from excommunication those who communicated with him, revived the ancient heresies of Liberius and Anastasius."

Text 10: Baudri of Bourgueil, *Second Poem on the Beguiling of Gerard of Loudun.*[67]
Date: 1098–1107?[68]

Nursed abundantly at your breasts, O Manegold,[69]
  (Though he is younger in age, he is almost older in the perfection of his learning),
When weaned from your bosom, he came to Angers,[70]
  — Gerard — bearing lofty words and plain.
By his glory he multiplied the glories of Loudun,[71]
  Teaching the arts with gentle affability.
Bourgueil envied Loudun when he was there,
  And, speaking blandishments, lured him away from the envied townsmen.
Even now Gerard tarries with his friend at Bourgueil,
  Until a mound must be raised for one and the other.
O would that neither death nor fate should separate them,
  Until the swan, once white, turns black,
And until the black raven flies off on wings of white,
  And until the Loire, flowing uphill, goes to Loudun,
And until the querulous cicadas fall silent — so long may they endure,
  And neither old age nor sorrow afflict them.

Text 11: Bernold of Constance,[72] *Chronicle.*[73]
Date: Before 16 Sepember 1100.[74]

1094. […] In the German lands many prodigious events took place. People hanged themselves, and wolves devoured many. Undoubtedly this took place by divine

---

[67] Baldricus Burgulianus, *Carmina*, ed. Karlheinz Hilbert (Heidelberg: Carl Winter Universitätsverlag, 1979), p. 77. Also *Les oeuvres poétiques de Baudri de Bourgueil (1046–1130): Édition critique publiée d'après le manuscrit du Vatican*, ed. Phyllis Abrahams (Paris: Librairie ancienne Honoré Campion, 1926), p. 109.
[68] Baudri was abbot of Bourgueil during these years. In 1107 he was elected archbishop of Dol in Brittany. See F.J.E. Raby, *A History of Secular Latin Poetry in the Middle Ages*, vol. 1 (Oxford: Clarendon Press, 1934), pp. 336–37; idem, *A History of Christian-Latin Poetry*, 2nd ed. (Oxford: Clarendon Press, 1953), pp. 277–78.
[69] *Carmina*, ed. Hilbert, p. 77: "Vberibus, Manegaude, tuis lactatus abunde…."
[70] Baudri studied at the cathedral school of Angers.
[71] There is a play on the Latin form of Loudun (*Lausdunum*) which echoes the word for glory (*laus*): "Laude sua laudes Lausduni multiplicavit."
[72] Also known as Bernold of St. Blaise (Sankt Blasien); see Text 2.
[73] *Bernoldi Chronicon*, MGH SS 5: 385–467, at 459–60, 461, 466.
[74] Ibid., p. 386. This is the day of Bernold's death.

vengeance, because they had neglected the divine law by not fearing to taint themselves with excommunication. Lightning from heaven also struck terror into many people, as in the monastery at Ottobeuren, where the larger crucifix and the choir-stalls of the monks, as of those not living according to a rule, were destroyed by a thunderbolt. Likewise in the greater church at Basel, a bolt of lightning struck the beam on which the crucifix was suspended at the very moment when many who were excommunicated had assembled there.

At this time Master Manegold of Lautenbach began to teach at the monastery of clerics at Marbach and chose to be one with the same clerics, who were living in community and according to a rule.[75]

In the Black Forest, in a place that was named after St. Blaise, the foundations were laid for the construction of a monastery in honor of the same saint, on 11 September. For God had so exalted that place and had inspired so many to profess vows there, that it was necessary they should found a larger building. [...]

In Alsace, Master Manegold of Lautenbach, with God's mercy, wondrously rekindled the Church's worship, which had been extinguished in those parts for a long time.[76] For as the long-lasting pallor of death that hung over them grew stronger, almost all the greater nobility and knights of that province crowded together upon him in droves. As they were absolved from excommunication through the power conferred on him by the Lord Pope, as well as from the rest of their sins, they did not hesitate to accept the penance he required for their absolution. All of these then faithfully declared their obedience to the Lord Pope Urban and immediately refused to accept the sacraments from simoniac and married priests. And Lord Manegold was the greatest cause of this obedience. For this reason he aroused great envy against himself among the perfidious. But he gave no thought to that, because he did not doubt that it was actually a most glorious thing to be despised for the sake of God.

1098. [...] Manegold, the venerable prior of the canons dwelling at Marbach, was held in captivity for a long time by Henry the King[77] because he refused to obey the schismatics who rejected the authority of the Church. For this reason the whole Church far and wide grieved for him.

---

[75] Ibid., pp. 459–60: "Hoc tempore magister Manegoldus de Liutenbach monasterium clericorum apud Marhbach instituere cepit, seque unum eorumdem clericorum communiter et regulariter viventium esse voluit."

[76] Ibid., p. 461: "In Alsatia magister Manegoldus de Liutenbach mirabiliter aeclesiasticam religionem, iam dudum in illis partibus omnino extinctam, Deo miserante reaccendit."

[77] Ibid., p. 466: "Manegoldus venerabilis praepositus canonicorum apud Marchbach degentium, a Heinrico rege diu in captione detentus est...."

Text 12: Pope Paschal II, *Letters and Privileges* 97.[78]
Date: 2 August 1103.

Paschal, bishop, servant of the servants of God, to his beloved sons in the church of Marbach professing the canonical life, and to their successors persisting in the same religious life, in perpetuity.

Just as no request is to be granted to those who demand what is wrongful, so too the petition of those who desire what is legitimate must not be denied. Wherefore we find no difficulty in accommodating the request that you and your prior, our most dearly beloved son Manegold, have petitioned.[79] Since indeed we follow in the footsteps of our predecessor of saintly memory, Urban II, we place you and all that is yours under the protection of the Apostolic See, and we furnish you with the authority of the present privilege. [...]

Issued at the Lateran, on the 2nd of August, by the hand of Equitus, the acting vice-chancellor, in the 11th indiction, in the year of the Lord's Incarnation 1103, and in the 4th [year] of the pontificate of Pope Paschal II.

Text 13: *The Book of Udalric*, No. 160.[80]
Date: 1109–1112.[81]

To my Lord Prior, as beloved as he is revered, D., the one who though poor is not a false friend, the one who is ragged after having spent such a long time in exile, warmly offers his ardent expression of faith, love, and devotion.[82] [...]

I am now in Paris, in the school of Master William,[83] who is the most accomplished instructor in every branch of learning of all the men of the present day whom I have known. When we hear his voice, we think that it is not a man who speaks but, as it were, an angel from heaven; for the sweetness of his words and the profundity of his

---

[78] PL 163: 116B–17B. See *Regesta Pontificum Romanorum*, ed. Philipp Jaffé et al., 2nd rev. ed., vol. 1, p. 715, no. 5949 (4442).

[79] PL 163: 116B–C: "Proinde tam vestris, quam charissimi filii Manegaldi vestri praepositi petitionibus non difficulter accommodamus effectum...."

[80] *Monumenta Bambergensia*, ed. Philipp Jaffé, Bibliotheca rerum germanicarum 5 (Berlin: Weidmann, 1869), pp. 285–87.

[81] Ibid., p. 286 n. 4.

[82] The identities of author and recipient are unknown.

[83] William of Champeaux, archdeacon of Paris. He resigned from this position ca. 1108 in order to found the house of canons regular at St. Victor, which he left in 1113 when he became bishop of Châlons-sur-Marne.

thought seem to transcend human ability.[84] When he was archdeacon and was favored practically above all others by the king,[85] he gave away all that he owned (this was last Easter) and removed himself to a certain impoverished little church for the purpose of serving God alone;[86] and there, afterwards, he devotedly and kindly taught anyone who came to him, free of charge and only for the sake of God, in the manner of Master Manegold of blessed memory.[87] The instruction that he now offers in the divine and human sciences is of such a high level that I have not seen or heard anything like it in any land during my lifetime. [...]

Text 14: *Fragment from a History of Francia*.[88]
Date: 1110 or later.[89]

When, therefore, the emperor[90] had been deprived of communion with the Church,[91] Pope Gregory appointed a certain Rudolf, of Saxon birth,[92] to reign in his place; however, he was killed by the emperor's dukes, who had lured him into battle.

After these events, the emperor sends messengers to the pope; again and again he offers a defense addressing the indictments against him. But since the pope would not revoke his sentence of excommunication, he marched on Rome with a great company of troops and besieged the city for some time.[93] When at last it was captured, in place

---

[84] For an alternative estimation of William's abilities as a teacher, see Abelard's account in his *Historia calamitatum*, translated by J.T. Muckle under the title, *The Story of Abelard's Adversities* (Toronto: The Pontifical Institute of Mediaeval Studies, 1964), pp. 15–18.

[85] Louis VI, King of France (1108–1137).

[86] Since it is uncertain when exactly William retired to St. Victor, we cannot use the phrase "last Easter" (*in preterito pascha*) to clarify the precise year in which the letter was written. It could have been written as early as 1109; it was, in any event, written before 1113, when William became bishop of Châlons-sur-Marne.

[87] Ibid., p. 186: "...more magistri Manegaldi beatae memoriae...." If this is a reference to Manegold of Lautenbach, as Jaffé assumes (*Monumenta Bambergensia*, p. 285 nn. 5, 6), the letter enables us to narrow down the range of years in which Manegold's death took place. Thus, when read in conjunction with Text 12, it allows us to suppose that Manegold died between 1103 and 1109/1112. See also Text 15, which indicates that Manegold died by 1119.

[88] *Historiae Franciae fragmentum, a Roberto ad mortem Philippi I. Regis*, ed. François Duchesne, in *Historiae Francorum Scriptores*, vol. 4 (Paris: Sebastian Cramoisy, 1641), pp. 89–90.

[89] The last report in the chronicle is dated 1110.

[90] Henry IV, Emperor (1056–1106).

[91] Henry was first excommunicated in 1076, was received back into the Church at Canossa in 1077, and was excommunicated again in 1080.

[92] Rudolf of Swabia (d. 1080).

[93] Henry's Italian campaigns lasted from 1081 to 1084.

of Gregory he installed as pope Guibert of Ravenna, who took the name Clement,[94] while Gregory fled to Apulia, where he tarried for the remainder of his life. Upon his death[95] he was buried at Salerno in the monastery of St. Matthew. In his place was ordained Desiderius, the abbot of Cassino, who took the name Victor.[96] When he died, he was succeeded by Odo (that is, Urban),[97] who was of Frankish stock. […]

Upon the death of William, glorious king of the English,[98] his son, also named William, inherited the kingdom as his patrimony.[99] His brother Robert received the office of count of the Normans. Their brother Henry, however, remained without position until the death of his brother the king.[100]

At this time, there flourished in both divine and human philosophy the masters Lanfranc, bishop of Canterbury,[101] Guido the Lombard,[102] Manegold the German,[103] [and] Bruno of Rheims, who afterwards led an eremitical life.[104] In dialectics there also were the following skilled logicians: John, who also taught that the same sophistic art was about words,[105] Robert of Paris,[106] Roscelin of Compiègne,[107] Arnulf of Laon.[108] The latter were followers of John and had numerous students of their own.

---

[94] Clement III (Wibert, or Guibert, of Ravenna), antipope (1080–1100). Wibert was installed at Rome in 1084.

[95] 25 May 1085.

[96] Victor III (1086–1087). There was a period of vacancy for one year between the death of Gregory VII and the election of Victor III.

[97] Urban II (1088–1099).

[98] William the Conqueror, King of England (1066–1087).

[99] William II (Rufus), King of England (1087–1100).

[100] Henry I, King of England (1100–1135).

[101] Lanfranc of Bec (1010–1089).

[102] "Guido Langobardus"; see *New Catholic Encyclopedia* 6: 842. François Châtillon identifies this individual as Guitmund of Aversa, without providing convincing reasons for this identification; see "Recherches critiques sur les différents personnages nommés Manegold," *Revue du moyen âge latin* 9 (1953), pp. 153–70, at 164.

[103] *Historiae Franciae fragmentum*, ed. Duchesne, p. 89: "Hoc tempore, tam in diuina quam in humana Philosophia floruerunt Lanfrancus Cantuariorum Episcopus, Guido Langobardus, Maingaudus Teutonicus, Bruno Remensis, qui postea vitam duxit heremiticam."

[104] St. Bruno (ca. 1032–1101), founder of the Carthusian Order.

[105] The identity of this figure is uncertain. See Étienne Gilson, *History of Christian Philosophy in the Middle Ages* (London: Sheed and Ward, 1955), p. 625 n. 88.

[106] Unknown.

[107] Teacher of Peter Abelard. He was accused of teaching the heresy of tritheism in 1092; the dates of his birth and death are uncertain (ca. 1050–ca. 1125).

[108] There is a brief poem in the *Liber Udalrici* entitled *Super Arnulphum Laudunensem*; see *Monumenta Bambergensia*, ed. Jaffé, p. 188, no. 99. Jaffé dates the poem to ca. 1100.

In the year since the Incarnation of our Lord 1096, stars were seen as though falling down from heaven in great numbers, like drops of rain, for several nights in succession. In the same year Pope Urban came to France and called together a very great council of bishops and abbots at Clermont in the month of November.[109]

Text 15: Pope Calixtus II, *Letters and Privileges* 38.[110]
Date: 30 October 1119.

Calixtus, bishop, servant of the servants of God, to his beloved sons in Christ in the church of Marbach, professing the canonical life, and to their successors persisting in the same religious life through the power of God's grace, in perpetuity.

The responsibility of our office urges us to be concerned for the state of the churches and to further what has been rightly established. For this reason we accommodate without difficulty the prayers of our son, the venerable Gerung, your prior. Since indeed we follow in the footsteps of our predecessors of saintly memory, namely, Urban II and Paschal II, we place you and all that is yours under the protection of the Apostolic See, and we furnish you with the authority of the present privilege. [...]

Issued at Rheims by the hand of Grisogonus, cardinal deacon and librarian of the holy Roman Church, on the 30th of October, in the 13th indiction, in the year of the Lord's Incarnation 1119, and in the first year of the pontificate of Pope Calixtus II.

Text 16: Gerhoh of Reichersberg, *Letter to Pope Innocent [II]*.[111]
Date: Early 1131.[112]

S[ecular Cleric]:[113] It may be the case that those who hate you tell lies about you, asserting that you have said things that you have not actually said. But we gladly lend an ear to anyone who says bad things about you, so that in some way we may erase and

---

[109] Actually in 1095.

[110] PL 163: 1130B–31C. See *Regesta Pontificum Romanorum*, ed. Philipp Jaffé et al., 2nd rev. ed., vol. 1, p. 788, no. 6763 (4949).

[111] *Epistola ad Innocentium Papam missa quid distet inter clericos seculares et regulares*, ed. E. Sackur, MGH Ldl 3: 202–39, at 232–33. Also printed in PL 194: 1375–1426, at 1415C–16B. Gerhoh relates a conversation between a secular cleric and a regular cleric; his own opinions can be identified with those of the regular cleric.

[112] MGH Ldl 3: 202.

[113] The Secular Cleric is addressing the Regular Cleric.

obliterate you from the land of the living, for the very sight of you is enough to cause us grief, especially since you are the only one who seems to find fault with us. This is what bothers us for the most part, that in the cloister in which you were educated, not one of your brothers sides with you.

R[egular Cleric]: Read the book composed against the slanderers of Gregory VII by Manegold, the former dean of our monastery, and you will find in it a proof based on the firmest authorities, with which we are in agreement, namely, that clerics who fornicate[114] as well as those who usurp interdicted offices are Nicolaites — and not only heretics with Nicholas, but also condemned with Ebio and Paul of Samosata.[115] With such arguments he defended Gregory VII, who was slandered by clerics of our land because he prohibited ministers of the altar who are fornicators not only from continuing to perform their office, but even from entering a church.

S.: The Manegold of whom you speak was himself a cantankerous man. Now he is dead, and we hope, moreover, that his book has been buried with him. We have heard that he was despised even by the fellow brothers of your cloister, and that even though the book was composed in defense of Gregory VII, it was not approved by him.

R.: Well, I myself do not consider the book as a whole to be authoritative, but I know that it had the approval of some Catholic bishops who were driven from their sees in the Wibertine schism[116] and found refuge at that time in the cloister of Rottenbuch. As to your idea that I am not in agreement with the canons regular who are my brothers, I reply that they actually had even higher praise for that Manegold, since they lauded the dean's defense of Gregory and regarded his writings as the utterance of a heavenly oracle, by which not a few found solace during the Wibertine schism, and by which the secular adversaries who opposed the Church were to a considerable extent refuted. Hence, since that time, the more rigorous brothers in the cloister of Rottenbuch have listened to that dean just as though he were still alive; for although he is dead, he still speaks through his writings and continues to detest the sacrifices of fornicators.[117] Recently, one of the brothers of that monastery wrote to me, saying, "It must be made known that priests who serve at the altar for payment in silver and gold are not only worshippers of golden calves, but they insanely adore Baal himself. […]"

---

[114] That is, married priests.

[115] Manegold, *Liber ad Gebehardum* 76, ed. Francke, MHG Ldl 1: 429. Gerhoh quotes this passage from the *Ad Gebehardum* earlier in his text (at MGH Ldl 3: 221).

[116] Named after Wibert of Ravenna, the antipope Clement III (1080–1100).

[117] That is, the sacrifice of the Mass by "Nicolaites" (married priests).

Text 17: Otto of Freising, *Chronicle, or A History of the Two Cities,* Prologue 5.[118]
Date: 1143–1146.[119]

And as I said above,[120] all human power and learning arose in the east and have begun to set in the west. With regard to human power — how it passed from the Babylonians to the Medes and the Persians, and from them to the Macedonians, and afterwards to the Romans, and then to the Greeks who adopted the name of Rome — I judge that enough has been said. It remains to be shown in the present work how it was transferred from them to the Franks, who dwell in the west. It is likewise with regard to learning, which was first discovered in the east, in Babylon, and from there was transferred to Egypt, to which Abraham migrated during a time of famine. Thus Josephus reports in the first book of the *Antiquities*, speaking of Abraham: "He brought arithmetic to them, and he was also the one who introduced them to astronomy. For before Abraham, the Egyptians were completely ignorant of these things."[121] The same author notes that learning was next brought to the Greeks in the time of the philosophers, in these words: "Having been transplanted from the Chaldees, these subjects were known in Egypt. From there, it is said, they reached the Greeks."[122] So writes Josephus. Afterwards, this learning was transferred to the Romans under the Scipios, Cato, and Cicero, and especially during the time of the Caesars, when the crowd of poets together sounded their various songs. Most recently it has appeared in the furthest west, that is, in the regions of Gaul and Spain, in the days of the illustrious teachers Berengar,[123] Manegold,[124] and Anselm.[125] Men divinely inspired were able to foresee the unfolding of these events, as though in a dream. We, however, do not merely believe, but are able

---

[118] *Ottonis Episcopi Frisingensis Chronica sive Historia de duabus civitatibus*, ed. Adolf Hofmeister, MGH Scriptores rerum germanicarum in usum scholarum (Hannover and Leipzig: Hahnsche Buchhandlung, 1912), pp. 227–28. The translation provided here is my own; cf. Otto of Freising, *The Two Cities*, trans. Charles Christopher Mierow (1928; repr. New York: Octagon Books, 1966), pp. 322–23.

[119] *Chronica*, ed. Hofmeister, p. xii.

[120] Prologue 1 (ibid., p. 8).

[121] Josephus, *Antiquities* 1.8.2. See *The Latin Josephus* 1: *The Antiquities: Books I–V*, ed. Franz Blatt (Copenhagen: Ejnar Munksgaard, 1958), p. 145; for a translation, see Josephus, *The Complete Works*, trans. William Whiston (Nashville, Tenn.: Thomas Nelson Publishers, 1998), p. 44.

[122] Ibid.

[123] Berengar of Tours (d. 1088).

[124] *Chronica*, ed. Hofmeister, p. 227: "…a diebus illustrium doctorum Berengarii, Managaldi et Anshelmi…."

[125] Probably Anselm of Laon (d. 1117) rather than Anselm of Canterbury (d. 1109), since Otto specifies the former twice in his *Gesta Friderici* (1.49, 1.52), but not the latter. See Otto of Freising, *The Deeds of Frederick Barbarossa*, trans. Charles Christopher Mierow (1953; repr. Toronto, Buffalo, and London: University of Toronto Press, 1994), pp. 83, 88.

to see clearly what was foretold, as we ourselves now perceive that the world, which they already said should be despised because of its mutability, is waning and drawing its last breath, as it were, in the final moments of its senescence.

Text 18: Arno of Reichersberg, *Shield of the Canons*.[126]
Date: ca. 1146.[127]

However, as someone wrote, "Nothing is in every part blessed"[128] — for, as I have said,[129] when peace returned to God's churches, secular pomp and the vanity of this world and concupiscence devoured me, I who am the order of canons, the firstborn of Rachel, as has been said; and rightly the heavenly Father, [like Jacob], lamented over me and said: *A most terrible wild beast has devoured my son Joseph* [Gen. 37.33]. Then at that time, as charity cooled and iniquity abounded, even Benjamin — that is, the monastic order — left his Father and set out on a sojourn into Egypt, which is this world, and the sorrow of Father Jacob was increased.[130] But behold, in our time, by God's consent, the order of canons has revived, and it has been announced to Jacob my Father that His son Joseph lives, and He has said, as though waking from a heavy sleep: *If my son Joseph still lives, it is enough for me; I shall go and see him before I die* [Gen. 45.28] — this is to say: "If I shall one day see my son, the order of canons, still living among my posterity, I shall not die."

But I, the order of canons, who have revived and flourish once again, cannot disclose in but a few words all that I have endured for the defense of ecclesiastical liberty at the hands of impious kings, now at the end of the ages. For in the time of Henry's schism, I was stricken by the darkness of death in the person of my beloved Erlembald of Milan, who was the prior of my sons whom they call "Patarenes."[131] I have endured persecution in the persons of the Roman pontiffs Gregory VII and Urban [II]; and I have been hunted down and imprisoned in the persons of Pope Paschal [II] and also his cleric, Manegold of Lautenbach,[132] and in so many others.

---

[126] PL 194: 1498C–99A.

[127] *Die deutsche Literatur des Mittelalters: Verfasserlexikon*, 2nd ed., vol. 1, cols. 458–62.

[128] Horace, *Odes* 2.16: 27–28. See Horace, *The Odes and Epodes*, ed. and trans. C.E. Bennett, The Loeb Classical Library (London and Cambridge, Mass.: William Heinemann and Harvard University Press, 1960), pp. 150–51.

[129] The speaker is the order of canons regular, personified.

[130] Genesis 42.1–43.15.

[131] See Colin Morris, *The Papal Monarchy* (Oxford: Clarendon Press, 1989), pp. 97, 113, 115.

[132] PL 194: 1499A: "…in Pascali papa ejusque clero, Manegoldo quoque Luterbacense, aliisque quam plurimis captivatus et incarceratus sum."

Text 19: *Necrology of Zwiefalten.*[133]
Date: Before 1150.[134]

1 January. Manegold.
4 January. Manegold, layman.
14 January. Manegold, layman.
2 February. Manegold.
7 February. Manegold, monk.
8 February. Manegold, of our congregation.
22 February. Manegold, layman.
5 March. Manegold, layman.
24 March. Manegold, lay brother of our congregation.
4 April. Manegold, layman [of] Roudorf.
19 April. Manegold, count [of] Hundirsingen.
23 April. Manegold, priest.
28 April. Manegold of Isiningin, monk.
29 April. Manegold, abbot.
20 May. Manegold, layman.
24 May. Manegold, monk.
20 July. Manegold, layman [of] Nifin.
7 August. Manegold, layman.
11 August. Manegold, layman.
2 September. Manegold, layman.
25 September. Manegold, monk of our congregation.

---

[133] *Necrologium Zwifaltense*, ed. Franz Ludwig Baumann, MGH Necrologia Germaniae 1: 240–68. The selections presented here include only the occurrences of the name "Manegold" that appear in the earliest version of the necrology. Although this source is in all likelihood irrelevant, I have included it here because some modern authors have assumed that the entry for 24 May refers to Manegold of Lautenbach; see Charles Hoffmann, "L'Abbaye de Marbach et le Nécrologe de MCCXLI," pp. 71, 167 (full citation at note 182, below); Édouard Sitzmann, *Dictionnaire de biographie des hommes célèbres de l'Alsace* 2 (1910; repr. Paris: Éditions du Palais Royal, 1973), pp. 232–34, at 233; François Auguste Goehlinger, *Histoire de l'abbaye de Marbach* (Colmar: Éditions Alsatia, 1954), p. 14. See also the Introduction, p. 31 n. 128, above.
[134] Baumann, ibid., pp. 240–41.

Text 20: *Annals of St. George in the Black Forest.*[135]
Date: ca. 1153.[136]

1094. A great many deaths. And the simoniac heresy was bitterly denounced by a certain Manegold.

1119. Wernher is elected abbot. Theoger [is elected] bishop of Metz, previously abbot of St. George.[137]

Text 21: Richard of Poitiers (Richard of Cluny), *Chronicle.*[138]
Date: ca. 1153.[139]

Henry,[140] son of Robert,[141] rules the Franks for 23 years.[142] Michael rules in Byzantium.[143] Henry II rules the Romans and Germans.[144] At the same time Sancho,[145] king of the Christians in Spain, bore the scepter. When he died, Fernando,[146] his son, received the reins of the kingdom.

In this time, the abbot Lord Odilo,[147] who governed Cluny for 56 years,[148] died. After this, Lord Hugh began to govern the same monastery;[149] he was renowned above others in birth, in almsgiving, and in the spirit of prophecy. [...]

---

[135] *Annales Sancti Georgii in Nigra Silva*, ed. Georg Heinrich Pertz, MGH SS 17: 295–98, at 296.

[136] Ibid., p. 295. See also *Repertorium fontium historiae medii aevi*, vol. 2 (Rome: Istituto storico italiano per il Medio Evo, 1967), p. 329.

[137] See Text 29.

[138] *Ex Richardi Pictaviensis Chronica*, ed. G. Waitz, MGH SS 26: 74–84, at 78. For a less abridged edition, see *Antiquitates italicae medii aevi*, ed. Lodovico Antonio Muratori (1738–1742; repr. Bologna: A. Forni, 1965), vol. 4, cols. 1075–1114, at 1085A–C.

[139] MGH SS 26: 74–75. See also Élie Berger, "Richard le Poitevin, moine de Cluny, historien et poète," *Bibliothèque des écoles françaises d'Athènes et de Rome* 6 (Paris: Ernest Thorin, 1879), pp. 43–138, at 56.

[140] Henry I, King of France (1031–1060).

[141] Robert II the Pious, King of France (996–1031).

[142] Actually 29 years.

[143] Presumably, Michael IV the Paphlagonian (1034–1041). There were two other emperors by the name of Michael during the years that Henry I was King of France, but they reigned very briefly: Michael V Kalaphates (1041–1042) and Michael VI Stratiotikos (1056–1057).

[144] Henry II, Holy Roman Emperor (1002–1024).

[145] Sancho III, King of Navarre (970–1035).

[146] Fernando I, King of Castile (1035–1065) and King of Leon (1037–1065).

[147] Odilo, Abbot of Cluny (994–1048).

[148] Actually 54 years.

[149] Hugh of Semur, Abbot of Cluny (1049–1109).

During this time Manegold the philosopher began to flourish in the German land; he was learned beyond all his contemporaries in letters divine and secular. His wife and daughters also flourished in the religious life, having an impressive knowledge of the Scriptures; and his aforesaid daughters taught their own students.[150]

Philip,[151] son of Henry, rules over the Franks for 45 years.[152] At Byzantium Alexius rules;[153] Henry III rules over the Romans and Germans.[154] [...]

Text 22: *Necrology of Schwarzenthann* (from *The Book of Guta and Sintram*).[155] Date: 1154.[156]

1 January.	[Col. 4] Manegold.[157]
7 January.	[Col. 2] Manegold.
9 January.	[Col. 4] Manegold, priest.
24 January.	[Col. 4] Manegold.
12 February.	[Col. 3] Manegold, priest.

---

[150] MGH SS 26: 78: "His temporibus florere cepit in Theutonica terra Menegaldus philosophus, divinis et secularibus litteris ultra cohetaneos suos eruditus. Uxor quoque et filiae eius religione florentes multam in scripturis habuere notitiam et discipulos proprios filiae eius predictae docebant."

[151] Philip I, King of France (1060–1108).

[152] Actually 48 years.

[153] Alexius I Komnenos (1081–1118).

[154] Henry III, Holy Roman Emperor (1039–1056). Henry IV (1056–1106) was only six years old when he succeeded his father, with his mother Agnes (d. 1062) as regent.

[155] *Le Codex Guta-Sintram: Manuscrit 37 de la bibliothèque du Grand Séminaire de Strasbourg*, ed. Béatrice Weis, 2 vols: facsimile and commentary (Lucerne and Strasbourg: Éditions Fac-similés, en co-édition avec les Éditions Coprur, 1982, 1983), commentary volume, pp. 81–113; facsimile volume, fols. 7v–76v. Schwarzenthann was a house of canonesses founded by the priory of Marbach.

[156] Ibid., commentary volume, p. 145 (article by Michel Parisse, "L'enseignement historique du nécrologe"). The manuscript is dated to the year 1154 by the scribe, Guta, canoness at Schwarzenthann; she identifies the illuminator as Sintram, canon and priest of Marbach (fol. 4r–v). Béatrice Weis edits Guta's statement and translates it into French and German on pp. 57–58 of the commentary volume. Although names were added to the necrology after 1154, the record of "Manegold, priest, master" on 24 May is among the original entries that were transcribed from a text now lost (see Parisse, ibid.: "Guta écrit en 1154 son texte introductif. Elle a, cette année-là, composé son nécrologe et porté tous les noms qu'elle a repris d'un catalogue antérieure.").

[157] The necrology arranges its entries in four columns. Column 1 contains canons of Marbach who were priests. Column 2 contains canons of Marbach who were not priests, as well as canonesses of Schwarzenthann. Column 3 contains lay benefactors. Column 4 contains friends of Marbach and Schwarzenthann whose precise relationship to the communities is not clearly specified. For this classification, see *Le Codex Guta-Sintram*, ed. Weis, commentary volume, p. 80.

6 March.   [Col. 3] Manegold, from whom we have the property at Uffholtz.
17 March.   [Col. 4] Manegold.
9 April.   [Col. 2] Manegold.
15 April.   [Col. 3] Manegold, [who gave us] two *sazzos*.[158]
1 May.   [Col. 4] Manegold.
24 May.   [Col. 1] Manegold, priest, master.[159]
24 August.   [Col. 1] Lord Gerung, prior of Marbach.[160]
6 September.   [Col. 2] Manegold.

[*The entries for 1–3 February, and all entries after 3 October, have been lost. The entries for 29–31 January, 4–7 February, and 1–3 October are mutilated.*][161]

Text 23: Wolfger of Prüfening (Anonymous of Melk), *On Ecclesiastical Writers*.[162]
Date: ca. 1165.[163]

Chapter 105. Manegold the priest, master of the modern masters, assiduously professed the truth, from which he could not be turned by either the blandishments or the threats of a schismatic king. To the contrary, in the strife that arose between Gregory VII and Henry IV, he labored to defend justice even unto chains.[164] There exists a letter of exhortation addressed to him by Ivo, bishop of Chartres.[165] He annotated the pages of a copy of the prophet Isaiah and wrote a continuous gloss on Matthew. He also wrote a most excellent work on the Psalter more precious than topaz and pure gold.

---

[158] An economic unit; see *Le Codex Guta-Sintram*, ed. Weis, commentary volume, p. 115.

[159] *Le Codex Guta-Sintram*, ed. Weis, commentary volume, p. 98: "Manegoldvs, presbiter, magister." Note that this entry marks the only Manegold found in Column 1, which contains priests and priors of Marbach.

[160] See Texts 15, 24, 25, 29.

[161] See *Le Codex Guta-Sintram*, ed. Weis, commentary volume, pp. 85, 113.

[162] PL 213: 981 (Ch. 105). Two other editions are less accessible: Emil Ettlinger, *Der sog. Anonymus Mellicensis De scriptoribus ecclesiasticis* (Karlsruhe: Druck der G. Braun'schen Hofbuchdruckerei, 1896), p. 91; Francis Roy Swietek, *Wolfger of Prüfening's De scriptoribus ecclesiasticis: A Critical Edition and Historical Evaluation*, Ph.D. thesis, University of Illinois at Urbana-Champaign, 1978, pp. 153–54.

[163] *Die deutsche Literatur des Mittelalters: Verfasserlexikon*, 2nd ed., vol. 10, cols. 1352–60, at 1355–58.

[164] Swietek, ibid., p. 153: "Manegoldus presbyter, modernorum magister magistrorum, strenuus veritatis assertor fuit, a qua nec promissis nec minis scismatici regis flecti potuit. Quin immo in dissensione illa que inter Gregorium septimum et Heinricum quartum fuit exorta pro tuenda iusticia laboravit usque ad vincula."

[165] See Text 5.

Text 24: *Annals of Marbach.*[166]
Date: Begun ca. 1210, later updated to 1238.[167]

In the year 1090, the bishops of Würzburg and Metz, and Berthold the duke of Swabia,[168] son of Rudolf the king,[169] closed their last days in faithfulness to St. Peter. In the same year the church of St. Augustine was founded at Marbach[170] by the illustrious knight, Burchard of Gueberschwihr,[171] whose helper and fellow worker was the most faithful Master Manegold of Lautenbach.[172] For indeed, this Master Manegold, with God's mercy, rekindled the Church's worship, which had been altogether extinguished for a long time in Alsace.[173] For as the long-lasting pallor of death that hung over them grew stronger, almost all the greater nobility and knights of that province crowded together upon him in droves, and they merited to be absolved from excommunication through the power conferred on him by the Lord Pope Urban. For this

---

[166] *Annales Marbacenses qui dicuntur: Cronica Hohenburgensis cum continuatione et additamentis Neoburgensibus*, ed. Hermann Bloch, MGH Scriptores rerum germanicarum in usum scholarum (Hannover and Leipzig: Hahnsche Buchhandlung, 1907), pp. 37–40, 44. Previous edition: *Annales Marbacenses*, ed. Roger Wilmans, MGH SS 17: 142–80, at 157–59.

[167] On the problems of dating the text and determining authorship and provenance, see Bloch, ibid., pp. vii–xxi (especially pp. xii–xiii), as well as his fuller study in "Die Elsässischen Annalen der Stauferzeit," *Regesten der Bischöfe von Strassburg* 1 (Innsbruck: Verlag der Wagner'schen Universitäts-Buchhandlung, 1908), pp. 49–124. Bloch believes that the annals were written by a canon in close association with Marbach, but not actually at Marbach itself (see his edition, p. xi). For additional scholarship on the *Annales Marbacenses*, see *Die Chronik Ottos von St. Blasien und die Marbacher Annalen*, ed. and trans. Franz-Josef Schmale (Darmstadt: Wissenschaftliche Buchgesellschaft, 1998), pp. 5–10. (Note that Schmale begins his facing page edition and translation of the *Annales Marbacenses* with the year 1152.)

[168] *Annales Marbacenses qui dicuntur*, ed. Bloch, p. 37: "...dux Alemannie...."

[169] Rudolf of Swabia, recognized by the Gregorians as the rightful king of Germany after Gregory VII excommunicated Henry IV in 1076; Rudolf died in 1080.

[170] The *Codex Guta-Sintram* (see Text 22) implies that the year was actually 1089. The scribe, Guta, notes that the codex was completed in 1154, "the sixty-fifth year since the foundation of the monastery of Marbach"—hence, 1089. Béatrice Weis provides a discussion and edition of Guta's statement in *Le Codex Guta-Sintram*, commentary volume, pp. 57–58. Bernold of Constance gave 1094 as the year of the monastery's foundation (see Text 11). The *Annales Marbacenses* distinguishes between the foundation of the church (1090) and the foundation of the monastery (1094).

[171] Gueberschwihr (alternative form: Gebersweiler) is approximately two miles south of Marbach.

[172] *Annales Marbacenses qui dicuntur*, ed. Bloch, p. 37: "Eodem anno fundata est Marbacensis aecclesia sancti Augustini a militari et illustri viro Burchardo de Gebeleswilre, cuius adiutor et cooperator fidelissimus magister Manegoldus de Luotinbach extitit." Cf. Text 30.

[173] The rest of this paragraph is nearly identical with part of Bernold's chronicle for the year 1094, except for the last clause, which echoes a passage from Bernold's entry for 1098 (see Text 11).

reason he aroused great envy against himself among the schismatics, so that he was haled before H.[174] and imprisoned by him for some time. […]

A.D. 1094. Master Manegold, with the help of Lord B.,[175] began to build the monastery at Marbach from its foundations and chose to be one with the same canons, living in community.[176] […]

A.D. 1096.[177] Hugh the archbishop of Lyons sent to Master Manegold the relics of St. Irenaeus the martyr,[178] which are preserved to this day with great honor in the church at Marbach. In the same year, Pope Urban convened the famous synod at Tours during the third week of Lent with bishops from numerous provinces. Master Manegold attended this synod and received from the apostolic lord the privilege of his protection for the church of Marbach,[179] in which he decreed, among other things, that no one is to be made prior in this place either by violence or cunning; the canons must install him by communal consent. […]

A.D. 1105. The church at Marbach, originally founded by Burchard, was dedicated by the venerable Gebhard, bishop of Constance, in honor of the bishop St. Augustine.[180] […]

A.D. 1120. Burchard, the founder of the church at Marbach, migrated from this light, and having been buried in the same church, rests in peace. […]

A.D. 1130. Gerung, the first prior of the church at Marbach, dies. He is succeeded by [Arn]old.[181]

---

[174] Henry IV.

[175] Burchard of Gueberschwihr.

[176] The concluding clause corresponds to a passage in Bernold's *Chronicon* for the year 1094 (see Text 11).

[177] Bloch's edition provides the year "MXCVI" (p. 39), whereas the older edition by Wilmans provides "1098" (p. 158). Since a typographical error is far likelier when it is a question of one Arabic digit rather than two additional Roman digits, and since the Council of Tours (reported here) did indeed take place in the year 1096, I have followed Bloch rather than Wilmans. Both editions are based on the sole surviving manuscript of the text (Jena, Universitätsbibliothek, MS. Bose q. 6, fols. 123–50).

[178] On the reputation of St. Irenaeus of Lyons as a martyr, see David Farmer, *The Oxford Dictionary of Saints*, 4th ed. (Oxford and New York: Oxford University Press, 1997), p. 250.

[179] See Text 6.

[180] That is, Augustine of Hippo (354–430).

[181] See *Annales Marbacenses qui dicuntur*, ed. Bloch, p. 44 n. *b*; and MGH SS 17: 159 n. *g*. There was some confusion among the sources in regarding Gerung, rather than Manegold, as the first prior of Marbach; see notes 187, 188, below.

Text 25: *Necrology of Marbach.*[182]
Date: 1241–1731.[183]

2 January. Anniversary of the Adm[irable] Reverend and Most Eminent Lord[184] Manegold, the first Prior of this house, once a Canon of Lautenbach and a most distinguished Doctor in sacred Theology.[185]

24 May. Manegold, priest, master, not here.[186]

4 July. Anniversary of the Adm[irable] Reverend and Most Eminent Lord Gerung, Prelate and second Prior of this house.[187]

24 August. Gerung the first prior, here, 1130.[188]

In the year 1241 this book was written by the unworthy priest Wernher. Grant, O Christ, I beg, that the name of Wernher, by whom this book is composed, may be inscribed with the just.

---

[182] Charles Hoffmann, "L'Abbaye de Marbach et le Nécrologe de MCCXLI," *Bulletin de la société pour la conservation des monuments historiques d'Alsace*, 2nd series, vol. 20 (Strasbourg: R. Schultz & Co., 1902), pp. 67–230. The selections presented here include all references to the name "Manegold" (there are only two) and to Manegold's successor, Gerung.

[183] Ibid., p. 166. The necrology was begun in 1241 (based on a previous source, now lost), and entries were added over the course of the next five centuries; the last entry was made in 1731.

[184] This formula was used to refer to the priors (later the abbots) of Marbach, and was added to the necrology only in the seventeenth century. (Other examples are offered by Béatrice Weis in *Le Codex Guta-Sintram*, commentary volume, pp. 81 n. 6, 84 n. 26, 86 n. 10.)

[185] Hoffmann, ibid., p. 181: "Anniversarium Adm. Reverendi et Amplissimi Domini Manegoldi primi Praepositi huius domus, olim Canonici Lutenbacensis, nec non in sacrosancta Theologia Doctoris eximij." This entry is written in a seventeenth-century hand, as noted by Béatrice Weis in *Le Codex Guta-Sintram*, commentary volume, p. 81 n. 6. There is no corresponding entry in the *Necrology of Schwarzenthann* (Text 22).

[186] Or possibly "Manegold the priest, our master here." There is disagreement on how to edit the manuscript. Béatrice Weis (*Le Codex Guta-Sintram*, commentary volume, p. 98 n. 24) suggests "Manegoldus, presbiter, Magister, non hic," against Hoffman's reading ("L'Abbaye de Marbach et le Nécrologe de MCCXLI," p. 198): "Manegoldus presbyter magister noster hic." The matter turns on how to expand the abbreviation "n." I have adopted Weis's "non" rather than Hoffman's "noster," since the former is more consistent with standard paleographical practice. Indeed, Hoffmann himself admits that his expansion is unusual; see "L'Abbaye de Marbach et le Nécrologe de MCCXLI," p. 168 n. 2. I am not aware of any evidence, archaeological or written, that indicates where Manegold was buried.

[187] This is written in the seventeenth-century formula. There is no corresponding entry in the *Necrology of Schwarzenthann* (Text 22). Note that the entry for 4 July contradicts the entry for 24 August. On the contradictory numbering of the priors, see Hoffmann, "L'Abbaye de Marbach et le Nécrologe de MCCXLI," pp. 160–61.

[188] Gerung is also identified as the first prior in the *Annales Marbacenses* (see Text 24, under the year 1130). The entry in the *Necrology of Schwarzenthann* (Text 22) for 24 August reads simply, "Lord Gerung, prior of Marbach."

Text 26: Alberic of Trois Fontaines, *Chronicle*.[189]
Date: After 1241.[190]

In the year 1060. [...] In the time of St. Maurilius, archbishop of Rouen,[191] Anselm, who was born in Aosta in Lombardy,[192] became a monk at Bec under the Abbot Herluin and the Prior Lanfranc, at the age of twenty-seven. [...]

It was considered above how world power passed from the Assyrians through various kingdoms to the Eastern Franks, that is, the Germans; similarly philosophy, that is, wisdom, devolved from the Chaldees through various peoples to the Gauls, that is, the Western Franks, in this way. For it was Abraham, coming from Chaldea, who first taught astronomy and arithmetic in Egypt. What he transplanted from the Chaldees to Egypt was then transferred from there to the Greeks, especially at Athens in the time of the philosophers; from there to the Romans under the Scipios; [then] Cato and Cicero were its keepers. After them it continued under the Caesars in the time of the poets, when Virgil, Horace, Ovid, Seneca, and Lucan flourished. From there to the regions of Spain, and most recently to the regions of Gaul in the days of the illustrious masters Berengar,[193] Manegold,[194] Lanfranc,[195] [and] Anselm.[196]

[189] *Chronica Albrici Monachi Trium Fontium, a monacho Novi Monasterii Hoiensis interpolata*, ed. Paulus Scheffer-Boichorst, MGH SS 23: 631–950, at 792–93. The text was first edited by Gottfried Wilhelm Leibnitz, *Alberici Monachi Trium Fontium Chronicon, e manuscriptis nunc primum editum* (Leipzig: Nicolas Förster, 1698), vol. 2, pp. 97–99. There are very minor differences between the two editions for the selections translated here.

[190] The last entry is for the year 1241. Scheffer-Boichorst offers an extensive discussion of the editorial questions that the text raises; see MGH SS 23: 631–73.

[191] On Blessed Maurilius, archbishop of Rouen (1055–1067), see *Lexikon für Theologie und Kirche* 7: 190.

[192] Anselm of Canterbury (1033–1109).

[193] Berengar of Tours (d. 1088).

[194] MGH SS 23: 793: "Inde ad Hispanias, nuperrime ad Gallias a diebus illustrium virorum, Berengarii, Managaldi, Lamfranci, Anselmi." Cf. Texts 14 and 17.

[195] Lanfranc of Bec (d. 1089).

[196] Although Otto of Freising, who clearly was Alberic's inspiration for this passage, had probably intended Anselm of Laon (d. 1117) at this point in his own text, Alberic probably had Anselm of Canterbury in mind here, as implied by the presence of Lanfranc in the list and by the biographical information on Anselm of Canterbury provided earlier in the text.

Text 27: Ptolemy of Lucca, *Annals*.[197]
Date: 1303–1308.[198]

A.D. 1090. Urban convenes a council at Clermont,[199] where it was decided that the hours of the Blessed Virgin should be said daily, and that on the day of the Sabbath there should be a solemn office in her honor. It is also said that here they formulated the preface of the Blessed Virgin for the Mass which we now sing.

At this time Anselm the abbot flourishes in England, a man wondrous in life and knowledge, who afterwards was made archbishop of Canterbury, without relinquishing his previous office.[200]

At the same time there flourished in Germany a certain philosopher named Mane-gold, whose wife and daughters were most greatly learned in philosophy.[201]

Text 28: *Necrology of Rottenbuch*.[202]
Date: 1490.[203]

2 February. Manegold.

21 March. Manegold, villager.

4 April. Lord Hermann, prior in Schlechdorff, once dean of this house, died in the year of the Lord 1451, and Gertrude his mother.

17 April. Manegold, priest.

24 April. Manegold, priest.

---

[197] *Die Annalen des Tholomeus von Lucca*, ed. Bernhard Schmeidler, MGH Scriptores rerum germani-carum, new series 8 (Berlin: Weidmannsche Buchhandlung, 1930), p. 21.

[198] Ibid., pp. xvii, xxvi–xxvii, xxxii.

[199] Actually in 1095.

[200] That is, he did not cease to be a monk. See *Die Annalen*, ed. Schmeidler, p. 21 n. 4.

[201] Ibid., p. 21: "Per idem tempus floruit in Theotonia quidam philosophus, cui nomen Menegaldus, cuius uxor et filie in philosophia fuerunt permaxime." Compare with Richard of Poitiers (Text 21).

[202] *Necrologium Raitenbuchense*, ed. Franz Ludwig Baumann, MGH Necrologia Germaniae 3: 109–15. The selections presented here include all references to the name "Manegold," as well as all explicit refer-ences to deans. Since only three deans of Rottenbuch are thus specified, it is clear that most of the hold-ers of this office were entered into the necrology without indication of their status.

[203] Ibid., p. 109. A number of the entries are dated. Since all dated entries up to the year 1490 are copied in the same hand, whereas entries bearing later dates appear in different hands, one may conclude that a previous exemplar was transcribed in 1490. The earliest of the dated entries is from the year 1210 (6 March); most are from the fifteenth century.

15 July. Manegold of Lautenbach [Luttenbach?]²⁰⁴ and his wife Irmelgart, and Peter the subdeacon and Conrad, both sons of theirs.

4 September. Manegold, lay brother.

11 October. Manegold, lay brother.

23 October. Walther, priest and dean of Schongau.

28 October. George Rapp, priest and dean of this house.

10 November. In the year of the Lord 1446 died the venerable father and prior Thomas de Diessen, once dean of this house.

19 November. Manegold.

Text 29: Johannes Trithemius, *Annals of Hirsau*; Wolfger of Prüfening, *Life of Theoger*.²⁰⁵

Date: 1509–1511 (*Annals of Hirsau*);²⁰⁶ 1138–1146 (*Life of Theoger*).²⁰⁷

[Trithemius's summary of Theoger's early life.]

Theoger was born in eastern Francia, which the ancients called by another name: Teutonica. His parents were of fairly humble status. Since he was an intelligent child and had received a soul as wise as Solomon's, he was sent to study letters in the manner of his kind. He received the finest education under the tutorship of a certain Manegold, prefect of the schools in the province of Alsace,²⁰⁸ a man who was not only most learned, but also of the highest moral integrity — one who was rightly called

---

²⁰⁴ Ibid., p. 113: "Manegoldus de Liutenpach et uxor eius Irmelgart et Petrus subdyac. et Cuonradus, ambo filii eorum." The index (pp. 480, 481) suggests that "Liutenpach" refers to Luttenbach in Oberbayern near Schongau, which is about 10 km from Rottenbuch. It may be noted that Luttenbach in Oberbayern is presently too small to appear on any but the most detailed maps of Germany. The editor shows no awareness that Manegold of Lautenbach was connected to the monastery of Rottenbuch. In any event, "Liutenpach" is a legitimate form for either Luttenbach or Lautenbach.

²⁰⁵ *Vita Theogeri, Abbatis Sancti Georgii et Episcopi Mettensis*, ed. Philipp Jaffé, MGH SS 12: 449–79, at 450–51, 476. The beginning of the *Vita Theogerii* has been lost; Jaffé has substituted in its place the summary of Theoger's early career found in Trithemius's *Annales Hirsaugienses* (for the year 1087). Wolfger of Prüfening is believed to have written the *Vita Theogerii*, as well as the *De scriptoribus ecclesiasticis* that mentions "Manegold the priest, master of the modern masters" (Text 23); see *Die deutsche Literatur des Mittelalters: Verfasserlexikon*, 2nd ed., vol. 10, cols. 1352–60, at 1358–59; Swietek, *Wolfger of Prüfening's De scriptoribus ecclesiasticis* (see above, n. 162), pp. 27–29. (Note that the modern German form of Theoger is "Dietger," but English and French scholarship tends to use the Latinate form.)

²⁰⁶ Klaus Arnold, *Johannes Trithemius (1462–1516)*, 2nd ed. (Würzburg: Kommissionsverlag Ferdinand Schöningh, 1991), pp. 149–54.

²⁰⁷ MGH SS 12: 450.

²⁰⁸ MGH SS 12: 450: "…sub magisterio cuiusdam Manegoldi, praefecti scholarum in Alsatiae provincia…."

both a Christian and a philosopher. He completed his studies in a brief span of time, yet he received a thorough training in every kind of science. For he was indeed remarkably skilled in every discipline of the liberal arts, and particularly accomplished in music. For when he later became a monk at Hirsau, he wrote a book on music which was not only useful but also very learned and elegant. He also produced a brief, but very useful and beautiful, commentary on the Psalter which demonstrates most clearly the powers of his intellect. He also wrote many stylistically refined letters to various people, as well as diverse sermons and homilies for monks.

After he had been in the company of his aforenamed teacher for some time and had received at once the best possible instruction in every branch of learning and in the beauty of moral perfection, he obtained permission to return to his family, who were extremely delighted by his erudition. He became a canon in the church of the holy martyr Cyriacus, a new house near Mainz. He always proved himself to be just, prudent, and moderate in all things, and he was the exemplar of all modesty and honesty. And because, as we have just said, he was most learned in every kind of science, the office of teaching was committed to him by the prior of the aforementioned church. Many attended his lessons daily for their education, and with the greatest diligence he instructed them fully, not only in the divine Scriptures, but also in secular letters.

Then some years later, having family business,[209] he came to William the saintly abbot at Hirsau for advice, not at all intending to become a monk. Yet at length he was inspired by the words of the most holy father, and his plans were redirected by divine compassion while hearing Mass celebrated by the man of God, who prayed for him. When he was about to leave, he suddenly changed his mind and took the vow of the monks. And thus with contempt for worldly honors and for all vanities, for love of Christ he became a monk, and soon he gave excellent proof of his future sanctity. Keeping watch in the fear of the Lord with the greatest solicitude, he sought nothing more than how to please Him and to prove himself before Him.

[*Book 2, Chapters 23–24 of the Life of Theoger, reporting events of the year 1118, following Theoger's election as bishop of Metz.*] And when they arrived at the monastery of Marbach at the end of the journey, [they found that] even there news of the old fellow[210] had gone before them. Wherefore the brothers dwelling therein, religious who were canons regular, came out in order to greet him as he arrived; and having struck up a melodious song, they received him with the fullness of joy and exultation. As it happened, amongst that chorus was the venerable Gerung,[211] who, as we mentioned in the

---

[209] MGH SS 12: 451: "…negotium habens familiare…."
[210] That is, Theoger.
[211] This Gerung is almost certainly Manegold's successor as the prior of Marbach. A papal letter of Calixtus II identifies Gerung as the prior of Marbach in the year 1119 (Text 15).

first part of this work,[212] had sent Theoger, still within the years of adolescence, to the venerable Abbot William at Hirsau under the pretense of learning about penance from him.[213] And now he[214] was advanced in age, his head flecked with white hair — which to Theoger was startling, for he had not seen him since the day of his conversion — and he[215] was happy to see the monk and priest, the pupil and guest.[216] The blessed pontiff Theoger also, still at a distance when he recognized the old man, was very happy.

"After they had gone inside and permission to speak had been granted,"[217] he drew near to him most cordially;[218] embracing him with both arms and covering him with kisses, he confessed that he considered him his apostle,[219] and that he had once been his captive, though it had been a wholesome kind of captivity. Then he[220] replied, "I am not at all sorry that I took such a captive, since not only has that captivity not harmed him, but it has actually conferred upon him so great a dignity of honor and glory that he first became a monk, then an abbot of monks, and finally by God's will he climbed up to the highest rank of priests." And the bishop spoke these words: "Nor, my apostle, was I ever sorry to have benefited from such a counselor, who has through his office amassed for himself his own rewards, and has found in me, with Christ's favor, the desired fruit of his pious effort."

At last this saintly bishop bid farewell, first to all the brothers, then to the one who was especially his own, his apostle as he would have it, and rejoined his flock at the monastery of St. George, his beloved house of virtue.

---

212 That is, the part now lost and imperfectly substituted by Trithemius's summary.

213 Without the context provided by the lost portion of Book 1, it is impossible to determine the precise meaning of this ambiguous passage. The rest of the selection here suggests that Theoger had once been Gerung's ward, presumably at the time when Theoger was studying with the renowned Manegold who is mentioned in Trithemius's summary. The Latin is as follows (MGH SS 12: 476): "Huic forte concentui venerabilis ille Gerungus intererat, qui ut in prima huius operis parte meminimus, Theogerum adhuc infra annos adolescentiae constitutum Hirsaugiam ad venerabilem Wilhelmum abbatem sub percipiendae ab eo poenitentiae specie destinarat."

214 That is, Gerung.

215 That is, Gerung.

216 MGH SS 12: 476: "Erat vero iam aetate adultus, et canis albentibus caput aspersus, ac mirum in modum Theogero, quippe quem a die conversionis eius non viderat ultra, iam monacho et sacerdote, alumno vel hospite laetabatur."

217 Virgil, *Aeneid* 1: 520.

218 That is, Theoger drew near to Gerung.

219 Possibly because Gerung had once sent Theoger to Hirsau, where Theoger found his ideal form of religious life. In this way Gerung, like an apostle, led Theoger to a deeper spirituality.

220 That is, Gerung.

Text 30: Heinrich Elten, Prior of Marbach (d. 1522).[221]
Date: 1502.[222]

And so, when Burchard began the work, and the individual buildings were built as was fitting, Master Manegold, a canon of the church of St. Michael of Lautenbach, gathered the brothers, of whom some were from Lautenbach, and others are said to have come from the mountain of St. Irenaeus the martyr near Lyons in Gaul. He undertook to organize a life of discipline following a rule at Marbach, and chose to be one with these clerics, who were living in community and according to a rule.[223]

Text 31: *Annals of Strasbourg*, forged by Philippe André Grandidier.[224]
Date: 1785–1786 (previously believed to have been written soon after 1207).[225]

A.D. 1090. The church of St. Augustine was founded at Marbach by the illustrious knight, Burchard of Gueberschwihr, whose most faithful helper and fellow worker was Master Manegold of Lautenbach.[226]

---

[221] Cited in Philippe André Grandidier, *Oeuvres historiques inédits*, ed. J. Liblin, vol. 3 (Colmar: Revue d'Alsace, 1865), p. 120; see also Hoffmann, "L'Abbaye de Marbach et le Nécrologe de MCCXLI," pp. 69–70 n. 4. This text does not play a significant role in recent studies of Manegold, but it has been included in this dossier because a number of older publications have drawn upon it.
[222] Ibid. (both locations).
[223] See Text 11.
[224] *Annales Argentinenses*, ed. Philipp Jaffé, MGH SS 17: 86–90, at 88. On the forgery, see Hermann Bloch, "Die Elsässischen Annalen der Stauferzeit," p. 21 (see note 167).
[225] The text was regarded as a product of the early thirteenth century (MGH SS 17: 86, 144) until Hermann Bloch discovered that it was a forgery of the late eighteenth century; see the preceding note.
[226] MGH SS 17: 88: "Anno Domini 1090. fundata est Marbach ecclesia sancti Augustini a militari et illustri viro, Burchardo de Gebelswilre; cuius adiutor et cooperator fidelissimus magister Manegoldus de Lutenbach extitit." Cf. Texts 11 and 24.

Index

II. Biblical Citations

This index records passages that are italicized in the Translation of the *Liber contra Wolfelmum* (pp. 35–68); it does not take into account Manegold's more oblique uses of Scripture, which are described in the Notes (pp. 69–92). Entries followed by numbers in parentheses indicate first the page of the Translation in which the passage occurs, and then (in parentheses) the page in the Notes where the text is referenced. Manegold's versions of biblical text sometimes vary from standard editions of the Vulgate, possibly because he was quoting from memory.

Old Testament

NEW TESTAMENT

III. Modern Scholars

IV. General Index

Tertullian, 81
Theodora, Empress, 117 n.
Theodoric of Verdun, Bishop, 4, 11, 18, 67–68, 91, 92, 109
Theoger, Abbot of St. George in the Black Forest, and Bishop of Metz, 27, 129, 137–39
Timaeus, see Plato
Tours, 15, 113, 114, 133
transmigration of souls, *see* soul
Trier, 67, 91
Trinity, 42, 44, 51; *see also* God *and* Holy Spirit
tritheism, 123 n.
Trithemius, Johannes, 27, 137, 139 n.

Udalric of Godesheim, 88
Ulrich (Oudalricus), prior of Rottenbuch, 114, 115 n.
Urban II, Pope, 15, 23 n., 113–15, 116 n., 117 n., 120, 121, 123, 124, 127, 132, 133, 136
Uriah the Hittite, 81

Victor III, Pope (Desiderius, Abbot of Monte Cassino), 20, 123
Vigilius, Pope, 117
Virgil, 39, 72, 79, 135
Virgil of Salzburg, 75
Virgin, Blessed, *see* Mary
Vita Theogerii, attributed to Wolfger of Prüfening, 27, 137–39
Vulgate, *see* Bible

Wenrich of Trier, 4, 11, 17, 18, 67, 91, 92, 109

Wernher, Abbot of St. George in the Black Forest, 129
Wernher, author of the *Necrology of Marbach*, 134
Wibald of Corvey, 25 n.
Wibert of Ravenna, excommunicated archbishop (*also* Guibert, *and* Clement III, antipope), 2, 4, 20, 64–65, 89, 90, 117, 123, 125
William I the Conqueror, King of England, 26, 123
William II Rufus, King of England, 123
William of Champeaux, 10, 25, 26, 82, 101, 121–22
William of Conches, 78, 79, 87
William of Hirsau, 138, 139
Wolfger of Prüfening, 23–25, 26, 27, 81, 89, 94, 131, 137
Wolfhelm of Cologne (Wolfhelm of Brauweiler), 4–14, 18, 21–22, 69, 79, 80, 81, 83, 84, 86, 87, 88, 91
world-soul, 13, 70, 71, 72
Worms, Concordat of, 12; Council of, 88, 89, 90
Würzburg, 132

Xenocrates, 39, 72, 73
Xenophon (Xenophanes), 39, 72, 73

Zeno, 39, 72, 73
Zilpah, 112
Zion, 108
Zwiefalten, monastery of, 31 n.; *see also Necrology of Zwiefalten*